# Urban Housing in the Third World

Geoffrey K. Payne

London: Leonard Hill
Boston: Routledge & Kegan Paul

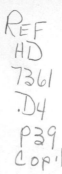

Published in Great Britain by
Leonard Hill
(a division of International Textbook Company Limited)
450 Edgware Road, London W2 1EG
A member of the Blackie Group


and in the U.S.A. by
Routledge & Kegan Paul Ltd.
9 Park Street, Boston, Mass 02108

First published 1977


ISBN 249 44149 7


Printed in Great Britain by Robert MacLehose and Co. Ltd
Printers to the University of Glasgow

*To Rita and our daughter Tania*

# Contents

# Preface

One of the major difficulties concerning the study of housing is that
every man is his own expert. At the individual or group level this is,
of course, an asset, since a house is the largest single investment most
people ever make, and control over it is essential if housing is to
reflect widely differing needs. Issues regarding the planning context
of housing are, however, more complex. The scale of urban
structures and the factors which condition them, all too easily
induce a sense of confusion or impotence, which is not helped by the
compartmentalism of disciplines such as geography, sociology and
planning. This problem is particularly relevant in the analysis of
housing and planning in regions currently experiencing rapid
urban growth. Under conditions of limited financial resources and
unprecedented population increase, the inability of conventional
concepts and policies to control, or even regulate the forms of
urban development, is already beyond much doubt. In such a
situation, it is vital that concepts are appropriate to the contexts in
which they operate, since housing is a structural urban problem as
much as an individual one, yet if conventional planning does not
have the answer, what are the alternatives? This problem forms the
motivation for the pages which follow.

In any such study, the definition of terms used is naturally an
important factor in determining the scope of material and regions to
be included. Such definitions have become the subject of changing
fashions and one rarely now sees reference made to 'modernizing
countries', since there is increasing doubt as to what constitutes
'modernity' and understandable disagreement about its merits. On
the other hand, terms such as 'developing country' are frequently
considered paternalistic and imply a movement from some assumed
'primitive' or 'backward' state towards one that is a more rational
and 'civilized'. Even the term 'urbanizing country', which is
relatively value-free, would not always be valid and in India, for
example, the proportion of the total population living in urban
areas continues to remain at a low and relatively stable level. The
term 'Third World' has therefore been used, despite its limitations,
as a general framework for selecting case study material. This is
because it incorporates the element of underdevelopment which is

an essential and common factor in the problems of countries
experiencing rapid urban growth and also because a large number of
such countries have themselves acknowledged the term as
applicable. It does not imply, of course, that all 'Third World'
countries share the same specific problems, or that modes and
concepts applicable to one would be relevant for another — it is
simply an heuristic device.

Similar care in the use of terms must also apply in discussing
the nature of housing settlement processes in this context. It is often
assumed, for example, that urban growth rates are 'excessive'; that
much development is 'unplanned', and that because the proportion
of urban populations employed in productive industry is small,
relative to the 19th Century experience in Europe, that the cities
are 'over-urbanized' and 'abnormal'. It will be argued, however, that
such assessments are not only too crude but are inappropriate, since
the ability of urban centres in the 19th Century to generate extensive
industrial employment was not unrelated to guaranteed access to
raw materials and to controlled markets for their processed goods.
These benefits were made possible to a large extent by the growth of
colonialism and other forms of economic exploitation and are an
integral part of the emergence of development in some parts of the
world and underdevelopment in others. In this respect, the cities of
the industrial West must *also* be considered 'abnormal', or 'over-
industrialized', since it is doubtful if they could have achieved their
economic growth rates if forced to rely solely upon local or regional
resources. If this is the case, the cities of the 'Third World' are simply
experiencing the negative aspects of the same process and it is
unreasonable, as Sovani has shown, to expect them to remain
islands of prosperity and full employment, in a sea of un- and under-
employment.

What is one to make of this in terms of housing and planning?
The focus of this book is geared primarily to those least able to help
themselves — the substantial numbers of the urban poor, whether
they be the indigenous urban population or migrants from rural
areas. This is partly because the more affluent are in a better position
to look after themselves, but more particularly because it is often felt
that the poor should not be in the cities in the first place, since it is
assumed that they are economic parasites and that any assistance
given to them in the form of housing or services will therefore only
attract more and increase problems still further. This argument,
however, fails to recognize that migrants generally move for *jobs*

rather than houses and that the urban poor make a collectively substantial, (if individually marginal), contribution to both urban and regional economies. In addition to this must be included their ability to use housing as a means of generating substantial employment and capital out of nothing, in order to improve their socio-economic position. It is therefore all the more unfortunate that existing official approaches restrict these achievements rather than support them.

There is, however, nothing inevitable about such a state of affairs. Planning and housing policies can be a powerful tool in helping reduce inequalities instead of reinforcing them and thus make a major contribution to development strategies. In order to do so, however, it will be necessary for planners, architects and policy-makers to learn from the poor, who generally constitute the bulk of urban populations, and work with them rather than to make arbritary assumptions and plan *for* people. Only then will it be possible to create planning frameworks which can maximize the capabilities of people to contribute to and benefit from development in its widest sense. Studies by a number of writers such as John Turner, have served to demonstrate clearly the capacities for self-help that the poor possess. Whilst I have adopted a somewhat different position on specific aspects of this approach it is not in any way to challenge the revolution in attitudes that it effected, but to explore its implications as a model for general application.

If the already large and rapidly increasing populations of cities throughout the 'Third World' are to obtain housing which can help them in their efforts to improve their socio-economic position, a great deal of reassessment of policies and priorities will be required. If this book can help in some way to create a climate in which more egalitarian, flexible and economic alternatives can be developed, then it will have been worthwhile.

Geoffrey K. Payne
London, 1976.

# Acknowledgements

It is a pleasure to be able to record the advice, co-operation and support received from a large number of individuals and institutions during the several stages of work which have led up to this book. At the outset, my gratitude goes to the Government of India for the award of a Commonwealth Universities Research Scholarship in 1970, to enable me to undertake detailed surveys of low-income settlements in Delhi. If my approach appears critical of official attitudes and policies regarding housing, I earnestly hope that this will be seen as honest and sincere comment on what is generally acknowledged to be a major urban problem and one that therefore justifies a number of alternative approaches. Whilst in India, I was greatly indebted to the staff of the School of Planning and Architecture, New Delhi, under whose auspices the fieldwork was carried out and Professor Bijit Ghosh, D. V. R. Rao and Cyrus Jhabvala gave freely of their advice and considerable experience during critical stages of the Delhi survey. A similar debt is owed to Dr. Ashish Bose of the Institute of Economic Growth, Delhi University, and the period of co-operation with Richard Weiss of the School of Architecture, University of California, was both fruitful and enjoyable. Perhaps most of all, however, I am in debt to the people in the Rouse Avenue, Maulana Azad and other settlements, who were prepared to tolerate my presence in their midst for so long, giving information and recording their experiences with a patience and insight which, more than any other factor, provided me with my real education in the field of housing and planning.

On returning to London, the Social Science Research Council kindly provided financial support to extend and complete the research. This work was undertaken at the Architectural Association School of Architecture who provided necessary administrative backing and services. The constructive criticism and advice of Patrick Crooke was invaluable at this stage.

I am grateful to Professor Rory Fonseca, Maurice Mitchell, Patrick Crooke, Mehmet Darie and Musée de l'Home, for permission to publish copywright material and to my publishers and to Tom Hancock for their help and comment in improving the text. I must, however, accept sole responsibility for the work as it now appears.

To Dorothy Harley and Verity Whitworth I offer my thanks for long hours spent typing a notoriously illegible manuscript and finally, but by no means least, the tolerance and help of my wife Rita, who has been largely responsible for enabling me to prepare this work for publication.

Geoffrey K. Payne, 1976.

PART ONE

# The Context of Urban Growth

# PART ONE
# The Context of Urban Growth

## 1.1 Introduction

To an ever-increasing number of people throughout the world, a secure and optimistic future is coming to be seen as synonymous with living in an urban area. The extent of contemporary urban growth is greater than at any other time in history and as yet shows no sign of slackening, so that the problems facing cities and those responsible for planning or regulating them are equally unprecedented.

Rapid urban growth is usually associated with periods of intense socio-economic or political change. This was true of the urbanization of European countries in the 19th century and the growth of cities in other periods. It is equally true today, though the context within which it is now occurring is very different. There are, of course, great variations in individual areas and these change quickly over time, but growth rates are highest in what are loosely termed underdevelped, developing, or 'Third World' countries. Until the last thirty years, most of these countries had relatively few large cities and the majority of the population lived in rural areas. Such cities as did exist were the centres of economic and political power, many of which were clearly linked to patterns of international trade directed from other countries. The cities served the interests of a small section of the local population and generally exhibited much higher environmental and amenity standards than the rural areas. Their physical growth, though sometimes spectacular, was generally capable of being controlled by conventional planning policies.

In the period immediately following World War II, however, this relatively stable situation began to change. As empires fell and changes in international trade modified the internal structure of national economies, the cities became the focus of refugees and migrants on a vast scale. Many of these established temporary or semi-permanent settlements in the urban fringe and waited for a

Figure 1.1        The value of marginal urban land along railways or canals
is demonstrated by this settlement in the central part of Manila, known as
the Tondo. (Photo by courtesy of Patrick Crooke)

*Figure 1.2    Inner city housing and commercial development in Guayaquil, Equador.* (Photo by courtesy of Patrick Crooke)

chance to gain some form of employment, whilst others filtered into rented housing in the central areas which provided greater accessibility. Pressure on the existing housing stock increased with the swelling populations and many people began to construct hutments in pockets of unused land left untouched by modern development, (see Fig. 1.1) whilst elsewhere whole areas were transformed into low-income rented housing (see Fig. 1.2). These processes had, of course, also occurred in the cities of Europe during the 19th century (1.1), but their scale within more recently urbanizing countries has exceeded anything experienced before. Gradually, both the unauthorized settlements and the over-crowded tenements have become permanent factors of the expanding cities and are growing more rapidly than any other form of development. As growth continues, mass invasions of land have occurred beyond the urban boundaries (and official control) so adding yet another variation to an increasingly complex situation (see Fig. 1.3).

The effect of these processes has been to transform the social and spatial structure of cities so that they reflect the dilemmas of the regions in which they are situated. Yet if this reality is presenting a major contemporary problem, it raises another which is at least as serious and even more elusive, that of interpretation. How should the fact of rapid urban growth within a context of increasing total populations and rural poverty be judged? In what ways does present urban growth differ from that of previous periods and are attempts to restrict it desirable or feasible? What roles do the migrants fulfil in the developmental process, and is housing a restriction upon, or support for, them? Finally, what are the major issues raised by the extensive growth of low-income settlements?

The answers given to these questions so far vary greatly according to the ideology of the writer or the way in which people are affected. Whilst the problems faced by major cities are very large, no cause is served, however, by misunderstanding the real nature of the processes involved, or applying inappropriate concepts to them. In this section, an attempt will therefore be made to describe the nature of contemporary urban growth and the various factors that have conditioned it, and to evaluate the relevance of current theories. It is therefore essential to classify the range of phenomena with which we are concerned.

It has become accepted in recent years that there exists such a thing as the 'Third World City' (1.2) and that this has distinctive features. Theories regarding these features have been interpreted

*Figure 1.3    Peri-urban land invasion typical of many throughout Latin America. This example at Arequipa, Peru, dates from the early 1960s. (Photo by courtesy of Patrick Crooke).*

either as the initial stages in the development of fully 'industrialized' or 'modern' cities, or as the spatial consequence of socio-economic underdevelopment according to the ideology of the writer. What is not disputed, is that such cities are fundamentally different, qualitatively and quantitatively, from the typical industrialized, capitalist city of the West with which they are so frequently compared. For example, the growth of cities in the United States and Western Europe during the 19th century took place at a time of structural transformations in the rural sector which led to the displacement of surplus agricultural labour when there was an increasing demand for such labour by urban based industry. There is little doubt that technological innovations based initially on labour-intensive methods provided the capability of meeting demands from greatly increased domestic and international markets in a way that dispersed rural-based sources of production would have found extremely difficult to achieve. Consequently, the economies of scale and concentration led to the creation of large factories and attendant workers' housing which characterized — and frequently still characterizes — the growth of the European industrial city.

So much is well known. What is seldom investigated is the relationship between the growth of such specific urban forms and the sources of their economic power. Some studies imply that cities generate their own surplus by the simple diversity and abundance of their products and that these surplusses are used for further growth (1.3). Yet this begs the question of the original organization involved and also fails to explain the complex relationships whereby resources can be obtained from one region of the world for processing in one specific city, in order to be re-exported abroad again as finished goods, as was the case of Manchester in the 19th century (1.4). Obviously, it is more than possible that there existed a link between the ability of Manchester to absorb such rapid increases in its working population and the expansion of trade due to the success of British colonialism and the captive markets which it provided. It is only recently that this 'colonial connection' has been studied, in spite of the obviously vital implications for the analysis of the historical link between industrialization and urbanization which it implies. In view of the lack of an alternative theoretical framework, the forms of urbanism analyzed in the wake of the Western industrial and urban revolutions slowly acquired the status of a universal norm.

Thus a myth has been generated about the Western industrial city — to name but one specific form of urbanism — which assumes it to be the outcome of a primarily regional or even a self-contained process of growth, absorbing surplus rural labour and putting it to more productive activities. The evolution of a large-scale service sector is assumed to be a progressive factor in such a process because of the specialization of the services provided, and the support they provide to the productive industrial sector.

Compared to this conventional image, the typical 'Third World City' is at the opposite end of the spectrum. Located in regions of even greater agricultural surplus labour than was the case with their 19th century Western counterparts, they have manifestly failed to develop an adequate industrial base to absorb even a modest proportion of the rural urban migrants who increasingly arrive in their midst. Instead, they create a marginal surplus as the result of limited capital-intensive industrial activity, (which is frequently foreign owned), combined with a mass of small-scale cottage industries. Whilst the former may produce goods of extremely high quality, they are usually geared more to the consumption patterns of a small middle class than to the creation of productive industry or a reinvestment of capital. The limitations established by this restricted source of surplus production are to some extent cushioned by the existence of a large-scale service sector into which a high proportion of the urban population are absorbed. This service sector, however, is very different from that of the typical industrialized city, in that it is characterized by relatively low levels of differentiation and technical expertise and consists primarily of petty traders, temporary labourers and unskilled artisans.

Clearly then, we are dealing with two very different types of urbanism, neither of which necessarily constitutes a complete typology. (In a number of writings, Pahl and others have noted the need for distinct theoretical frameworks in order to make possible the understanding of different types of city produced by varying social and economic systems (1.5)). That the Third World city therefore justifies an appropriately distinct theory cannot reasonably be doubted, especially since all the evidence of rapid growth rates leading to populations in some conurbations in the region of twenty million people or more, are frequently discussed. It is vital that we know much more about the nature of the processes generating such rapid urban growth and the ways in which it manifests itself, if we are to translate more relevant theories into a framework which can lead to action of a type which will be socially just and economically feasible. There is very little time in which to achieve this if current projections regarding available energy and food resources are to be equated in any meaningful way with increasing population (in both urban and rural areas) in some parts of the Third World (1.6).

Before it is possible to undertake such an analysis, however, it is essential to outline briefly the historical factors which have conditioned the evolution of contemporary urban forms, their associated socio-economic structures and their urban-rural context. This analysis makes certain assumptions which need to be stated at the outset. It is considered, for example, that the increase in economic growth in certain parts of the world during the latter part of the 19th century and the similar creation of underdevelopment in others is not unrelated; in fact an attempt will be made to show from the existing literature that the achievement of 'development' or more accurately economic 'take-off' was an integral consequence of the creation of underdevelopment and that they should be considered as mutually supportive rather than exclusive processes (1.7).

The starting point for this analysis, therefore, will be the growth of cities at historical phases which are critical in the evolution of such development or underdevelopment, and this is taken as being coincident with the establishment by Western Europe and North America of the international trading structures and their associated metropolitan economies. This approach does not draw what may, justifiably, be considered as a necessary distinction between the various forms of colonialism and other equally critical factors such as dependency, economic and cultured colonialism or imperialism. However, since the central objective of the study is to concentrate on the impact of foreign influence over societies and economies as they operate at the urban level, the reader is recommended to refer directly to the literature specifically concerned with this subject. For the present purposes, colonialism is therefore intended to represent the most extreme, but not untypical, form of foreign intervention and control of other countries or regions. Since this is closely linked with the parallel growth of colonialism, the latter has been taken as a convenient guideline. Changes in the status of many Third World countries since achieving independence are therefore seen as constituting a logical consequence of previous phases. This analysis is not, of course, new in itself, but it has yet to be fully explored in terms of the analysis of urbanization and urban growth in the Third World. If it is a valid concept, our understanding of the Third World city may require considerable revision with an equal effect on the study of housing.

## 1.2  Historical Factors

### 1.2.1  Pre-colonialism

Many of those regions and countries which are, today, generally accepted as underdeveloped have achieved remarkably high states of economic and social development at earlier stages in their history and were themselves in control of large areas of neighbouring regions; the old civilizations of South and Central America are obvious examples.

Unfortunately, however, the lack of adequate or reliable data for periods preceding the 19th century makes it extremely hazardous to infer details about spatial distributions of population or about the nature and extent of urbanization. It is evident that settlement patterns associated with this period ranged from fully developed metropolitan centres to small isolated villages and even included a large number of nomadic tribal societies. Generally, however, the number of urban settlements was remarkably small (1.8) and most countries were essentially agricultural in their economic base. Naturally, the architecture and technology varied according to the climate and social structure of each area, but groupings of individual units would be associated with what Gideon Sjoberg identifies as the 'pre-industrial city with its clearly defined social groups but mixed land use patterns' (1.9).

A good example of such a country can be found in the case of India. (In this context India refers to the Indian sub-continent, since contemporary national boundaries in the region are a modern innovation. Although there was a clear distinction between areas ruled by the Moghals and the Hindu Kingdoms in the South, both groups were, or became, indigenous, whereas the British involvement did not follow this pattern.) Prior to contact with European traders, India as a whole was an exporter of many products to East Africa and elsewhere and was, of course, linked on the overland trade routes through to the Hindu Kush and to China and Europe, through which luxury products like silk and spices were transported. There was therefore a flourishing trade link in existence which integrated parts of the economies of many Asian societies by providing their elites with goods which they could afford and which led to the development of sophisticated labour-intensive industries producing high-grade products for domestic and export markets.

Settlement patterns naturally reflected both this trading and productive pattern and also the priorities of various dynasties. Cities therefore existed either as productive and processing centres, such as Dacca; served main trading routes, such as Lahore; were centres of political power such as Delhi and Fatehpur Sikri; or grew up around places of pilgrimage. Since the trading routes were mainly overland, cities whose economic base depended upon them were generally located at strategic points for the interchange of goods heading for different locations and similar criteria applied to political centres. Places of pilgrimage, however, were less predictable in their location and need not be considered together with the other types, especially as their permanent population was often relatively small and was only swelled for specific occasions.

Indian cities therefore expressed a coherent order which was the result of internal regional factors, in which the achievements and products of the socio-economic system were re-invested within the area. No doubt there were varying degrees of exploitation by cities of the rural areas and this may have become harsh on occasion; the general rule, however, was for surplus produced in the area to be reinvested and not exported. There is no reason to suppose that early trading patterns with European countries to any significant extent impeded or threatened this process of internal growth. On the contrary, the Moghals appear to have regarded such trade as mutually beneficial for many years.

Another example of an internally generated and sustained growth process in what is generally acknowledged as an under-developed region is that of West Africa. As Weeks has demonstrated (1.10), both Ghana and Nigeria had developed dynamic economies which adapted in a positive (i.e. income-increasing) manner to the expansion of world trade during the 18th and 19th centuries. A cash economy had developed and was well able to exploit the benefits of international trade for internal development. Mabogunje (1.11) has shown that such internally generated economies produced a large number of dynamic and socially cohesive urban settlement patterns.

Unfortunately, there is a shortage of studies on pre-colonial economies and settlement patterns which makes it difficult to extend such an analysis. It is interesting, however, that both these examples indicate that prior to the influence of external forces, these regions were flourishing and dynamic. How, then, did they start on the path which was later to lead to under-development and their contemporary difficulties?

## 1.2.2  The Impact of Colonialism

A simple but useful answer to this question is provided by a number of writers who make the distinction between trade and control (1.12). Thus, whether a country was incorporated into a colonial structure *or not,* its penetration by expanding European capitalism generally, became a major liability. Colonialism was often necessary in stabilizing a situation of complete dependence, and where it did occur it was perhaps the formal recognition of the new relationship between the metropolitan centre and its dependency, thereby implying the additional existence of administrative, legislative, military and social control. Colonialism remains, therefore, a convenient if loose term for the analysis of historical processes which linked the growth of European and later North American capitalism with the creation elsewhere, and to varying extents, of under-development (1.13). This structural transformation usually began in modest ways with the establishment of trading ports and agency houses, though in the case of the Spanish intervention in South and Central America force was employed from the outset.

Such a process has perhaps been most fully analyzed in the case of Central and South America, where a number of writers have challenged Western interpretations regarding the rise of capitalist economies and their relationship to those of under-developed countries. Whilst acknowledging that contacts between the two did not occur in a uniform manner, Furtado, for example, claims that within the newly dominated countries, the result was always the same and hybrid structures were created, part tending to behave as a capitalist system, part perpetuating the features of the previously existing system (1.14). He continues, 'the capitalist enterprise penetrating into a previously inhabited region with an archaic *(sic)* economic structure, does not become dynamically linked with the latter, for the mass of profit it generates does not become integrated into the local economy' (1.15). In an analysis of the relative degrees of development throughout the Americas, Frank goes further and claims that the 'super-exploitative character of European capitalism ensured that the greater the wealth available for exploitation, the poorer and more underdeveloped the region today and the poorer the region was as a colony, the richer and more developed it is today' (1.16).

In Africa, the situation has been subject to less comprehensive analysis, but such studies as have been undertaken arrive at similar conclusions. Weeks, for example, has observed how local dynamic responses to the expansion of the world trade in Ghana and Nigeria were eroded and eventually suppressed by foreign interests. He argues that contrary to popular Western assumptions, both economic growth and urbanization had started well before the arrival of foreign traders. He states that thousands of workers migrated from North to South to work for cash wages in cocoa and kola farms of coastal Ghana and western Nigeria every year during the 19th century and earlier, but by 1890 British bureaucrats and businessmen were said to be complaining of the lack of labour and attributed the shortage to 'the African's cultural or racial characteristics' (1.17), though he quotes Hopkins (1.18) to show that in fact this was more likely to be due to the low wages offered and the appalling working conditions. The point of Weeks' argument is, however, that rather than modernizing the African economy as has been claimed, such intervention represented a straightforward process of transferring control of lucrative trade from local to foreign hands, and that this was achieved by restricting the commercial fields into which indigenous businessmen could operate, and more importantly denied them access to colonial metropolitan markets, administrative favours and international financial institutions, and inhibited links with shipping enterprises (1.19).

A further example can be cited in the case of India, where several writers, including Marx (1.20), have described how the Indian economy was transformed from an exporting to an importing one and how this was eventually made dependent on that of Britain.

With the installation of railway links between raw material producing areas and the ports of Bombay, Calcutta and Madras, the way was open at an early date for the rapid exploitation of India's resources (1.21). The expansion of the cotton trade in particular occurred at great speed and jute also became in great demand in Europe. (An additional incentive to such investment and increased production, especially of cotton, was the outcome of loss of exports from North America at the time of the Civil War). By 1847 Bombay employed 2000 dockworkers and grew rapidly. This was because Indian unprocessed cotton goods were being increasingly sent to England for processing, following the virtual exclusion of processed goods from the British market. They were then made into twists and finished goods and re-exported to India where they saturated the market and were able to undercut the price of locally produced articles. This induced dependence had therefore directly contributed to the development of economic and in particular industrial growth in Britain and made possible the ability of its manufacturing cities to absorb surplus agricultural labour, whilst at the same time destroying the handloom and other indigenous industries in India and generating a state of underdevelopment from which the sub-continent has never recovered.

If these examples are acknowledged as containing an element of the reality of this process, many areas of the world which have *become* underdeveloped can be seen to have arrived at that state not merely because of their economic exploitation as such, but because they contributed materially to the economic growth and development of their exploiters. In other words, as Bernstein has noted, 'the analysis of underdevelopment is inseperable from that of development' (1.22).

It would be incorrect or naive, however, to suppose that the international flow of resources and rewards which characterized this process, operated exclusively at the national level. Such a macro-economic analysis fails to explain how such a situation was maintained in a relatively stable form for many years, or why such countries have experienced obstacles to development after achieving national independence. It is therefore necessary to examine briefly the internal or domestic transformations which resulted from colonialism and their effect upon such dependent countries.

The importance of this 'internal' factor is the subject of a rapidly expanding literature which focusses primarily on the Latin American experience, where it is now commonly regarded as a major element in the maintenance of dependency status, especially in its more recent periods. Such a development can be seen in the reaction to the early work of Frank, who has been criticized by Santos for failing to acknowledge the extent of internal transformations and for arguing that 'the capitalist system arises like a central star which exploits a system of satellites and sub-satellites which in their turn exploit those lower down in the system of internal exploitation linked to the international system' (1.23). Santos concludes his summary of Frank's thesis with the view that 'the process under consideration, rather than being one of satellization as Frank believes, is a case of the formation of a certain type of internal structure conditioned by international relationships of dependence' (1.24).

In reply, Frank himself has acknowledged other critics who have argued that it would be more accurate to state the relations of exploitation in terms of social classes. In defending his position in a later work, he refers to previous emphasis upon just such an approach and elaborates it at some length (1.25).

The increasing recognition of internal transformations effected by externally generated processes, goes a long way towards explaining the ability of metropolitan powers to maintain political stability with relatively limited manpower. Although such a process was by no means restricted to colonial states, it is in the colonial system that it could be seen at its most extensive form in the creation of new social classes, which were often the product of intermarriage or inter-breeding between settlers and the local population. Whilst their creation was rarely official policy, such groups served the valuable functions of acting as intermediaries between colonial representatives and the local population and were encouraged to identify closely with their metropolitan heritage through the system of education and job opportunities which were open to them. Thus, the increasing differentiation of social classes served to maintain social friction and reduce the possibility of the indigenous population uniting in opposition to the representatives of the colonial power; Davis has provided an illustration of Spanish policy in this respect (1.26). This was not, however, the only means of maintaining social and political control, though it was perhaps the most obvious. In many regions, such a policy was complemented by the elevation of existing social groups to positions of privilege and leadership which effectively compromised their interests between their own society and that of the metropolitan power. Rodney (1.27) illustrates the lengths to which British administrators in Africa went in order to win the loyalty of tribal chiefs in areas under colonial control, whilst the patronage of the Indian royalty extended by the Raj, virtually rendered it incapable of acting as the focus of discontent or revolt. Colonial policy frequently varied between these and other methods, or encouraged both or all at the same time according to circumstance.

Whilst such analyses have advanced our understanding of the historical origins and socio-economic consequences of colonialism, the same cannot be said however, for the analysis of urbanization and urban growth. It is not uncommon, for example, for major texts on this subject in underdeveloped countries to restrict discussions of historical (and in particular colonial) aspects to a paragraph or two and to then dismiss them in summary fashion. By omitting full analysis of the impact of colonialism on urban settlements, it has consequently become difficult to explain how urbanization in 19th century Europe was achieved and similarly to understand the reasons for the extreme variations from this situation in contemporary patterns. Yet if it is accepted that colonialism contributed to economic expansion and therefore to industrialization and urbanization in Europe, it would seem irrefutable that the industrial cities which grew at this time were greatly indebted to colonial sources for their raw materials and to colonial markets for their produce. Many writers would appear to argue that it was either technological innovation or some internally generated dynamism that has been responsible for the particular urban structure characterized by Sjoberg as the industrial city (1.29).

It is hardly surprising that such a myopic and a-historical perspective fails to impress, or that it has been any more convincing in analyzing urbanization in underdeveloped regions. There are signs, however, that the 'colonial connection' is slowly becoming recognized as a major force in the generation of settlement patterns which had a specific historical function and which have since become the basis of urban growth throughout the Third World.

In one of these studies, Weeks relates the socio-economic impact of colonialism in West Africa to an analysis of the changes it induced in the forms of urban growth. He claims that these took one or two basic forms, the first of which is called a 'colonial urban transformation', defined as the situation wherein foreign bureaucracy and enterprise were imposed upon a pre-colonial area and by its control transformed the process of urbanization, and the second of which he terms a 'European urban creation' wherein 'urban areas grew up in an environment without any significant degree of urbanization in pre-colonial times' (1.30). He cites examples of the former as Lagos, Ibadan and Kano in Nigeria, Mombasa in Kenya, Zanzibar in Tanzania and most of the cities in North Africa, whilst the second includes Jos and Port Harcourt in Nigeria, Nairobi in Kenya, Lusaka in Zambia and Dar-es-Salaam in Tanzania. Weeks goes on to argue that in the former case, urbanization proceeded in a context within which the indigenous labour force possessed traditions of urban craftsmanship, commercial expertise and entrepreneurial skills which brought them into direct conflict with Europeans in trade, particularly import-export commerce. In such situations he holds that the advantages held by the foreign enterprises restricted the expansion capability of such areas, although those producing only for the domestic economy were less harmfully affected and continued to supply the increasing low-income population. In settlements created by the Europeans, the lack of a local craft industry and service sector, led to the importation of other ethnic and tribal groups from other regions, so that the unskilled indigenous population who migrated to such settlements were unable to fill vital economic roles and these niches were occupied by Asians and other imported groups (1.31).

This disruption of existing settlements was also experienced in India, where Marx claimed that Dacca's population dropped from 150,000 in 1824, to 20,000 by 1837. (Because of problems of data collection at the time, these statistics must be regarded as highly unreliable, though there is little reason to doubt that the observation was valid.) Nilsson relates how Lahore, once occupying an area seven times that of its original size, quickly shrank back within its walls, as overland trading patterns were supplanted by maritime routes. New colonial urban settlements in India were generally of the 'urban creation' type and Bombay, Madras and Calcutta were all built up from the original residency towns *(sic)* established in the 17th and 18th centuries. Only Delhi, which was again to become capital in the early 20th century, can be considered as an urban transformation.

King has proposed a further typology for colonial settlements which is concerned with what may be termed 'composite' cities. By selecting Delhi as his reference he is, of course, dealing with a special case, in which the two exist side by side, yet in an uneasy relationship. Their combination is itself considered to constitute the 'ideal-type' colonial city (1.33). King holds the elements of this settlement to be, first, the area of the indigenous settlement, sometimes predating the colonial era and sometimes conforming to the characteristics of Sjoberg's pre-industrial city, or occasionally a small town or village which grew as a result of its proximity to the incoming colonial power. The second element was that of the 'modern' western or European sector, which he labels the 'colonial urban settlement'. A third element is also acknowledged as an occasional variant in which migrants brought in by the colonial power from adjacent regions would be accommodated. This last element is seen as particularly common in the Far East and in a modified form in parts of Africa (1.34). King's studies incorporate a wealth of empirical evidence, and he brings this to bear upon the various levels of urban development to explain the manner in which this colonial factor is all pervasive. Even individual house designs and methods of aggregation are shown to reflect, to an extraordinary degree, the rigid socio-economic structure which was developed to reinforce the new order (1.35).

In much of South America, South Asia and Africa, these socio-economic factors resulted in an equally fundamental change in settlement patterns with a reduced importance for cities in the continental interior and the growth of port cities, as overland routes were supplanted by maritime trade. Such urban growth was not generated, therefore, by internal processes, but was linked to the expansion of colonial or foreign trading interests — as these flourished, so did the cities. In this sense, such centres could be termed 'colonial urban dependencies' and represent a specific urban type which forms a major element in the initial growth of many contemporary cities throughout the Third World. No two cities were, of course, the same, and even those which manifested all these characteristics, were also much more than *just* that. In some cases, such as Bombay, continuous attempts were made by the colonial power to encourage local economic activity and this was later to become extremely successful. Even the more openly exploitative situations also manifested great diversity and often offered local groups greater opportunities than other economic sectors. This does not, however, change the main issues being discussed.

The 19th century can therefore be seen to have witnessed the growth of colonialism as one means of enforcing and protecting the benefits of international trade to the favour of a small number of expanding capitalist countries throughout the world. Whilst the general characteristics of this have been assessed in detail elsewhere, it is worth repeating at this point that the consequence of this creation of development and under-development, as integral aspects of the same process, can be clearly observed also in the analysis of urban settlements. The creation, during the process of under-development, of well developed urban systems, the high levels of infrastructure which they offered and the efficient communications networks of which they formed a part, made them a natural focus for later growth. We can now move in to examine how countries have been struggling with varying degrees of success to free themselves

B

from that past and what impact this process has had upon urban development and housing settlements.

## 1.3     Contemporary Processes

To the majority of underdeveloped countries, whether they had experienced direct colonialism or not, it became increasingly clear by the 1960s that the barriers to development or even to economic growth in its crudest sense of increased GNP, lay increasingly in the nature of international terms of trade and the limited opportunities which existed for increased exports or foreign exchange earnings. Whilst specific approaches to development varied enormously, their effect was distressingly similar; the majority of Third World countries were manifestly unable to even approach, let alone achieve, economic 'take-off', and continued to be tied to large-scale aid and international loans, many of which they could not hope to pay off, and which were frequently designed to benefit foreign corporations wishing to improve their flow of trade (1.36). In addition, the scope for initiating much-needed domestic reform programmes was reduced because of the control exercised by the loan-donors.

The situation facing many countries at present is therefore arguably worse that at any point in their history, in that the gap between the wealthy countries and the rest is larger and more visible, whilst the ability of the Third World to transform international economic structures has, with the notable exception of oil-producing countries, proved so far to be limited. It remains to be seen whether the recent emergence of Third World economic groupings may be able to reverse this trend in the future, but it will still be some considerable time before such changes can be expected to result in a radical improvement in the economies of most countries. Meanwhile, the socio-economic imbalance created during the process of underdevelopment persists. Indigenous elites who control large proportions of national wealth and resources, frequently also exert great influence over entrepreneurial and policy decisions and therefore strive to maintain and increase imbalances rather than reduce them. Such processes only serve to illustrate the claim by Frank *et al.* (1.37) that dependency patterns and underdevelopment operate across class as well as national boundaries.

With social and regional disparities large and increasing, the tendency has therefore been for trends which emerged in the 1950s to continue in the 1960s and 1970s, as both people and capital moved from areas of low productivity to those where the rewards were greater and more secure.

## 1.3.1  Demographic Factors

These imbalances have also become more extreme because they apply to more people. Reductions in mortality rates due to improved public hygiene and medical services have been so dramatic that there is now little difference between those of developing and developed countries (1.38), whilst there is little evidence of a widespread decline in fertility rates. Thus, overall population growth has been marked, though, as Demeny has shown, this can be achieved by various combinations of birth and death rates. In Latin America, the number of births per 1000 population (the crude birth rate) was 37 in the early 1970s and the number of deaths per 1000 (the crude death rate) was 10, yielding an annual increase of 27 people per 1000 or 2.7%. In Africa a similar growth rate of 2.6% resulted from much higher birth and death rates (45 and 20 respectively) whilst Asia, (excluding China) had a growth rate of 2.4% resulting from a birth rate of 39 and a death rate of 15 (1.39).

Similarly, the evidence does not indicate a substantial variation in fertility rates between urban and rural areas, so that the theory of urban living being associated with decreasing fertility cannot be supported (1.40). Population growth in both urban and rural sectors therefore continues at a high rate, though in some cases, the predominance of young families of child bearing ages migrating to the cities, indicates a change in the age structures within both rural and urban areas, which may well reduce the rural growth rate in the future. Any such change would still effect only a marginal reduction in the total increase of the rural population by the end of the present century however, and a reduction of fertility rates would equally have only a minimal impact on the potential rural labour surplus, since those who will be seeking employment within the next twenty years have already been born.

Two points require explanation regarding these data. The first is that in many areas, the actual rate by which urbanization is taking place is not only lower than is commonly envisaged, but in many areas such as India, it has virtually stopped. Thus the 1961 census in India indicated that the proportion of the total population living in urban areas was 17.98% out of a total population of 439 million, whilst in 1970, the proportion had increased by a minute 1.89% to 19.87% of a total of 547 million. The situation in Latin America, although varying to a great extent over time and from one country to another (not to mention variation due to changes in the definition of the term 'urban' and modifications of urban boundaries), also indicates that the rate of urbanization is less than generally assumed (1.41). It must be acknowledged that many African countries are, however, greatly exceeding these figures and are urbanizing at an extremely high rate, but this has to be seen in relation to the fact that they started to urbanize at a later period and the total population base is generally smaller (1.42).

Urbanization, then, is not the threat to the development or even the stability of the Third World that it is often assumed to be and many projections which indicate that the majority of the World's population will be living in urban areas in the near future, are open to serious doubt (1.43).

The second point which needs to be considered, however, relates to the question of scale already mentioned and the fact that the majority of the populations of underdeveloped countries still live in rural areas. Although the minimal 1.89% increase in urbanization in India over a period of ten years may represent a stabilization in the regional distribution of the total population, what it conceals is the absolute numbers involved. Thus, this small percentage increase effected an expansion of the total urban population from 78.9 million in 1961 to 108.78 million in 1971, representing an increase of 29.88 million or 37.83% (1.45). In South America, where both the existing degree of urbanization and its growth rate are higher (though where total populations are relatively much smaller), an increase in the proportion of urban to total population averaging 11% resulted in an absolute urban population increase of approximately 35.6 million between 1940-1960 (1.46). Finally, in Africa, the annual urban population growth rate was 10% for the twenty-year period 1940-1960 giving a total urban population of 19.4 million, an increase of 13.7 million (1.47).

Naturally, any attempt to extrapolate trends from these data must be done with great caution, as there is considerable variation in both the percentage growth rates and the numbers of people involved between one country and another, and even where these are similar, different conditioning factors need to be considered. However, it can be seen from the demographic evidence that Asian rates of urban population increase are generally lower than those of Africa and South America but that the numbers of people involved are much greater, yielding extremely high urban population increases throughout the Third World.

Another factor which requires mention is that the distribution of this increased urban population is not equally spread over settlements of each size. There is a tendency in almost all cases for the cities, (generally defined as settlements with populations in excess of 100,000), to attract a substantial proportion of rural-urban migrants and for the major cities (one million +) to exceed the medium sized cities and towns. Thus, the growth rate of urban areas is frequently proportional to their size and the scale of opportunities which they are able, or appear able, to offer. It is this phenomenon which has given rise to increasing concern over the fate of many large cities in the Third World and which has led a number of observers to project city populations of over 50 million as an inevitability within the near future (1.48). Whilst there is an obvious danger of projecting present trends into the future when dealing with such dynamic pressures and large numbers, even the most conservative estimates indicate the number of people living in the urban areas of the Third World as almost 1500 million by the year 2000 (1.49). The similarly increasing growth of rural populations provides an even more disturbing element in attempting to assess the implications of such trends upon the attempts at development or even survival within many regions. Already, several cities have exceeded a population level of five million and no slackening of their growth rate is indicated by the available evidence. These primate cities have therefore become a major feature in the complex socio-economic processes characterizing underdeveloped societies. They do not, however, always dominate growth rates completely, and in a number of countries, medium sized cities now appear to be expanding at an increasing rate. This trend has been interpreted as possibly being 'a compound of slower growth rates for large urban centres of the richer developing countries as urbanization approaches or passes the 50% mark, and still rising growth rates of big cities in countries at early stages of development, particularly those where total population growth rates have not yet "peaked" ' (1.50). In larger countries, regional variation in terms of economic development further compounds these factors; India, by no means one of the wealthier developing countries and one in which the population growth rate has certainly not yet reached a peak, nonetheless reflects a situation in which medium-size cities are growing rapidly, and where the largest city, Calcutta, confounds popular assumptions since its annual growth for the period 1960-70 was only 1.8% (1.51).

This more dispersed pattern of growth does not, however, generally extend to the smaller size of urban areas and it is evident that the major urban centres will continue to dominate the migration and population growth trends of the Third World for at least the near future, even though it may gradually be reduced (1.52).

### 1.3.2  Socio-Cultural Factors

Similar variation and complexity exist when considering the *manner* in which such processes operate within different parts of the Third World. Thus Mayer's study *Townsmen and Tribesmen* in East London (1.53) provides a highly relevant frame of reference for the analysis of urbanization in many parts of Africa, where tribal groupings have been overlaid by more recent economic class groupings, but by no means replaced by them, The complex change in peer group structures and the different levels at which tribal and other structures, such as the emergence of recent national status interact, can therefore be understood most easily in terms of the changes induced since tribal structures were all-pervasive. Thus the predominance of urban social groupings on a fragmented tribal pattern reflects the manner in which various sub-groups react to the socio-economic changes affecting them, and the environment in which they live and work. The lack of private land ownership in the tribal villages, where land is traditionally communally owned, has led to urban settlements of an almost village-like pattern (1.54) in which the builders often consider their actions as perfectly legitimate, because they are unaware of the concept of private land ownership which has evolved in the cities.

Such factors are not equally valid, however, in other parts of the Third World, nor do they operate in similar ways. The historical consequence of Spanish rule in many parts of South America, for example, has resulted in the presence of various mixed-race groups as well as the indigenous Indian populations, all of which are affected by, and react to, rural-urban dichotomies in different ways. It is still possible, however, to gain more understanding of these processes in terms largely of socio-economic class structures than would be possible in the case of Africa, as the large body of literature bears witness. The prevalent element of political and economic

motivation in many of the land invasions organized by the poor of
major cities throughout South America also supports such an
argument.

Since the literature on various South American countries is
perhaps more comprehensive than for any other part of the Third
World, there is a danger that the processes existing there may well be
inappropriate for other areas such as Asia where cultural factors are
arguably even more crucial to an understanding of the context of
urban growth than they are in Africa. Both McGee (1.55) and Dwyer
(1.56) have described and analyzed the impact of cultural, ethnic and
social forms in influencing the nature and extent of urban growth in
Asia. In his study of Kuala Lumpur, McGee indicated the way in
which the ethnic balance between Malayans, Indians, and Chinese
was maintained more or less intact throughout the main years of the
city's growth (between 1947-57), and that the basis of settlements
within the city also followed the lines established after colonial rule
had ended. Though class groupings did exist, they were as variations
within the ethnic domain.

This predominance of socio-cultural factors is equalled or
exceeded in the case of India, where rural attitudes and behaviour
have been conditioned for centuries by the interaction of religious
and social structures as expressed in the caste system. Although caste
is essentially a Hindu concept, it has also penetrated, to some extent,
other minority social groupings such as Christians and Buddhists
and has considerably affected the way in which the rural population
has reacted to the regional imbalances generated since
Independence. It has undergone significant internal changes and is
no longer necessarily the dominant conditioning force in the social
structure, but it still permeates domestic life and is particularly
pervasive in the rural areas (1.57). Whilst the 'vertical' segregation of
society is extremely rigid and exploitative in terms of benefiting
some groups more than others, it is mitigated by means of the
Jajmani system of caste patronage, by which low-caste villagers have
traditionally recognized rights to food, clothing and money at
religious festivals, and of work for which their caste may make them
suited. Thus the Wisers, in a sensitive study of village life in India,
found that although the upper caste exerted great influence over the
others, their power was enforced from below as well as above, since
any threat to the security and welfare of caste patrons was resented
equally by the lower castes as constituting a threat to them also
(1.58). The mutual independence of caste groups within the rural

areas has reinforced the fears of change on which the whole structure of rural life depends. Even methods of farming serve to reinforce this security consciousness (1.59).

It is hardly surprising, therefore, that one sees less evidence in India of the type of migration that characterizes the Latin American literature, or that the forms of urban growth which are generated within different countries reflect these distinctive socio-cultural influences.

### 1.3.3  Socio-Economic Factors

A major distinction between contemporary urban growth and that of previous periods is that levels of per capita income and resource provisions are significantly lower than those available during the 'urban revolution' of the 19th century. The scale and intensity of rural poverty combined with the effects of agricultural mechanization and forms of capital formation have ensured that a significant proportion of the ever increasing rural population will be unable to sustain itself within existing constraints, so that continued high urban growth rates can be confidently expected. Even the immediate introduction of changes in the structure of Third World economies is unlikely to lead to any early reversal of this trend, since rural development is an essentially long term consideration requiring widespread and sustained investment in order to achieve results.

Since the majority of Third World countries have evolved within mixed or free-enterprise economies, the locational behaviour of industrial and commercial units are a major influence upon the regional distribution of resources and opportunities. The existence of large urban areas, with the access to large market outlets, skilled labour, communications and infrastructural services which they provide, have proved a strong attraction to such activities.

The continued concentration of the small but influential private sector of industrial and commercial activity predominantly in the major or medium-sized cities (with the obvious exception of mineral extraction and forestry), has therefore resulted in these cities receiving a large share of limited capital investment. Consequently, they have also attracted a major share in the allocation of resources for services and infrastructure provision. With the existence of a limited number of major cities in many Third World countries, there has been a tendency, therefore, for new private sector industry to locate itself in them because of the relative ease with which connections can be made to the available services. For existing industry seeking to expand, it is also generally easier (in the absence of tax inducements or other incentives), to remain in the same area since the cost of moving existing plant to new locations would be high.

Private sector initiative is not, however, the only influential factor in the focus of resources in urban centres. The increase of national and regional government functions in either economic, administrative or political areas, has led in most countries to the expansion of public sector employment and investment. Although in a number of notable instances, this has led to the formulation and establishment of new national or state capitals (such as Chandigarh or Brasilia), in the vast majority of cases it has led to the growth of public sector activity in existing major cities.

Whilst the initiatives of these sectors by no means completely coincide, their combination has resulted in continued heavy investment being made in urban areas. Rural-urban economic imbalances have not been reduced as a result and average urban per capita incomes are generally several times greater than those available in the rural areas. Such indices, of course, do not reveal the complex variation in income distribution patterns in either rural or urban areas nor the fact that many aspects of rural life are outside the cash economy altogether, but the evidence suggests that even the lowest income groups are significantly better off in the cities.

Since it is generally in the existing major cities that incremental costs of additional activity are lowest and the opportunities for employment or profit greatest, it is these centres which have attracted the greatest number of rural-urban migrants. The combination of urban investment and incomes together with an increasing surplus labour- force in the rural areas, have both contributed to their further expansion. This process can be expected to continue until either the increased urban labour force is so great that widespread un- and under-employment reduces per capita incomes to the level prevailing in rural areas, or until rural employment and real per capita income opportunities match those of the city. The precedents for the latter are few and only China, Tanzania and a handful of others, can claim a degree of success. All the evidence therefore points to a continuation of existing high urban growth rates throughout the majority of Third World countries.

The phenomenal increase in urban populations that this has already generated has not been simply of a quantitative order, however, for with the numerical increase has come a qualitative transformation of the cities and their social and spatial structures.

Originally established during the period of colonial rule or the ascendency of foreign trading networks, these cities served the interests of the metropolitan economies, and in return became relatively prosperous. As such they provided a natural attraction for what was later to emerge as the domestic middle-classes. For these groups, the cities were islands of prosperity in a sea of rural poverty and 'backwardness', from which they invariably recoiled.

The inroads made by rural-urban migrants have served to challenge this situation and have drastically and permanently changed the socio-economic structure of the Third World city. This transformation was achieved in no small way by the growth of informal economic structures which were primarily labour-intensive and proved capable of generating modest but real incomes for a substantial proportion of the increasing urban population. Several writers (1.60) have amply demonstrated that the informal, service or tertiary sector as it is also termed, has evolved a complex relationship with both the urban capital intensive (formal) sector, and the rural 'bazaar' peasant sectors. McGee argued that the ability of this sector to act as a safety valve in absorbing rural-urban migrants, is heavily dependent on the close ties it has with the peasant sector and showed what happened if the capitalist system were to expand to such an extent that it effectively penetrated the whole economy and threatened this relationship. He cited pre-revolutionary Cuba and contemporary Puerto Rico as examples in which, 'capitalist penetration was so comprehensive that the areas left outside of the commercialized market economy were minute. The rural sector had been as thoroughly commercialized as the urban. By the early decades of this century, the agricultural sectors of both countries had been predominantly geared to capital-intensive cash-crop production in the company estates, which also controlled the commercial crop-growing peasants producing for the sugar centrales — the companies' "factories in the field" ' (1.61). Similar assessments by a number of authorities on this subject are also reviewed by Wilsher and Righter (1.62). McGee went on to claim that such a process was a major factor in breaking down the ability of the urban informal sector to cushion the otherwise extensive rural-urban imbalance and creating the pre-conditions for the Cuban revolution, and that the opportunity of migration provided the means of preventing such a situation in Puerto Rico. He concluded that 'the traditional urban service sector is heavily dependent upon the existence of a traditional rural productive base. When (and if) that base is penetrated and largely replaced by another system of production, the urban bazaar, lacking a course of supply for a great part of its activity, will be weakened if not destroyed as an indigenous involuted system. Secondly, the growth — or even the continuted existence — of the urban bazaar system in the Third World city, is not a self-contained process — it is ultimately dependent upon the activities and policies of the capitalist sector. Under conditions of continued penetration of the traditional structure — whether in the city or the countryside — the capitalist modes of production and/or appropriation, its capacity to assess labour would fall and the polarization between the modern capital-intensive sector and the unemployed urban lumpen-proletariat would come out into the open'. The origin and growth of the urban service sector can be seen from this and other evidence (1.63) to comprise a major element in the urban *and* regional economies of the Third World and have therefore achieved what no other sector has so far been able to, namely the absorbtion of large numbers of the urban population, many of whom have had little experience or training for non-agricultural activity of any sort, yet who have been able to adjust quickly to the opportunities available and acquire substantially greater incomes than was possible elsewhere.

Nonetheless, the interaction of these so-called dual-economies should not conceal the great disparity of opportunities and resources which exist *between* the rural and urban areas and within them. The fact that the Third World city is populated by a majority of extremely low-income people can be seen, from the evidence of studies in a large number of countries, to indicate that although urban per capita incomes, even amongst the lowest economic groups, are considerably greater than in the rural areas, there is an inequitable distribution within the cities which produces large-scale *urban* poverty. Thus, in India, a survey by Sovani shows the proportion of urban population with incomes in excess of Rs.500 per month in the four of the largest cities (Delhi, Calcutta, Bombay and Madras) is at the most 3.20%. Sovani also pointed out that a prominent feature of the income distribution is the very large proportion of earners in the lowest category of Rs.00-50 in most cities and towns and these figures do not include the un- or underemployed (1.64). Estimates also indicate that 78% of the urban population have a monthly expenditure of less than Rs.31 and for 48% it is less than Rs.19 (1.65).Whilst India may represent one of the most extreme examples of urban poverty, gross inequalities in urban income distribution can be found throughout the Third World.

### 1.3.4  Conclusions
The pressures contributing to contemporary urban growth in the Third World can now be seen to be so widespread and entrenched that any reduction in the near future must be considered unlikely even if radical measures were adopted. China, with the greatest degree of success so far in stabilizing urban growth and redistributing resources on a regional basis, has yet to fully control the size of major cities and this has been the outcome of efforts over many years. Countries without the commitment or controls available to China cannot, therefore, expect to be able to slow urban growth rates for some time, since there are limitations to the control which public sector initiatives can have upon the desire of private sector industry and commerce to concentrate in the main urban centres.

In this context, the movement of migrants to these cities represents a rational and resourceful process. Such has been the scale of movement, that the entire social, economic and settlement structures of cities have been transformed and even conventional concepts of 'urban' have been brought into question. We can now look at the evolution of such concepts to see what relevance they have in the present situation.


## 1.4     Western Theories and Third World Realities

Despite the extension history and influence that cities have exerted over man's development, it is only comparatively recently that they have received comprehensive analysis. Concepts evolved from empirically observed processes in one context have therefore not infrequently been applied to those in which they are partially or totally inappropriate. This consideration is particularly important at the present time, when urban growth is assuming unprecedented proportions and forms. These changes, and the urban pressures they have generated, have led to a widespread view that contemporary urban growth must be restricted and 'planned' if development strategies are to be achieved, a view which is traditional to those concerned with urban planning at either the theoretical or operational level. If this is so, it is vital that the nature of the processes to be 'planned' are fully understood and the implications of 'planning' and the concepts upon which it is based are explored.

Whilst the range of such concepts covers a wide spectrum, economic and social factors can be clearly distinguished as constituting two major bases upon which urban theories have developed.

### 1.4.1  Economic Factors in the Analysis of Urban Growth

The association of urbanism, and of cities in particular, with economic growth dates back as far as writers such as Ibn Khadun in the 14th century (1.66) yet comprehensive studies had to wait until the industrial/urban revolutions of the 19th century to gain wide currency. At this time, the obvious connection of industrial cities, in Britain and elsewhere, with economic development led to the general association of a link between urbanization (as defined in the demographic sense of an increase in the proportion of population living in urban areas relative to the total population), and industrialization, (similarly defined as the increase of population employed in industry, relative to the total population employed in other sectors), and between both of them and economic development. Whilst these characteristics could certainly be seen to co-exist in the 19th century, it does not follow that they are automatically interdependent, since industrialization is certainly possible without urbanization, and urbanization is conceivable without industry.

However, studies of the economic role of cities tended to regard them as the 'engines of economic development'. Thus Hoselitz (1.67) has argued that 'Commerce, financial institutions, industrial establishments, governmental bureaucracies and advanced educational and intellectual training facilities all require an urban climate in which to develop and flourish'. Sjoberg (1.68) has drawn a similar conclusion by claiming that 'Economic development, it seems clear, demands expansion of the urban sector', and McGee (1.69) has listed other writers such as Berry, Rostov and Hirshman, as supporting a similar approach.

That urban growth was invariably inter-related with the economic growth of Western Europe and North America during this period is perhaps self-evident, so that it was only a small step towards regarding it as a necessary *precondition* for economic development. Cities in the industrialized West therefore became associated in the minds of many analyists as 'natural' vehicles for development. Yet few of these writers acknowledged the influence of colonialism or less direct means of control in contributing to the ability of such cities to achieve sustained economic growth. Similarly, they gave scant attention to the fact that the benefits of rapid economic growth were far from equally distributed. The pressure of both structural and regional imbalances in the early stages of growth were acknowledged by writers such as Hoselitz, who considered them an acceptable price to pay, on the assumption that the overall growth that resulted would trickle down to the slower-growing, non-capital intensive sector (1.70).

The benefits afforded to the 19th century city through trade did not, however, trickle down fast or far. Manchester, widely accepted during the mid-19th century to be the model city of the future, nonetheless embodied great extremes of wealth and poverty as was studied by Engels in the 1840s (1.71). In some of the first great social and environmental studies to be conducted in major cities, Engels described in detail the working and living conditions of the industrial working class, yet as Harvey (1.72) was to observe over a century later, his work was bypassed by mainstream thought in sociology and other environmental disciplines until Harvey himself revived it.

If countries with the built-in advantages of Britain during the 19th century were unable to successfully distribute the benefits of economic growth to include the vast proportion of the urban population, or to resolve inequalities in housing provision, it is perhaps unreasonable to expect countries whose economies do not exhibit sustained growth to be able to do so. Yet despite the differences in context between 19th century Manchester and the contemporary Third World city as already discussed, it has become generally accepted that cities are synonymous with economic development and industrialization (1.73). Many countries made such factors the basis or at least, a major part, of their development strategies, though few were explicit about the exact manner in which cities should be developed to fulfil such roles, or the relationship between rural and urban areas that was desirable.

When the resulting forms of urban growth became apparent, they gave rise to a theoretical reassessment which attempted to explain the divergence between industrial urbanism and that occurring today in the Third World.

Central to these theories was the concept of 'over-urbanization'. This has been defined in a number of ways, but is generally accepted as indicating a higher degree of urbanization than is justified by the degree of industrialization (1.74). It was considered particularly relevant as a conceptual framework in Asian countries (1.75). In such analyses, the historical experience, of both urbanization and industrialization patterns in certain developed countries, are elevated into a norm and the relation between the two indices (of population concentration and economic activity) at different times are used as a measure of normality (1.76). These indices are then measured in terms of 'push' and 'pull' factors, in which migrants are considered to be pushed out of rural areas because of transformations in the agricultural sector, and pulled into the urban areas to expand the non-agricultural sector. In the normal, Western experience, these factors contribute equally to effecting a change of both occupation and distribution of population and at each stage the population in both sectors is considered to be gainfully employed.

In a state of 'over-urbanization', it is normally assumed that the 'push' factor becomes larger whilst the economic 'pull' factor of the cities is reduced, because of the lack of productive employment opportunities. Migrants are therefore assumed to move from 'low-productive agricultural employment to yet another sector marked by low-productivity employment' (1.77). It is a short step therefore to considering that if the cities are 'over-urbanized', and that this is due to 'excessive' rural-urban migration, then it is the migrants who are responsible for the pathological deviation from conventional European and North American norms. With urban administrations under great stress to cope with expanding major cities, this concept was naturally attractive and implied that if it was possible to 'contain' migration, the cities would be more able to fulfill their economic potentialities in generating growth. Increasingly widespread calls for the control of rural-urban migration have, in fact, emerged from many parts of the Third World, though attempts to actually implement such policies have been restricted by the lack of adequate policing and the fact that in some countries freedom of movement was enshrined within constitutions. In Indonesia, however, entry permits were at one time required for residence in Jakarta, though Wilsher and Righter (1.78) considered that its effectiveness was doubtful. And in Puerto Rico a temporary permit system was also introduced, but was eventually abandoned.

Perhaps more typically, however, the desire to consider migrants as the cause rather than the victim of regional socio-economic imbalances has led to an attitude of benign neglect on behalf of public and private agencies towards their needs and welfare once they have taken up urban residence. This will be examined in detail in a later section, but at this point we can note that despite the evident disparity in the regional contexts of urban areas in the 'developed' or 'underdeveloped' countries at any historical stage, the former has been used to formulate a model of what the latter should become. Yet as Sovani has indicated, 'the only reason for regarding the situation in a few developed countries as the norm for the rest of the world seems to be nothing better than the fact that today they are developed economies. But even if we judge other developed countries at some point of their development, we will find that they did not conform to this standard' (1.79). He goes on to argue that compared to the rest of the world, it would be more accurate to say that these countries are *over*-industrialized and *under*-urbanized, and concludes, 'that there is unemployment in the urban areas is true, but can the towns and cities remain dry islands of full employment and very high labour productivity in a sea of rural unemployment and under-employment?'

The role of migrants in the changing forms of urban development does not appear from the evidence to be as negative as the 'over urbanization' theories would indicate. The World Bank study of urbanization claimed that throughout under-developed countries, 'unemployment amongst migrants of a few years residence is generally noticeably lower than urban averages' (1.80), and detailed studies confirm this. Bose and Sovani (1.81) both provide data on employment rates for migrants and indigenous urban populations which indicate that the former are generally more gainfully employed. In Delhi, Rao and Desai (1.82) found that whilst 4.2% of the working force in resident households was unemployed, only 2.7% of the working force in migrant (excluding refugee) households was unemployed. In yet another study, Zachariah (1.83) has argued that migrant labour was a significant factor in the growth of Bombay.

Throughout the Third World, similar findings have been reported by World Bank sources (1.84) so that migrants have consistently shown themselves not only more capable of gaining employment than indigenous urban populations, but have succeeded in generating substantial savings which are used to supplement the incomes in the rural areas (1.85).

It could, of course, be argued that migrants do not gain employment immediately upon arrival in the cities and that until such time as they are able to do this they exist on rural savings which acts as a drain on rural income by transferring it to the city. This argument, however, overlooks the processes by which migration operates. Laquian, reported by Wilsher (1.86) emphasized that migrants were likely to arrive in the city as one of an already-established family or regional community. In Turkey, Kapil and Gencaga (1.87) found that complex rural-urban networks existed, by which migrants were channelled from one sector to the other and that these formed an integral element in the socio-ecomonic structure of Ankara.

It is now evident that kinship and other networks provide a highly efficient method of selecting potentially successful migrants and helping to establish them in the cities at little cost. A reassessment of popular assumptions of migrants as economic parasites reducing the development potential of the cities, would therefore seem to be more than justified. The problems of the expanding cities can, in fact, be more accurately related to the application of inappropriate and inadequate concepts based upon the Western experiment. As will be shown in Part 2, migrants and the urban poor have become a scapegoat for the failure of planners to formulate a more appropriate and economically more realistic basis for the development of urban settlements.

### 1.4.2 Social Factors in the Analysis of Urban Growth

With the notable exception of Engels and the work of social reformers like Robert Owen (1.88) the analysis of social and environmental processes, as they operated in the large cities of industrializing countries, had to wait until the early part of the present century. Much of the ground work on which these later ideas evolved, however, was based upon the sociological writers of the 19th century such as Maine, Durkheim, Tonnies and Weber. The basis of their various approaches was formed by binary constructions of polar opposites in the rural and urban areas, and used with each category (1.89). These typologies, whilst based upon qualitatively distinct criteria, did contain a common thread. They were all concerned with the theoretical and empirical implications of the growth of urban industrial society as it contrasted to the small-scale rural communities. In our present discussion, two points regarding Tonnies are of particular interest: the first is that he shared the romantic view of rural life as described by Comte to constitute man's 'natural' habitat and the second is that he conceptualized the social transformations involved in the creation of industrial urban society in the form of a polar type dichotomy (1.90). This approach was to be reinforced and elaborated by a number of later writers analyzing the urbanizing societies of Europe and North America and will be seen to feature prominently in the emerging writings on under-developed societies.

A further, major contribution to the study of social change in this context was that made by Durkheim, whose distinction between 'mechanical' and 'organic' solidarity was based upon the analysis of social relations resulting from changes in the division of labour. With the increased differentiation and division of labour in more 'advanced' societies, Durkheim held that the basis of social solidarity changed towards relations based upon greater interdependence and diversity and that as one type of solidarity advanced, so the other regressed (1.91). In this process, there was considered to be a threat of 'anomie', or a state of 'normlessness', as the individual was forced, by increasing diversification, to develop inhibitions towards social contact that significantly reduced social cohesion and could result in social breakdown. Durkheim's approach also exerted a great influence on later studies of social change in Western industrial societies and its use was to be even more widespread when studies of under-developed societies were initiated.

Of all these writers, one of the most influential, however, was Robert Redfield. Using the polar-type constructs of Tonnies and Durkheim, his studies of Yucatan in Mexico, were a major landmark in comparative analysis and established him as the author of the rural-urban continuum. No doubt this influence can partly be explained by the fact that of all theorists, Redfield conducted a large amount of field work which enabled him to relate his continuum to a practical methodology.

His typology assumed that folk of rural areas were 'small scale, isolated, inarticulate and homogenous, with a strong sense of group solidarity' (1.92). As with Comte, the limitation of Redfield's work is that it was constructed from a romanticized view of traditional village life and viewed the social structure of the city in a negative manner, in which old values died but were not replaced by others.

He considered, for example, that the villager's life has 'depth' whilst that of the urbanite is relatively 'shallow' (1.93), and that 'knowledge obtained by villagers more easily falls into an order than that of urbanites'. The possibility that such knowledge may be of a more restricted nature than in the city was not considered and Redfield even suggested that 'it is in the most isolated villages that the ways of living exhibit to their greatest degree an interaction of parts and inner consistency' (1.94).

Faced with the obviously complex and changing social structures of early urbanizing countries, it was not unnatural that cities appeared to maintain less social organization or 'inner consistency'; the fault was, of course, that instead of forming the basis for a new methodology, Redfield expanded the anti-urban bias latent in earlier studies and equipped later writers with the means of evaluating it. However, if Redfield gave less consideration to the urban end of his scale, the balance was amply made up by his contemporary, Louis Wirth. Although he also took the folk society as his datum, Wirth concentrated on classifying the urban characteristics. He was well aware that any worthwhile definition needed to be general enough to cover all types of cities — pre- and post-industrial, growing and dying, etc. — and that the manifestations of the 'urban way of life' reached out into the rural areas (1.95). However, his well-known definition of a city (1.96) as a 'relatively large, dense and permanent settlement of socially heterogenous individuals' was so general that it was difficult to use in any operational sense.

In formulating his theories, Wirth drew heavily upon the earlier work of Durkheim. He claimed that with the growth of urban life, 'whereas the individual gains, on the one hand, a certain degree of emancipation or freedom from the personal and emotional controls of intimate groups, he loses on the other hand, the spontaneous self-expression, the morale and the sense of participation that comes with living in an integrated society. This constitutes essentially the state of 'anomie' or the social void, to which Durkheim alludes in attempting to account for the various forms of social disorganization in technological society' (1.97). In the same paper, he developed the concept of 'social disorganization' as an innate characteristic of urban life and viewed cities from the position of a person new to them (1.98).

Wirth's eminence at a critical stage in the evolution of urban studies has perhaps made him susceptible to a critical reaction which imputes a sociological naivety into his work which Pahl rightly claims did not exist (1.99). However, despite the view of Wirth's sister that he greatly preferred cities to rural life as a result of childhood experiences (1.100), he remains responsible for the association of cities with social disorganization, for whilst he believed that conflict between normative values, which he held to be common in cities, represented a state in which society was *un*organized rather than *dis*organized (1.101), he claimed that disorganization *does* exist when the city is contrasted with 'the more or less integrated communities from which its inhabitants typically are recruited and with the relatively organized character of social life that obtains in the smaller constituent segments of the urban community itself' (1.102).

There is evidence that towards the end of his life, Wirth himself developed serious doubts about the validity of his typology (1.103), and Bannister has observed that 'whilst there is value in Wirth's hypothesis, it is a decidedly lopsided view of the city, rooted in the strained particularistic experience of American urban experience during World War I, the large scale South European immigration of the 1920s and the Great Depression' (1.104). Support for the concepts developed by Wirth was, however, an outcome of a series of urban studies undertaken in a city which particularly fits Bannister's description, Chicago. In the context of Chicago's growth during the 1920s and the increase in organized crime and social conflict, the school of sociological ecologists led by Park, Burgess and Zorbaugh, identified 'problem areas' which were regarded as major threats to the stability of urban society as a whole. Alienation, instability and high rates of criminality, disease and vice were observed, and Zorbaugh in particular (1.105), linked the existence of a physically 'run-down' environment with similar social characteristics and implied that slums threatened the general ethos of society by harbouring 'anti-social' (i.e. criminal and radical) elements.

The influence of such ideas pervaded Western urban sociology for many years and only recently have writers such as Pahl and Harvey drawn attention to the need for a new theoretical framework. Pahl, for example, has roundly criticized the descriptive work of the Chicago school and its failure to consider the socio-economic context of urban growth (1.106), whilst Harvey (1.107), in similar vein, has contrasted the work of Park and Burgess with the more critical analysis of Engels and lamented the stronger influence that the former had on the development of urban theory. Finally, by seeking to lay the foundations for a sociological definition of the city, but by omitting to analyse its socio-economic context, the Chicago School sought universality from what was a particularistic basis, and are guilty therefore of ethnocentrism.

This criticism becomes particularly relevant, of course, in the analysis of urban growth within societies in which the context is significantly different, such as socialist or underdeveloped societies. In the case of the latter, these essentially Western concepts immediately became applicable to the problems of extreme rural-urban dichotomies, rapid urban growth and social change and the unprecedented development of unauthorized housing settlements. If urbanism in the West represented a retrograde step from what was assumed to be man's 'natural' habitat, the community, and if the slum or the ghetto of Chicago was a pathological deviation from the alternative form of social solidarity that the city represented, it was only a short step to assuming that in the rapidly expanding cities of the Third World, these aberrations existed to an even greater degree. A pattern has therefore emerged which lays strong emphasis on the links between rural-urban migration, slum or 'squatter' housing and the increase of major urban problems. Such attitudes must be held to represent an element of middle-class revulsion at the lowering of environmental values and the impact of urbanization (1.108), and the social effect of urban growth has even been held to have corrupted life in the villages (1.109).

Avila, in his study of four Mexican villages (two of which were also those studied by Redfield), Lewis in his studies in Mexico, and Gusfield in his analysis of tradition and modernity in India, all drew conclusions that the rural-urban continuum was inadequate to explain the complex nature of urban social change and the effects this has on the rural areas and migrants from them. Their conclusions indicated a more positive relationship between social change and social organization, partly by showing how even so-called traditional societies are dynamic and continually evolve within themselves and in response to external influences, and also how migrant communities within large cities do not necessarily develop symptoms of 'social disorganization'. Avila, for example, found that the popular conception of villagers passively contemplating outside events was unjustified and that 'they have been active promoters and development seekers very much interested in working towards a better life' (1.110). He concludes that 'the first major factor that emerges — and in all likelihood the most important one — is that growth starts from within' (1.111). Even where external factors such as national educational expansion, land reform and changes in employment patterns combine to influence the internal organization of villages, it does not follow that disorganization results. Beteille, in his study of Sripuram, in Tanjore, has shown that traditionally factors such as caste, class and power networks tended to run in the same grooves, whereas the changes brought about by these external factors had, in the words of Dahl (1.112) produced 'a change from a system of cumulative inequalities to one of more dispersed inequalities', or in Beteille's own terms (1.113) replaced a closed social system with an open one.

Finally Gusfield (1.114) has pointed out the fallacy of associating traditional structures with rural areas and of urban culture as weakening them and he shows that, in many instances, change has in fact resulted in a strengthening of traditional ties and customs. There is increasing evidence also, that migrant communities in the urban areas manifest adaptability and organizational behaviour and studies by Lewis in Mexico City found that migrants maintained stable family life and 'traditional' forms of mutual support far more than was expected (1.115).

Lewis used the evidence from these and other studies in Tepoztlan, to expose both the suspect theoretical basis and ethnocentric bias of the rural-urban continuum and argued that 'the problem posed by Redfield, namely what happens to an isolated homogenous society when it comes into contact with an urbanized society, cannot possibly be studied in a scientific way because the question is too general and the terms used do not give us the necessary data' (1.116).

The emphasis of research until the early mid-1960s was therefore to a large extent concentrated upon eroding or refuting the basis of the rural-urban continuum. If Lewis assisted in hastening its demise as a generally accepted theoretical framework, he did, however, propose another concept which was to prove almost equally difficult to evaluate (and therefore to confirm or refute). In the introduction to the *Children of Sanchez* (1.117), he associated poverty with a stable and persistent way of life passed down from generation to generation along family lines. His term 'the culture of poverty' which this represents, has now become as accepted a term in sociological research as were the earlier concepts of Wirth and Redfield. Whilst he associated this with 'modern' nations (1.118), his definition is broad (or vague) enough to include the detribalizing countries of Africa and the 'courtyard culture' of migrants in Mexico City, so that it can only be assumed that the concept is also applicable in any country undergoing rapid urbanization. This is inevitably what followed and a large number of studies sought to develop or test the concepts in a large range of contexts (1.119).

That cultural traits associated with cycles of deprivation exist is undoubtedly true, but by emphasizing this cyclical nature it fails, as Mangin has observed, to account for change in a situation where change is the norm. It also implies that although migrant and other low-income sections of the urban populations manifest 'stable and persistent' social organization, it is limited to ensuring the survival of the group and is insufficient in itself to induce upward mobility or a measure of social dynamism. Thus as Mangin states, the Lewis concept is more sophisticated than the social disorganization thesis, but still assumes that the lower class, the poor and the blacks are a deviation from an urban norm and that it is therefore they, rather than the more powerful part of the culture or the social structure, that need to be changed (1.120). Whilst Lewis was therefore largely responsible for leading urban sociology out of a theoretical impasse, he made it easier to continue regarding migrants as 'marginal or unurbanized' groups and therefore to perpetuate their present predicament by reinforcing existing prejudice against them.

At about the time Lewis was writing, major changes in urban growth processes were taking place within both developed and underdeveloped societies. These consisted in the accelerated trend towards suburbanization in many economically advanced countries, and in the increasingly rapid concentration of population *within* the major urban areas of the Third World. Ethnocentric concepts, evolved from the experience of the industrialized countries, were therefore increasingly inapplicable and the work of Mangin and Turner provided seminal contributions towards creating an awareness both of this different context and also of the social and economic roles that migrants and the other sections of the poor played in urban areas. In his studies of Lima, Mangin noted that there were strong distinctions *within* the urban poor and that the self-generated settlements of squatters exhibited much greater social cohesion and morale than inner city 'slums'. More recent evidence indicates that even Mangin's studies have seriously underestimated the degree of social organization existing in slums and squatter areas. A number of case studies in various locations have all shown that, even in the inner-city areas, inhabitants have acted in rational and resourceful ways to safeguard their interests. Chana and Morrison, for example, found that in Nairobi squatters in the Mathare Valley area were able to achieve a high degree of community organization to offset the exploitation of middle and lower middle class groups who were building hutments for rent at inflated levels (1.121), whilst in Zambia, Andrews, Christie and Martin (1.122) have indicated not only that social organization existed to a high degree, but that the environment created, formed an appropriate and recognizable structure for the way of life it supported.


## 1.5   Conclusions — Urban Growth and Settlement Patterns


The development of theory in both social and economic aspects of contemporary urban growth has now, to a large extent, eroded the worst excesses of ethnocentric concepts evolved previously within Western contexts. Interestingly, this process can be seen to have initiated new perspectives within the main body of Western theory itself (1.123) and thereby given it new vitality. Unfortunately, however, this process has made only limited headway within urbanizing countries in changing traditional assumptions regarding the negative economic role of migrants and the existence of social disorganization or 'anomie'.

Such views are held primarily by influential middle class groups to whom rapid urban growth is seen as a threat to their own interests and to society as a whole. Such views have not led, however, to a re-evaluation of the role of cities within the development process and their association with economic growth is still largely accepted; it is the *form* of growth which is the focus of critical attention, and which is seen as 'unplanned', 'chaotic' or 'uncontrolled'. Thus the anti-urban bias of early Western theory (not completely refuted by Lewis or even Mangin) has been transferred into an anti-migrant bias at an operational level. Proposals for resolving the problems this is seen to create, therefore, frequently involve the creation of 'ring' towns or 'satellite' cities (1.124). In many cases, such programmes are supplemented by attempts to initiate rural development or expand existing towns or small cities, so that agricultural and non-agricultural sectors can be integrated and the rural population provided with economic opportunities without having to move location. This approach to decentralization, however valid in itself, generally pays inadequate attention to the high cost of providing the necessary infrastructure on a sufficient scale to offset the attraction of cities (1.125) and consists essentially of an attempt to reduce urban 'surplus' labour rather than to provide viable rural alternatives; in short to decentralize labour without a similar decentralization of capital or other investment.

Such approaches are occasionally justified because of assumed prohibitive costs of servicing large urban areas. Thus, India's fourth Five Year Plan states 'beyond a certain limit, unit costs of providing utilities and services increase rapidly with increases in the size of cities. In the ultimate analysis the problem is that of planning the spatial location of economic activity throughout the country. A beginning must be made by tackling the problem of larger cities and taking positive steps for dispersal through the suitable creation of smaller centres in the rest of the area' (1.126). This recognizes that industrial growth need not necessarily result in urban growth and that the objectives of industrialization and decentralization are theoretically consistent with the need to generate growth and distribute its benefits as widely as possible. The assumptions regarding urban costs on which the need for decentralization is based are, however, highly debatable. It is in fact an open question as to whether any such costs exist or, if they do, whether they are offset by increased benefits. There is little empirical data on which to confirm this, (none is offered in the Plan document), and what recent evidence is available indicates that no such conclusion can be drawn (1.127). If this is so, it would appear that the motive for decentralization as expressed, springs from a bias against urban growth at least as much as from a desire to benefit rural areas.

This is not to detract in any way from the urgent need for radical and far-reaching programmes of rural development. It does indicate, however, that in a market or mixed economy (and even to a certain extent in socialist, command economies), that growth is inevitable, even if urbanization itself is not. It also highlights the very real problem facing regional planners and policy makers regarding the means of financing programmes to reduce regional economic imbalances and achieve rural development (as opposed simply to rural growth). If, as seems likely, investment per unit capital yields a higher and quicker return in urban areas, it is naturally tempting to invest scarce infrastructural and other resources in these areas, in order to generate the surplus necessary for policies of decentralization. The extent to which this should then be reinvested in urban areas or used for regional development is, of course, a central dilemma which can only be resolved in individual instances. It is possible that public sector inducements can lead to voluntary dispersal of economic activity in the private sector through forms of tax concessions, licensing controls and land grants, etc., and many examples of such schemes can be cited. It remains doubtful, however, to what extent they can effect a significant redistribution of non-agricultural activity, since in such economies the capacity of public sector initiative to control the locational behaviour of the private sector is limited by its inability to control capital formation (1.128).

Policies to restrict the growth of the major urban areas through rural development or more dispersed urban growth must be seen, therefore, as having limited potential within the context of most developing countries. Unless labour, or population, dispersal is matched by equal regional and social dispersal of capital and other resources, it will be impossible to resolve the fundamental problems of the rural areas or provide people with viable alternatives to urban migration. China, with centrally controlled economic planning and a long-term commitment to such policies, has made the greatest progress towards achieving this objective. Yet even here, the extent to which urban growth has been effectively controlled is by no means certain (1.129). If this is the case, the likelihood of such objectives being achieved in situations with a reduced commitment must be extremely limited.

Whatever development strategy is adopted, rapid growth of existing major cities can be predicted for at least the foreseeable future, particularly in countries with large rural populations. The scale and pace of growth therefore demands an appropriate theoretical framework if it is to be regulated. Yet the continued influence of theories based upon the historical or contemporary experience of industrialized Western countries has inhibited the formulation of such a framework and served the vested interests of a small proportion of the urban population. A theoretical duality has emerged which accepts the traditional link between cities and economic growth, but refuses to recognize the implications which this has in a situation of underdevelopment. Only when this is replaced by more realistic approaches will it be possible to initiate

economically feasible and socially just forms of urban growth.
Housing and settlement planning are a central element in any such
reassessment since they play a major part in assisting or restricting
the ability of people, particularly low-income groups, to contribute
to and benefit from the development process. With these criteria in
mind, we can now look at cities in more detail.

PART TWO
# Urban Development and Housing

# PART TWO
# Urban Development and Housing

## 2.1    Cities, Incomes and Housing

It is now possible to examine the various factors which condition the form of urban development within the major cities and the influence these have upon housing for the low income groups.

One of the most significant variables in terms of urban form is the distribution of employment and incomes in terms of the nature and extent of urban poverty. Employment patterns vary widely from. city to city and also with time. However, it is generally true that the inability of the small capital-intensive sector to absorb the available labour has created a dichotomy in employment patterns in which a small highly·skilled and well-paid group co-exists with a large semi- or un-skilled and low-paid group. Un- and under-employment is high and a recent World Bank survey indicates that, allowing for variations in definition, unemployment is more often above 10% than below and, in some countries, more frequently is over 20%.For large cities, the position appears worse than in the smaller urban centres and in some major African cities estimated unemployment exceeds 30% (2.1). Although the report indicates that the situation has actually worsened over the last two decades, it states that it is by no means clear whether it is any better in the rural areas, and quotes a recent ILO estimate that even allowing for a decline in participation rates, the total labour force of developing countries will expand by at least 25% between 1970 and 1980 (2.2), with particular concentration in the urban areas, so that the future does not offer much hope of an immediate improvement.

So far, one of the mechanisms which has enabled the already vast numbers of urban migrants to be absorbed into employment has been the growth of the service sector, but it must be an open question whether this will be able to absorb greater numbers without substantial encouragement. As has already been seen in McGee's analysis (2.3), the so-called economic 'dualism' represented by the modern and service sectors, is by no means as clear as was originally assumed and it now seems that they are in fact closely related. There remains a great disparity between them, however, in terms of incomes; as the World Bank study observed, 'average Gross Domestic Product (GDP) in the major urban cities may be three to five times that of rural areas with a somewhat lower differential for the smaller towns. Even allowing for higher prices in the towns, the gap is wide and on somewhat scant evidence, appears to be widening. A similar situation of polarization of resources has developed within the urban centres with a small and increasingly wealthy group separated socially and often physically from the poorer mass of the population . . . present trends and the pressures of population and labour force thus indicate a further worsening of income distribution during the near future at least. Sharp gains in the small modern sectors of both rural and urban areas will be paralleled by more rapidly rising numbers in the more traditional sectors.' (2.4).

The difficulty of obtaining reliable data on incomes and the impact of inflation on specific figures makes individual examples of doubtful relevance. However, the observation made in the World Bank study is confirmed in the case of India, where Sovani found the following pattern:

Distribution of Monthly Income of Earners in Different
Cities in India (2.5)

| Rs | Calcutta | Delhi | Hyderabad | Madras |
|---|---|---|---|---|
| 0-50 | 32.61 | 15.99 | 56.44 | 39.51 |
| 51-75 | 23.71 | 17.83 | 13.72 | 15.60 |
| 76-100 | 19.48 | 20.35 | 10.37 | 17.79 |
| 101-150 | 13.45 | 18.78 | 7.28 | 14.14 |
| 151-250 | 5.70 | 15.51 | 6.73 | 6.54 |
| 251-500 | 2.70 | 8.34 | 3.81 | 4.60 |
| 500 + | 2.35 | 3.20 | 1.65 | 1.82 |
| | 100.00 | 100.00 | 100.00 | 100.00 |

Since the figures do not include the unemployed, this imbalance would, therefore, in reality be increased even further.

Similar evidence is found in Turkey where Avcioglu has shown that 32% of the National Income is obtained by only 1.5% of the population (2.6), and in Nairobi similar disparities in income have been obtained by Tribe (2.7).

The extreme polarization in urban incomes that this and other similar data suggest, and the evidence that the situation appears to be getting worse rather than better, is one of the most obvious indications of the social and economic problems facing the major urban centres of the Third World. It is not, however, the only sign. There are also great inequalities in the distribution of resources, services and opportunities generally and these are possibly increasing still further, thus perpetuating themselves over generations and making it increasingly difficult for those in the low-income category to improve or even maintain their position. Harvey, in his study of the effects of external economies upon social processes and spatial form in urban systems (2.8), considers that certain groups, especially those with financial resources and education, are able to adapt far more rapidly to a change in the system, and he argues that these differential abilities to respond to change are a major source in generating and perpetuating inequalities. He concludes that differential disequilibrium in the spatial form of the city can thus redistribute income. In general, the rich and relatively resourceful can reap great benefits while the poor and necessarily immobile have only restricted opportunities. This can mean a quite substantial regressive distribution in a rapidly changing urban system, (2.9). In Harvey's estimation, the political, financial, locational and organizational mechanisms normally employed to regulate such inequalities, are themselves less open to influence by the less fortunate groups, so that they are unable to effect structural modifications in the distribution of real income, and public sector planning policies which could effect such changes, (particularly in the field of land use planning and public transportation) in order to improve accessibility to resources, generally tend to reinforce existing trends.

The socio-economic consequences of this analysis were originally considered in relation to the situation in developed countries, but the greater extremes in the differentials and the scale of urban growth in the Third World makes them even more problematic. In most major cities, ample evidence exists not only of extreme inequalities in the distribution of, and access to, resources and opportunities but in their perpetuation.

c

The large proportions of existing low-income groups are continuously being swelled by the arrival of additional migrants, the majority of whom are in the low-income category. Thus the existence of luxurious villas alongside large settlements of hutments, made from mud-brick or waste materials, is a typical phenomenon; in situations of great scarcity the provision of high quality services for some means the complete absence of them for many. Many writers have catalogued the scale and nature of deprivation.that exists and Dwyer (2.10) lists case studies from many countries of the Third World.

Since the shanty, slum or squatter housing areas (however these are defined) are increasing at a far greater rate than any other aspect of urban physical development, they are therefore becoming, or have already become, the dominant form of urban settlement (2.11). In Malaysia, unofficial estimates suggest approximately 35% of the population (representing 250,000 people) of the capital Kuala Lumpur, live in squatter settlements and even official figures acknowledge over 180,000 (2.12) and in Lusaka, one in every two of the population is a squatter (2.13), whilst Dwyer suggests that a fifth of the population of Rio de Janerio lives in favelas with poor levels of services (2.14). In Calcutta occupancy rates for housing indicate that more than two-thirds of the families live in one room *or less* (2.15), approximately 200,000 people live part, if not all, of their lives on public pavements without any shelter or public services such as water or sewerage, and an estimated 1.75-2 million people (equivalent to 25% of the population) live in one-storey hutments called *bustees* (2.16). In Bombay, over 600,000 people live in hutments (2.17) and even more live in *chawls,* or multi-storey tenements (2.18).

There is no need to catalogue further the extent of urban poverty and deprivation that exists. What is perhaps even more disturbing, is that despite such conditions people remain in the cities rather than return to their villages, because economic opportunities are generally worse still in the rural areas. It is in this context that the issues of urban development in the urbanizing world must be faced.

## 2.2    Differential Change in Settlement Patterns

With the cities experiencing such rapid growth and fundamental transformations of their socio-economic structures, their spatial forms have had to absorb new needs and pressures on an increasing scale. With great variations in their historical and economic context, it is obviously dangerous to generalize concerning the intra-urban relationship between social and spatial structures. The low density cores and high amenity values of many colonial cities, for example, contrast with the compact heterogenous character of many cities built in response to more indigenous needs. Even so, a number of factors have contributed to enable a tentative analysis to be made by contrasting these two types.

## 2.2.1  Egalitarian and Inequitable Frameworks

As was shown earlier, the spatial form of colonial cities frequently reflected the structure of colonial society and its relationship to that of the indigenous population. The administrative military and other services were therefore related to residential districts in such a way that easy and direct access was provided for the local elite, and decreasing ease of access (and of status) for the social groups lower down the hierarchy. As such, the colonial city in its extreme form is the example *par excellence* of the spatial reinforcement of privilege and the in-built discrimination against the less fortunate. It is particularly ironic that the actual *nature* of such cities with their low-densities, generous provision of services and facilities and garden city qualities are in part the outcome of liberal social philosophy within parts of colonial society itself. In Britain, for example, the atrocious living and working conditions of the industrial cities led reformers such as Ebenezer Howard and William Morris to evolve urban settlements in which all members of the population would have direct access to green open space, social services and employment, without suffering the squalor of the large cities. In their various writings, they laid the foundations for the early New Towns movement in Britain. In the colonial countries, however, such concepts were used to provide these advantages for the relatively small populations of colonial society and their servants and served therefore to reinforce their position of privilege.

When such cities, or others with similar large spatial inequalities in the distribution of resources, became the focus of rapid growth, however, the influx of low-income migrants led to large scale peripheral settlements of hutments. These accommodated people who sought work in either the small centrally located government or business areas, or in the high middle-income residential areas. In other cases, small groups of migrants moved into undeveloped pockets of land within the central areas and built settlements along railway lines, roads, or rivers, in positions that offered the minimum threat to local official regulations and maximized access to employment and other resources.

Nairobi, Lagos, Lusaka, Delhi, Quito and a host of other cities can be considered to have followed this pattern. As rural-urban migration gathered momentum and increased the numbers and proportion of the urban low-income groups, pressure on the inner city housing increased dramatically, creating high density, badly serviced areas adjacent to commercial districts and areas of middle and high-income housing. The consequent impact upon environmental quality, pollution levels, and provision of services

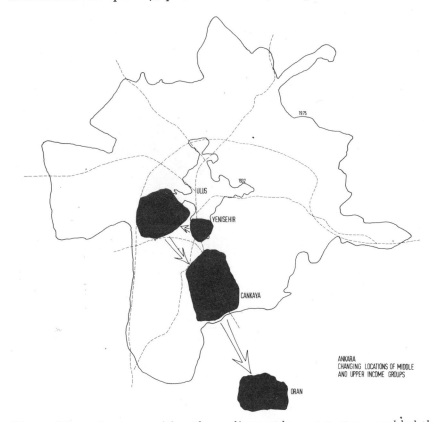

*Figure 2.1      In many cities, the earliest settlement pattern enabled the upper income groups to enjoy central locations and an attractive environment. As the cities have grown, however, these groups have moved progressively outwards from the city centres. This pattern can be seen, for example, in Ankara and in many other expanding cities.*

led, gradually, to the withdrawal of wealthier groups from their previously prestigious locations, towards new suburban locations free from overcrowding and deteriorating living conditions, but still having direct and easy access to the central areas. This trend was greatly assisted by the expansion of public and more especially private transport. Naturally, these groups were more able to meet the recurring costs of transport that were required, and Amato (2.19) illustrates how upper income groups in Bogota and Quito moved from the central locations they had occupied up until the 1930's into the then suburbs, by-passing middle income areas. As the cities continually expanded to encapsulate them, so these groups continually moved further out. Delhi, perhaps the ideal example of such processes, has witnessed the growth of large suburban areas for middle and upper-income housing, though the old centrally located bungalow compounds built for the British senior officials and Indian maharajahs, are now occupied by India's present political and administrative leaders. Similar processes also occurred in Ankara in the years following its growth as national capital.

The point is, of course, that the original urban form provided the affluent minorities with built-in advantages, and that when major changes were induced because of in-migration or other factors, it was the same groups who were most able to exploit the changes to their benefit, by using their capital to develop new areas in the suburbs and their influence to gain the required levels of servicing and communications to the centre. Less fortunate groups, however, were forced into living at high densities in the central areas where expansion of business or industry, or even the programmes of road construction, all threatened them with removal. Alternatively, they were offered subsidised housing in the suburbs at rents which, even when subsidies were heavy, generally proved beyond their means. Consequently, those who had sufficient capital, but who were denied access to officially approved housing because of high costs and standards, joined the movement to the suburbs and established large-scale settlements on the periphery of the urban areas on land which was unattractive to the more affluent. As studies in many parts of South and Central America have shown, the low-income population with stable employment have been able to organize autonomous settlements of almost urban dimensions in their own right on the urban peripheries. Whilst others have moved into housing in the old legally built areas of tenements or compound housing, or squatted in publicly owned pockets of land near the

Figure 2.2    The scale of many self-generated, low-income settlements in many parts of the Third World often exceeds the area of formally planned development. In Guayaquil, the suburban areas have developed out into the marshland of the River Guayas and access to housing is by a network of raised catwalks. As the settlement is extended the land is filled in and housing improved. (Photo by courtesy of Patrick Crooke)

centre. (In some older cities, the impact of the railways effected this transformation at an earlier stage in their growth.) It remains true, as Harvey has claimed, however, that the ability of middle and upper income groups to exploit changes in the urban system is much greater than for the poor, so then inequalities in the social and economic structure are reinforced by urban development, as determined by market forces and conventional planning policies.

Within cities of longer standing and developed to meet indigenous needs, the socio-spatial form usually exhibits a marked deviation from this and has adapted in different ways to the problems of urban growth. Although there are few studies of such cities, those by Mabogunje and Bray of Yoruba towns, by Fonseca of Old Delhi and Al-Azzawi of Baghdad, illustrate clearly the essential distinctions between them and the social and spatial segregation of the typical low-density colonial city. In the case of Old Delhi, approximately one million people live within the old city walls of Shahjahanabad, as it was known prior to British rule. The city is of extremely high density and has a mixture of land uses with specialized economic activities along specific streets, thus the silver-smiths, leather workers, brass foundries, dyers, and swordsmiths all had their own quarters and bazaars which have existed for several centuries. In a perceptive study, Nilsson (2.21) describes the early growth of the city and quotes Bernier, the 17th century traveller as observing that, in the spaces between are open shops where, during the day, artisans work, bankers sit for the despatch of their business and merchants exhibit their wares. Within the arch is a small door, opening into a warehouse, in which these wares are deposited for the night. The houses of the merchants are built over these warehouses, at the back of the arcades: they look handsome enough from the street and appear tolerably commodious within; they are airy, at a distance from the dust, and communicate with the terrace-roofs over the shops in which the inhabitants sleep at night. Scattered between these areas were a large variety of public buildings the Jama Masjid (Friday Mosque), other smaller mosques, hammam (baths), caravanserais, markets for grain, fruit, vegetables, salt, cattle and slaves, (2.22). As the later study by Fonseca (2.23) showed, the crafts developed under Moghal rule still exist and operate within a similar spatial context. Fonseca describes this as follows: 'The entire city may be described as a bazaar with peaks and dips as one moves from primary to secondary to tertiary streets. Retail and wholesale outlets, forming large agglomerations, are concentrated on primary streets, sometimes penetrating partway into secondary streets. Bazaars in secondary streets form smaller agglomerations and tend to specialize in single items, while bazaars in primary streets are more diversified in the items they retail. The actual production and storage of artifacts and other utilization items occurs in interior courtyards and alleyways away from primary streets — the exception occurs when workshops are immediately to the rear of shops fronting on the main streets. Thus, production, storage and service centres are either immediately behind the retail outlets, or a short distance away set into residential areas. A flow of merchandise is triggered by small groups of workers dispersed through the city. Production accumulates in the courtyards, moves in accretions down lanes in handrawn vehicles, or on the backs of doubled-over men, to distribution centres along secondary streets, whence it filters up to the bazaars. Wealth resulting from this production flows in the reverse direction completing the circle' (2.24).

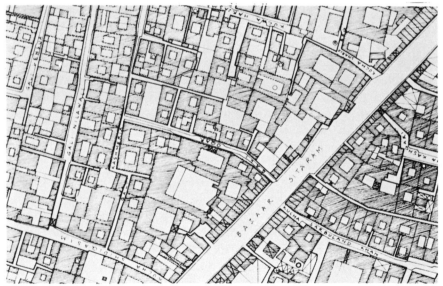

*Figure 2.3      The pattern of Old Delhi showing the way in which goods and people flow from one area of activity to another. Despite the high density, 25% of the ground area consists of courtyards.* (By courtesy of Rory Fonseca)

The high density and symbiotic character of this spatial and socio-economic structure therefore operates to the generally mutual benefit of all sections of the city's population. Social identity is assured through the association of occupational areas termed

*Figure 2.4   A chowk. Such spaces form an integral part of the social and spatial structure, yet take up a surprisingly small area.* (Photo by courtesy of **Rory Fonseca**)

*mohallas,* and even when an individual achieves upward social or economic mobility he tends to remain in his mohalla, or at least maintain strong links with it. With the city built at very high densities, small open spaces naturally assume particular importance and the series of *chowks,* which often consist of little more than a widening of the street, or a set back to accommodate a valuable shade-tree, become major social foci where tea-shops are located where old men smoke and chat and where children play (2.25).

The complexity and richness of this spatial fabric is admirably suited to the local climate (most main streets are oriented east-west to avoid direct sun and maximize local breezes), and the high densities reduce travel distances. It is therefore infinitely more advantageous to the needs of the poor, who can obtain direct and easy access to the same facilities and services as are available to other more fortunate groups and where the interaction between these groups reduces social polarization and maximizes cohesion. As Fonseca states, 'the indigenous city is attractive as a working example of a high density, self-contained community deriving its great strength from the fact that its spatial structure is a logical outgrowth of viable sets of social and economic rules governing group and individual behaviour. The charge that it is a slum is not without substance: parts of it are over three hundred years old. However, to equate the state of physical disrepair with the spirit of the community is political myopia, leading to endless conflict between the authorities and the community. The garden city environment of New Delhi may suit the life-styles of the planners and politicians, but one must question whether it has any meaning to the low-income indigenous population, (2.26).

In a similar study conducted by Al-Azzawi, consisting of a detailed survey of the traditional house and urban forms of Baghdad, the author comes to very similar conclusions to Fonseca. The close inter-relationship of the individual built unit with the communal built form, may appear unplanned and chaotic to the untrained observer, but represents a complex interaction which was generally true of cities throughout Islamic society. The fine 'mesh' of the urban form permitted gradual but continual change to take place without in any way affecting the ability of the total spatial structure, or the community it supported, to keep functioning. The disruptive effect of contemporary Western influence in the city, is shown to have destroyed this sophisticated urban form and replaced it with one which is both economically and climatically inappropriate.

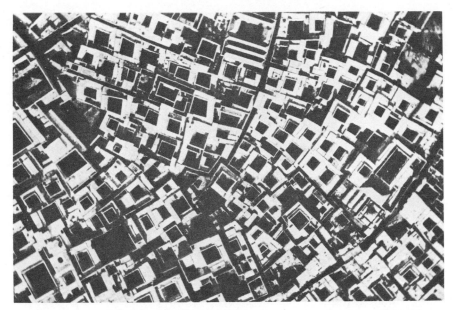

*Figure 2.5    Islamic settlement forms have always achieved a sophisticated, human and economic form whilst still enabling individual units to take a number of possible forms. This view of Marrakesh, in Morocco, is typical of the older sections of many cities built under similar influences.* (By courtesy of Musée de l'Homme, Paris)

Finally, in separate analyses of traditional Yoruba cities by Mabogunje (2.27) and Bray (2.28) the authors describe the similarly compact and heterogeneous nature of the spatial form and its role in inducing the economic growth of the Yoruba population.

In South and Central America the decimation of the indigenous population destroyed the continuity and coherence of any traditional social or spatial structures, but the other instances cited all clearly reveal that those settlements created by indigenous societies throughout areas of what now constitutes the Third World, obviate the main problems of socio-economic polarization and inequitable distribution as described by Harvey in the case of the typical city in industrialized capitalist societies.

When rural-urban migration or natural increase led to population expansion in such areas, the existing high densities and opportunities for peripheral growth throughout the settlements made it relatively easy to absorb new members and also to put them into the predominantly labour-intensive labour market. Although there was a limit to the extent to which additional numbers could be absorbed, the *process* of growth did not favour one group any more than another.

### 2.2.2. Modifying Factors

It would be wrong to extend this comparison further, since the examples available are limited and the majority of cities manifest a combination of settlement patterns. More significantly, the fact that low-income groups now generally constitute the majority of the urban population has greatly modified the extent to which socio-economic disparities are reinforced by the urban spatial form. Because of their voting power, it has often become more attractive for local political leaders to canvas support from the block or mass votes they offer, than from the small and isolated electorate in the low-density, high-income areas where these are fewer. In many cases this has led to incitement not to pay rents or other dues (2.29); in others it has led to covert — or even open — political support for land invasion and new popular settlements (2.30). In others it enabled squatters and other sections of the urban poor to obtain at least *de facto* recognition which provides a measure of a security and has enabled them to receive public water supplies and sanitation, street paving and lighting, electricity and other services (2.31).

These varying attitudes have fluctuated greatly over time and from country to country, depending partly upon the ideology and commitment of the government and the extent of deprivation involved. Thus, in the period immediately prior to and just after the 1971 presidential elections in Chile (when Allende came to power) extensive land seizures and settlement occurred with political support. In a thorough analysis of this period, LeGates (2.32) states that 'almost all the Tomas (land seizures) were by Comites De Los Pobladores Sin Casa (committees of poor persons without homes), were organized by political parties. Land for the Tomas was also chosen with a fine eye. Often public land was chosen. The land is distributed throughout Santiago though a majority is in the poorer communes and on the fringes'. Whilst the majority of these Chilean and other popular urban developments in South and Central America were achieved by political support of a fairly radical nature, and similar examples can be found elsewhere (2.33), this is not always the case. Such development can often be considered as a radical means to a relatively conservative end, or even a slow and continuous process which never intends to challenge the existing ethos of society, but seeks simply to enable the urban poor to gain access to urban resources and services. In their analysis of Las Colinas, in Bogota, Solaun, Flynn and Kronus (2.34), for example, found that subsequent to the establishment of the settlement and the increase in individual and group security which it afforded, the cohesion of the settlers and the influence of their radical leadership was reduced drastically (albeit with official encouragement).

Throughout Asia, the nature of political intervention and its implications have not been subject to the same intensity of investigation as it has in Central and South America, but it would appear to operate on very different lines. McGee, for example, shows how in Kuala Lumpur the traditional and migrant areas of the city were not politically active but did give support to opposition parties which operated within the parliamentary structure and sought to improve their position democratically (2.35). In India, it appears from observation that the majority of low-income areas in the cities vote for the ruling Congress Party and that this has resulted in improvements to the physical environment of such areas even when this is in blatant contradiction to the Government's own master plan.

It is therefore necessary to beware not only of imposing ethnocentric models based upon the urban experience of the industrialized Western countries, but also from other countries *within* the Third World, where the fact of underdevelopment may be the only common factor. It does nonetheless appear that political intervention on behalf of the urban poor has succeeded in modifying what would otherwise be even greater extremes of inequitable resource distribution. It is another question as to whether this in any way constitutes an actual improvement in the position of the poor, or whether it has simply served to prevent social unrest leading to open conflict; what *can* be observed is that the political structures of the Third World city have induced a shift in the way that urban development actually takes place, irrespective of official plans and policies. Where this gap between political or socio-economic realities and planning policies is large, and the attempt to impose an inappropriate order upon the processes prevails, the results may well prove counter-productive and the credibility of planning will be limited; where the gap is small, and pragmatic approaches accepting the limitations in resources and the realities of urban growth prevail, it is more likely that plans will achieve their intended objectives.

Before leaving this subject, it is necessary to return to the original discussion of social and economic polarization which seems to be occurring in major cities. If the gap between the income groups is already extremely large and if rural urban migration leads to a continued increase not just in city size, but in the proportion of urban populations living in the low and very low-income categories, the role of planning in either reinforcing or helping to redistribute incomes and resources is central to the whole question of urban growth and of development itself.

## 2.3    Ethnocentrism, Classcentrism and Housing Policy

In part 1 it was shown how concepts of urbanization borrowed from other contexts have been applied within the Third World in the interests of a small section of the population. Despite the crisis of confidence that the planning professions are facing in the Western countries, where these concepts originated (2.36), similar processes can still, unfortunately, be observed at the level of urban planning and housing policy.

The extent of urban settlement growth has not, however, made cities amenable to such approaches and many institutional structures have been ill-equipped to cope. Pre-occupation with the physical aspects of planning, rather than their socio-economic context, has led to widespread attempts to impose inappropriate forms of 'balanced and ordered' growth. Similarly, although many countries have initiated great innovations at both policy and action levels, few have yet evaluated their relevance at anything beyond the experimental project scale.

### 2.3.1   Housing Standards and the Deficit Myth

An example of this uncritical acceptance of inappropriate concepts can be seen in the estimates of housing need and what might be termed the 'deficit myth'. Thus the housing shortage for the whole of India has officially been estimated at about 83.7 million units (2.37) in 1968 and it is thought that this has been increasing by approximately 1 million a year since. Of this total, 11.9 million of the 'deficit' is located in urban areas, of which a large proportion is needed in the major cities. It is perfectly true, of course, that the vast majority of existing pucca (or permanent) housing is inadequate for normal family life, and in the four major cities of Calcutta, Delhi, Bombay and Madras, 75.8% of all housing consists of one room and only 10.5% of all their populations had more than two rooms (2.38). Housing, and the lack of it, ranks therefore as one of the greatest urban problems and Rosser has argued that it is in fact that greatest single cause of environmental deterioration (2.39).

Whilst these statistics reveal an undeniably acute lack of acceptable shelter provision, estimates of housing deficit should be viewed with extreme caution. As statistics, they represent arbitrary definitions as to what does and does not constitute a house. In India, such standards are still influenced by the legacy of the colonial period and current buildings regulations for Delhi were established by the British in 1915, at a time when the need for economy was hardly a major concern. Yet in spite of the totally different context existing by the 1950's, it was still felt possible to claim that 'standards have been established by various committees and technical missions . . . recommending the two roomed house with adequate sanitary and other facilities the barest minimum if the normal aspiration of healthy living is to be achieved. These standards cannot be lowered, whatever the community, whatever the location and whatever the economic situation in the country. Substandard housing is but a step towards the slums. Deliberate substandard housing will defeat the very purpose of housing, as it will lead towards the creation of future slums. The basic standards must be adhered to at all costs, (2.40).

It is hardly surprising that if such measures of adequacy are used in the context of Indian urban housing as described above, the vast majority of existing units will be deemed as unacceptable or uninhabitable, yet the assumption embodied by such standards omits any other criteria of acceptability as may be perceived by the poor themselves and leads to the conclusion that if such figures were correct 360 million, or nearly two-thirds of the entire population, would be homeless, assuming a household size of only 4.0 people. If one subtracts the numbers of permanent dwellers in many large cities who are literally homeless, it is immediately apparent that the population of both urban and rural areas does have shelter of a type and that this generally reflects the means and priorities of people within existing constraints. Deficit estimates therefore reflect more accurately the way in which adequate or 'minimum' housing is defined than they do the nature of housing shelter as it actually exists. Equally, the standards of new housing that such policies indicate as constituting the minimum acceptable standards, are generally well above anything that the poor can afford. The cost of the high space and construction standards imposed raises building costs beyond those which are tolerable even with heavy subsidies. Official estimates for providing housing to such standards in India were in the region of US $47,000 million in 1968 (2.41), whilst a more recent study, quoted by Bannister (2.42), projected a cost of US $43,000 million, which Manchar (2.43) has estimated as requiring requiring 30% of the total national capital investment against current official allocations in the public sector outlay for the Fourth Five Year Plan of only 1.5%.

Clearly this is unacceptable, and a similar analysis of estimated demand at existing official standards would in all probability reveal similar shortfalls in the available resources in many other countries. As Turner has observed (2.44) 'unattainable standards increase the demand for and the cost of slum housing and worsen slum conditions'. Deficit estimates as indicators of such problems have the further limitation of being static estimates and as such are unable to assess the rate at which new housing is entering the market, how much is being improved to a state at which it is considered (officially) to qualify as acceptable, or conversely, at what rate existing sound housing is deteriorating into a state which is considered unsuitable for habitation. In short, they are unable to express, let alone explain, the dynamic nature of shelter provision within a situation of socio-economic change and rapid urban growth.

### 2.3.2  Slum Clearance and (Problem) Relocation

A number of other examples of inappropriate policies can also be cited. Slum clearance and urban renewal programmes, which held great sway in Europe and North America in the 1950's and 60's, also form a central feature of housing and planning policies in many Third World cities. Thus the violent evictions and removals of people from the intramuros areas in Manila was carried out under official auspices and supplanted more peaceful and organized attempts to effect a similar relocation (2.45). In Kuala Lumpur, there has long been press and official condemnation of 'shanty' and other 'slum' housing areas and calls for their removal in order to make room for development projects (2.46) and to clear what was regarded as a serious threat to the city (2.47).

Similar examples can be found in most major cities, even where increasing attention is being given to the socio-economic and environmental advantages of rehabilitation. Although Calcutta has announced a major bustee (hutment) improvement scheme, the project was far from achieving complete official enthusiasm. In 1971, the Mayor, for example, attacked such proposals in strong terms, 'a lot of money is being wasted in the so-called bustee improvement scheme, it is an attempt at tinkering with a problem that needs a drastic remedy. An attempt is being made to whitewash one of the basic causes of the trouble in Calcutta. The bustees are the breeding grounds of lawlessness. Mere palliatives will not be enough' (2.48). Yet the self-evident fact is that the more successful slum clearances are, the more shelters they demolish and the greater the housing shortage becomes. Slum clearance and relocation policies do just that — they relocate and do not change or improve the housing or other conditions of the poor, even though they may remove them from view — in most cases the problem is even made worse. Thus in Delhi, 50,000 families were moved from their central locations in the late 1950's and given serviced plots of 25 sq yards in the urban preperiphery where they could construct temporary houses until the authorities could provide permanent housing. However, the disincentive this gave to investment and the inability of the households to remain in the periphery led to approximately 25% of them selling their plots illegally and returning to locations near their place of employment (2.49). The original plots were then developed to a high environmental level by their new (and generally middle-income) residents and proudly displayed by the authorities as evidence of the success of their policies. In fact, of course, valuable resources had been used in developing the suburban sites which either benefitted more affluent groups or were inappropriate for their intended residents, and the problem was simply re-created back in the central city.

Slum removal is therefore inconsistent with a situation of real housing shortage, as it already exists and as it will continue to grow. It makes absolutely no contribution to reducing or removing that shortage and only serves to use large amounts of capital investment to effect a marginal improvement in quality, much of which does not in any case accrue to the benefit of the poor. Abrams (2.50), with considerable experience in housing studies, noted as long ago as 1964, that 'in a housing famine there is nothing that slum clearance can accomplish that cannot be done more efficiently by an earthquake. The worst aspects of slum life are overcrowding and excessive shelter costs. Demolition without replacement intensifies overcrowding and increases shelter cost. It may also increase squatting and thereby quickly create slums that are more stubbornly enduring than those removed . . . Continued residence in slums may be a necessity for some time to come. In Singapore, the Improvement Trust had long been clearing slums as well as building some housing, but it soon came face to face with the consequences of its slum clearance policy, when those who were displaced proceeded to squat'. Abrams adds in a footnote that it was likely that such plans would be cancelled as a result. If this type of policy cannot be executed successfully in the context of relative prosperity and low population growth prevailing in Singapore (2.51), it is hardly likely to be valid in situations of low per capita incomes, scarce resources and rapid urban growth.

### 2.3.3  Models of Urban Planning
With the need to create new state and regional capitals, and with the existing cities frequently doubling their populations every ten or twelve years, many governments have called upon the services of foreign consultants with international reputations to assist in the preparation of planning policies and guidelines. In South Asia, *all* the national capitals and some of the state capitals have been designed by such architects and planners; Lutyens and later the Ford Foundation consultants were active in Delhi, Kahn in Dacca, Doxiadis in Islamabad, Corbusier/Mayer/Fry in Chandigarh; in Africa and much of the Middle and Near East similar situations prevail (Accra, Baghdad, Ankara, Kuwait City, etc., all have, or have had, foreign planners). Whilst recent projects indicate a greater appreciation of the socio-economic, climatic and cultural factors which condition the context of urban growth, this has not always been the case, and even present plans are frequently based upon forms which *reflect* inequality rather than *compensate* for it.

A prime example of such planning is presented by the case of Chandigarh, intended by Nehru as 'symbolic of the freedom of India, unfettered by the traditions of the past . . . an expression of the nation's faith in the future' (2.52). The city was planned to fulfill the need for a new capital for the divided state of Punjab and following the preparation of the master plan, Corbusier and Maxwell Fry were appointed to execute it (2.53). However, several major modifications were made to the plan and Corbusier is largely responsible for its final form. The central criticism of plans must be that they represent valid solutions to Western and particularly European planning problems, but are totally inappropriate for India climatically, socially and economically.

The clearest indication of this can be seen in the selection of a dispersed grid as the generator of the city's form. Such a solution is ideal for a population with a high car ownership ratio, but is disastrous for one in which it is minute; it also makes efficient public transport, an essential requirement for any Third World city, very difficult to achieve. As was shown in the discussion on Old Delhi previously, the traditional spatial form resolved these problems with a dense and compact city centre with very little suburban development (2.54), permitting short journeys to work and a mixture of land uses and social groups. The Chandigarh plan reverses this, but with few benefits. Land-use zoning techniques, in fact, are used to isolate the capital complex, one of the city's main employment areas, outside the city on the opposite side to the housing for low and middle income groups (2.55), so that the low-grade clerks must cross the city to get to work, but senior officials, (most of whom are the car owners), live in areas directly adjoining the secretariat complex. The spatial segregation of income groups is so complete that it is a popular joke that if you tell a taxi driver the income of a friend, he can take you to the house without knowing the address.

Despite its innovations in the housing sectors and the visually impressive design of the capital, it is doubtful therefore if Chandigarh was in fact ever conceived by its planners as a social experiment (2.56). As Gupta has noted, it may have effected an amelioration of the wide disparity between upper and lower echelons of society, but this has largely been as a result of weakening the old religious caste barriers and replacing them with equally formidable economic ones (2.57).

Such examples are not restricted, however, to projects initiated by foreign consultants. Brasilia is a prime example of a city based upon an inequitable framework, yet this was designed by Brazilians themselves. Moreover, the relevance of such criticisms is not restricted only to the planning of new cities. Invariably, planning and housing proposals for existing major cities consist of a mixture of zonal, density and transportation proposals in the main tradition of Western methods. The briefs for such programmes often make it difficult or impossible to relate proposals to their regional or socio-economic context, but even so, such plans tend to be myopic in character and view the cities themselves as the exclusive areas of study. Often insufficient attention is given to their role in national or even regional development, despite the fact that growth is as much due to regional interaction as to natural increase.

Master plans are, in any case, extremely poor vehicles for regulating the dynamic processes of urban growth. When given the status of legal documents, the attempt to understand change becomes impossible and plans are apt to become a parody of reality. The concept of some static future state as expressed in target population figures also frustrates the ability of such programmes to ever achieve their objectives, since cities in urbanizing countries are not likely, in the foreseeable future, to approach anything like a 'stable state'.

The continued application of Western assumptions in urban development has inhibited a re-evaluation of issues in Third World countries which has only served to further exacerbate already intransigent problems. As a result, the consequences of planning and official intervention have frequently produced or intensified the very situations they were intended to prevent or relieve. Thus the provision of high-cost, high-quality mass housing, has made it impossible for the poor to gain access and forced them into seeking alternatives which are generally of the type plans attempt to remove; the recurring costs of subsidising such housing then reduces the budgets available for servicing or improving these alternatives and so the polarization of urban society continues.

In this sense therefore, the ethnocentric' bias of imported models has become a 'classcentric' bias. Plans and programmes reflect the values and aspirations of the middle and upper class elites regarding problems of environmental quality, pollution and the fear of social disorganization, which are naturally of less concern to the urban poor. The fact that many planners and architects are trained in the universities of Europe and North America, or are susceptible to their influence, has not helped to change this situation.

The empirical data for more appropriate models are already available and only waiting to be recognized throughout the cities of the Third World there are settlements and entire cities which were developed to suit indigenous needs, and which enabled all social groups to contribute and benefit from urban life. These by no means necessarily represent ideal forms, and many of them have now deteriorated physically. The spatial structures which they generated, however, may well provide an object lesson in methods of using limited land and capital to achieve a socially acceptable and economically viable urban environment, which would be able to absorb more of the urban migrants than conventional low density, segregated land-use methods can achieve.

The main limitation to the application of such approaches perhaps lies in their association with tradition and hence 'backwardness', especially to a society that is pursuing programmes of 'modernization'. No doubt for a limited number of affluent countries such as those exporting oil and other similar resources, it will be possible to pursue such approaches with some success and to achieve Westernized urban structures. Leaving aside questions regarding the appropriateness of such plans for these societies, it is unlikely that similar strategies will be feasible for many Third World countries, or whether in fact they will continue indefinitely in the West itself. If such is the case, there is every reason to at least reconsider the merits of alternative planning models which extract the more positive and appropriate aspects of indigenous spatial structures and incorporate them into contemporary strategies. This *should not* in any way be thought of as encouraging a planning approach which accepts underdevelopment as a permanent or inevitable state, but rather a realization that the actual *path* taken by the West is unlikely to be available to most Third World countries, even assuming that economic growth in some form is possible. With Western planning increasingly becoming aware of its theoretical and operational limitations, a more socially appropriate and economically viable approach to urban planning would be more likely, in the end, to make development in its widest sense a feasibility.

## 2.4     Low-Income Settlements and Their Analysis

The combination of high urban growth rates, inappropriate policies and inequalities in distribution of resources, has created situations in which a large proportion of urban populations are unable to afford conventional 'minimum' dwellings. Whilst estimates must be regarded as tentative, a recent World Bank survey (2.58) of six selected cities indicated that this proportion varied between one- and two-thirds of the total population in each city.

When these limitations are added to the fact that much of the housing which *is* available to low-income groups is either of an unsuitable type or is too far from employment areas to be tolerable, the numbers of people effectively excluded from housing programmes can readily be imagined. Throughout the expanding cities, such people have been thrown onto their own resources and forced to generate alternative methods of financing, organizing and building housing settlements.

The nature and implications of these alternatives have been the subject of an increasing literature during the last five years, yet relatively little is yet known regarding the types of housing process involved.

The early pioneering studies of Turner and Mangin (2.59) tended to focus attention upon the distinction between the dynamic, organized nature of the large squatter invasions on the periphery of major cities such as Lima, and compared them to the centrally located slums of high density hutments or tenements. In an early paper, Turner (2.50) addressed himself largely to upper or middle class Peruvians or foreigners and sought to show that whilst the Corralon, or inner city housing, had no future and that it crystallizes out into a typical labyrinthian complex of slum courts which can only deteriorate until eventually they are eradicated, the Barriada or peri-urban squatter settlement will develop, albeit slowly, into a typical working and lower middle class suburb (2.61).

Mangin came to much the same conclusion when discussing the work of squatters in Lima: 'The differences in morale between squatter settlement dwellers and slum dwellers in Lima is impressive to even casual visitors and seems to me to be largely due to the fact that the squatter settlements were formed by organized invasions, have internal community organizations with elections, and reward talent, initiative and courage' (2.62). This distinction borrows heavily upon that made by Stokes (2.63) between the economically stagnant 'slums of despair' of the very poor and the 'slums of hope' of the dynamic and upwardly mobile groups and the link between this and Turner's approach is increased by the emphasis that both put upon the importance of security of tenure in encouraging improvement by the Barriada-type groups.

The highly organized and resourceful squatters discussed by Turner and Mangin in subsequent studies, particularly in the descriptions of the Pampa De Cuevas settlement (2.64) represent major achievements of popular action in housing and planning.

The effect of communal autonomy did much to give the squatters 'a confidence and strength that enables them to become a functioning part of the same society that opposed them' (2.65).

The influence that these seminal studies had on the understanding of popular housing or, as Dwyer refers to it, 'spontaneous settlement', achieved a revolution of attitudes that now enables us to appreciate the rationality and the positive character of such processes. Subsequent studies by a large number of writers have all tended to confirm these findings and the movement to provide infrastructural support through rationalized versions of similar processes, such as sites and services programmes, has now been initiated on a large scale (2.66). At the same time, appreciation of the merits of personal and group autonomy have led to the development of such ideas at a more generalized and comprehensive level. In a later work, Turner (2.67) expanded the theoretical and policy discussion of user control in housing by comparing locally or individually controlled systems which he classified as 'open' with those which are authoritarian, centrally controlled or 'closed' and adds that in the more extreme and relatively common cases of housing built or administered by public institutions or private corporations, all decisions are subsumed by a central directorate or administration (2.68). This typology thus permits the inclusion of studies of varying housing needs and means of resolving them, for the complete range of income groups in any type of context. Turner emphasises that in some situations, such as when housing the aged or infirm, an open system is wholly inappropriate that a closed system is frustrating for a growing family with savings and also that to obtain a valid policy in most situations, a judicious mix of the two is required (2.69). He has no doubt, however, as to which of the two is considered the most desirable and productive. Thus, 'in principle if not in practice, the greater the degree of centralization or the larger the scale of the housing operation, the less economic it becomes, except in times of crisis or when the hierarchy system is essential for the generation of basic resources' (2.70). He continues 'those who assume that they know people's demands better than the users themselves, or those whose interests are best served by this assumption, will naturally favour authoritarian, closed systems. In contrast, those who assume that the user is the best judge of his own demands (as distinct from his rights), will try to limit their participation to the administering of services which guarantee the supply of land, materials, tools and skills to the users, together with credit for purchase of those elements. He will therefore support open systems, in which the output is the product of a dialogue between rule makers and game players without which there can be no existential freedom' (2.71). Finally, Turner suggests elsewhere in his argument that the mixture of responsibilities mentioned above should, in fact, be interpreted in favour of a pre-eminence of group or individual controls: 'if housing is treated as a verbal activity, as a means to human ends, as an activity rather than a manufactured and packaged product; decision-making power must of necessity, remain in the hands of the users themselves. I will go beyond that to suggest that the ideal we should strive for is a model in which the users, as a matter of economic, social and psychological common sense — are the principal actors' (2.72).

In a still more recent study (2.73) these ideas of urban housing provision systems are carried forward to the analysis of settlements and urban planning. The same distinction is maintained between locally and centrally controlled policies and the argument is advanced that 'it is clear that the cities the poor build' and their informal economies, order themselves differently from those that are planned and administered by central agencies. The more traditional systems controlled from the bottom up, employed by the mass of the people in the world's exploding cities, are based on lateral information and decision networks that are totally different from the vertical and hierarchic organizations of large scale works and services. When these centralized systems are used to house the poor, their scale and the limitations of management, rule out the essential variety and flexibility of housing options. Even if the planners were sensitive to, and could have access to, the fine grain information on which local housing decisions were made, it would be administratively impossible to use it. Housing can only be supplied from the top down in large lumps' (2.74).

These quotations reflect the evolution of a number of ideas from one of the most influential of contemporary housing analysts. It is worthwhile, therefore, to discuss them more fully in order to highlight certain central issues.

In the early studies of the popular housing movement, the need to emphasize the rational nature of popular settlement was primary and the need to distinguish between the Barriada and the Corralon was therefore understandable. The distinction, however, had the unfortunate implication of many earlier studies which assumed the existence of social 'disorganization', or as it became in later and more sophisticated studies, 'social marginality' in the inner city housing areas. Whilst Mangin himself drew attention to this problem in the work of Lewis, (2.75), the Lima studies are in fact, guilty of the same fault and omit the fact that the nascent squatter organizations actually started in areas like the Corralones, even though for obvious reasons, they were unable to initiate appropriate changes there. It is highly debatable in fact whether the Corralones will inevitably deteriorate as 'slums of despair' or whether they will continue to supply Barriadas of the future and provide an optimal settlement in terms of location and cost for the less upwardly mobile. The distinction between the two types also overlooks the fact that by local standards the Barriada settlers were not particularly poor. In his description of the Pampa de Cuevas Barriada, Turner in fact quotes Mangin to the effect that 'the majority of its inhabitants are young families with more or less steady incomes. They are poor, but represent the average rather than below average wage-earning sectors, and as the rate of physical improvement of the average dwelling indicates, they have maintained an appreciable rate of upward mobility' (2.76). He is therefore describing the situation and actions of a specific section of low-income groups who were able to offset the additional transport costs against the obvious advantage of a well-built house and the security and investment potential it affords. For them, squatting provided an opportunity to circumvent a housing market that inadequately met their needs, but such a solution would be unlikely to help the mass of people remaining in the Corralon.

The same distinction in terms of socio-economic status of many Barriada-type settlers is made by Fichter in the preface of *Freedom to Build* where he states 'It must also be said that much of the case material in this book suggests the possibilities of greater autonomy in housing is based upon relatively strong, upwardly mobile families. The hopeless poor, therefore, may well remain just as much a dilemma after this book as before it' (2.77).

For the substantial number of people at lower income levels, with unstable employment or without economic mobility, such an approach to housing is obviously less applicable. Yet despite this, and the varied political ambitions of the Barriada settlers, Turner considered them to represent a social and political alternative for the mass of the poor. He therefore saw the inhibition to such alternatives in the existence of institutionally determined standards and methods and argued that 'the loss of administrative control over urban

settlement and the frequently chaotic conglomerations of inadequate structures which make up the greater part of contemporary
city growth in the modernizing countries, are a product of the gap
between values and norms required by the governing institutions
and those imposed on the people by the circumstances in which they
live' (2.78).

If it is accepted, however, that the suburban Barriada option, as
it existed, was only really appropriate for the upper strata and
improving lower income group (2.79), it is not completely adequate
to condemn official institutions as the main source of frustration,
though conventional planning and housing structures and policies
fully deserve such criticism. As has been shown earlier, official
attitudes are far from permanently hostile and even the Lima
squatters took care to get some official support before acting (2.80).
Even if the local institutions concerned with housing had
sanctioned the original Barriada settlements, they would not
necessarily have met the needs of all the lower income groups and
would manifestly have been inappropriate for the poorest, because
of their distance from the city and its employment areas. This
implies a more structural character to the housing problem in which
institutions are a contributing factor, but by no means necessarily
the major obstacle to more equitable solutions. As such, the early
writings underestimated the role played by the inner city slums or
'bridgeheader' locations, and laid the basis for the later studies in
which alternatives were to be seen as local autonomy versus
institutional control.

Since its supply is normally controlled by market forces, there is
an inbuilt barrier to low-income groups which is of a more
structural nature than the activities and attitudes of housing
institutions. Thus, even when authorities have attempted to adopt
egalitarian measures through programmes such as sites and services
projects, it has generally only been possible to develop them on a
limited basis or in suburban areas where land costs are lower, and
where only the upper-low or middle income groups can afford to
live.

Naturally, the growth of unauthorized settlements has greatly
distorted the normal functioning of a land market system and it is
possible that in many cities there is a dual land-market economy,
depending on whether settlement is legal or illegal. Even then, the
complexity of marginal situations (such as when housing is illegally
constructed on land for which legal titles, but no planning

permission exists), makes this difficult to analyse with any certainty. Thus, whilst the ultra-low income groups of Calcutta are forced into central areas to obtain accessibility and in South America the inner city slums accommodate the poorest groups, the comparatively recent appearance of a land market in Ankara, made it feasible for even the lowest income groups to accept long journeys to work and high travel costs, in order to obtain available land in the outer urban areas (2.81), though even then, many others still lived in the inner city areas.

Harvey's analysis of the relative inability of the lower-income groups to compete equally, therefore, applies to the Third World city as much as to that of the developed capitalist economies, though with the reservation of changes wrought by dual-market systems. In his analysis, Harvey discusses the work of Alonso and Muth (2.82), and shows how 'the bid-rent curve for the poor is characteristically steep, since they have little to spend on transportation and their ability to bid for the use of land declines rapidly with distance from the place of employment. The rich group on the other hand, characteristically has a shallow bid-rent curve, since its ability to bid is not greatly affected by the amount of money spent on transport. When put in competition with each other, we find the poor group forced to live in the centre of the city and the rich group living outside it (just as Engels described it). This means that the poor are forced to live on high rent land. The only way they can adjust to this, of course, is to save on the quantity of space they consume and crowd into a very small area. The logic of the model indicates that poor groups will be concentrated in high rent areas close to the city centre in overcrowded conditions' (2.83). Harvey does not, however, conclude that this is the inevitable form of urban growth and he cites the work of Lave (2.84) who points out that, 'the structure of the city will change if the preferences of the rich group change. If congestion costs increase in the central city, for example, and the rich decide that the time and frustration are not worth it, then they can easily alter their bid-rent function and move back into the centre of the city. Various city structures can be predicted depending on the shape of the bid-rent curves, and it is perfectly feasible to find the rich living in the centre of the city and the poor on the outskirts. In this case, the poor are forced to adjust, for example by exchanging time for cost-distance, so that they expend large quantities of time walking to work in order to save on transport costs, (a condition not unknown in Latin American cities)' (2.85). As Harvey concludes, 'all this means that the rich group can always enforce its preferences over a poor group because it has more resources to apply either to transport costs or to obtaining land in whatever location it chooses' (2.85).

In any discussion of housing settlements and urban development as a whole, the analysis must question the relevance of attacking institutions *per se,* and even where such criticism is valid it is, according to Harvey, partly because the institutions are themselves a product of the system in which they operate (2.87). Considerable modification would therefore seem to be required of Turner's approach when discussing the macro-level of urban housing policy and land use. In developing the idea of individual and group independence from institutional control at all levels, there is a great danger of enabling those who are advantageously placed to exploit new opportunities, to do so at the expense of those who are less fortunate. This, as Wilsher and Righter have noted (2.88) is tantamount to a return to *laissez faire,* in which 'the doctrine of self-help is deeply attractive. It appeals to everyone's belief in human ability, neighbourliness, ambition and good sense, as solvents for the most intractable difficulties (yet), it also, less nobly encourages people to believe that there is nothing much to worry about, that the less interference there is with natural forces the better, and that everything will sort itself out in the long run' (2.89).

Thus, although Turner is anxious to avoid any association with *laissez faire* approaches, his analysis is extremely susceptible to that interpretation and by attacking institutions rather than the structures which generate them, and implying that reform of one can be achieved without a total change in the other, he is only offering a partial solution. Similar reservations regarding the general applicability of self-generated settlements have been voiced, for example, by Cardona who has argued that 'however much I recognize that the change of attitude is very important, and that the squatter settlement achieves a lot of things that the urban reformers were not able to effect — for instance, obtaining land for the mass of the people — legalisation poses problems. *With the creation of the 'stayer' types and their families, not only do I fear, but I actually see a lot of people working hard, in Peru for instance, to develop the idea of the evolution of the squatter settlement. The danger, if they persist, is this: governments will again start to avoid their responsibilities'* (2.90).

It is worth asking of course, what those responsibilities are. Turner is quite clear on this point and states that 'higher authorities and larger, supra-local organizations should not carry out housing schemes at all. The assembly of components — of sites, services and the building of dwellings — must be done in small units. The provision of many components, however, depends on municipal or central agencies, although most may be shared. Access to the basic elements and resources, on the other hand, can only be ensured by central government action, whether by direct socialism or effective controls over commercial uses and transactions. Central planning and local controls are complementary in this view, which argues that all government housing sections should strive to increase local control. Its own part should be restricted to settling and maintaining performance standards, taking responsibility only for those parts of the infrastructure beyond the powers of local groups to handle' (2.91).

Elsewhere, Turner indicates that the provision of land is one of the major factors in this respect (2.92) and this brings us back to one of the central problems of the land market mechanism discussed previously. If, for instance, a local authority or housing agency accepted this premise, it would still find it difficult in the majority of cities, to obtain land on the required scale and in the required variety of locations, to enable all sections of the population and particularly the urban poor to benefit. The extremely high cost of urban land, particularly in the Third World where speculation frequently gives it a distorted and artificial value, means that public intervention may even result in a reduction of the volume of land available in the remaining areas of the private sector, thus forcing up prices even higher and placing the public sector in an ambivalent position. This has actually occurred in Delhi, where an attempt was made in 1959 by Delhi Development Authority to initiate a 'land freeze', in order to limit speculation and establish a revolving fund to buy land at 'current market prices' and develop it for a variety of activities such as low-income housing. (The revolving fund was intended to use capital, raised initially from the Government, to purchase land from private sources and then to auction a proportion of the acquired land to repay the debt and provide capital both for further purchases of land and for the building of low- and middle-income housing.) However, as Bose has pointed out, the time taken to negotiate for, buy and make available land, created a shortage which forced land prices up (though this would probably have occurred even without such a delay), and eventually tempted the Authority to join the ranks of the speculators (2.93). He even claims that this was a major factor in the sudden growth of squatter settlements at that time. The main point is, however, that even with perfectly laudable motives and well considered proposals, the intervention of public authorities or institutions, in an economic structure which does not permit easy influence or control, may well be inadequate at best, or counter-productive at worst. The limitations of public sector initiatives or inducements to influence the locational behaviour of the private sector in terms of regional location, can therefore be seen as equally valid within urban areas as they are at regional levels. In the case of Lima, which Turner cites and also in the further case of Ankara, the more egalitarian character of housing provision is the result either of the absence of a land market mechanism or its reduced strength. The situation does not prevail in all cities and the Delhi authorities quickly abandoned the revolving fund scheme when this became obvious. It must be accepted, therefore, that substantial difficulties are involved in assuming the ability of authorities to fully complement the role of local control as a means of effecting more socially, economically and environmentally desirable housing. It may well, therefore, be necessary to remove the market mechanism from the sphere of land-use and exchange within the major cities. The significance of this for social, economic and political structures, is inevitably far-reaching, yet as Barbara Ward has observed, in discussing the possible urban strategies and policies needed to make the planet habitable in the future, 'none of this work is possible without control over land use, without an end to urban speculation, without the highest possible priority for the citizens' work and shelter. In societies in which there is no commitment whatever to social justice, no such controls are possible and I doubt whether they are going to survive' (2.94).

Urban land, land use and land availability are therefore indissoluable from questions of urban housing, particularly in the Third World city (2.95). It is here that the greatest numbers of people are living at the lowest income levels and in areas with some of the highest land values, so that only by comprehensive changes of priority will it be possible to effect the scale and extent changes required. If planning and housing policies are to compensate for rather than reinforce urban poverty, such changes will also be required in terms of the provision of essential services and facilities. The scale of change can, however, only occur at the structural level and not at the local or individual level, since it is the structures themselves which are the impediments to progress. The squatter settlements which have formed the basis for an understanding of self-help housing and planning are, in fact, only representative of a particular socio-economic group operating in a particular urban context. It has already been observed that a substantial proportion of the urban population — even in the somewhat more affluent areas of Latin America and certainly in most parts of Africa and Asia — are well below this economic level and are therefore dependent to a much greater extent upon public sector assistance of one form or another.

The validity of existing self-generated settlements, as typified by the Peruvian examples, is also limited to some extent by their low density and the dispersed and realtively expensive urban structure they imply (2.96). Yet higher density settlements are frequently dismissed even by writers sympathetic to the Barriadas and Dwyer has joined Juppenlatz (2.97), in condemning the 'excessive' density, 'chaotic' building patterns and 'almost total disregard for the provision of any community space whatsoever' (2.98) and he quotes with approval from Khan (2.99) to the effect that 'every available foot of land has been built upon so that instead of streets and roads, there are narrow and winding lanes which provide the only approach to houses'.

Clearly the recognition accorded to the Barriadas of rational, resourceful and positive planning and building has not yet been extended to the very poor in the inner cities, and the views of Lewis, the early writings of Turner and Mangin and the ghosts of Redfield, Zorbaugh and Wirth are still all with us. It is perhaps advisable in this context, to assess the extent to which such assumptions are justified and what role such settlements, and the communities that create and sustain them, fulfill in the urban areas as a whole. Only then can we hope to be able to evolve models which can provide a basis for understanding the various needs of all sections of the urban poor and lay the basis for new structures and methods which can hope to assist them in their own efforts at development.

In the next section an analysis will be made of two such communities in the central areas of a large Asian city, Delhi. The people — and the context in which they live — are not, of course, any more typical of Third World housing by the poorest income groups than would be the case with any other case study. However, the great difference that they manifest from the more clearly observed South American studies, may perhaps throw more light upon the range of processes involved.

PART THREE
# A Case Study of Delhi

# PART THREE
# A Case Study of Delhi

## 3.1    Formal and Informal Settlement Processes

Because of its strategic position controlling movements between the
north-west frontier areas of India and the fertile valley of the River
Jumna, Delhi has been the seat of numerous dynasties controlling
Northern India. It is in fact several cities, all overlapping and
intermingling, of which only two are active today. The Moghal
walled city of Old Delhi is the older of these two, the Lutyens' capital
of New Delhi being the other. Together, they epitomize the extreme
forms of colonial and indigenous type cities with the high density
mixed land-use patterns of the old settlement contrasted against the

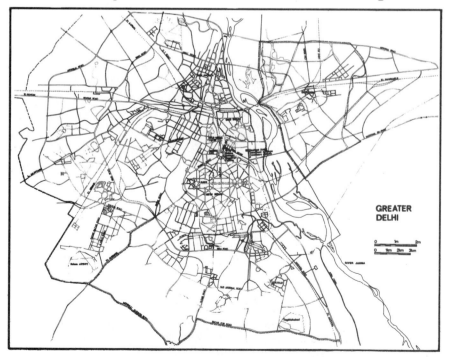

*Figure 3.1*

low density, socially and functionally segregated plan of the new, with the commercial centre at Connaught Place situated mid-way between the two.

The rise in population induced by the re-establishment of Delhi as the national capital was not felt immediately, partly because of the long construction period involved. (Until 1911 Calcutta was the capital of British India, and Delhi was not actually inaugurated until 1931). The partition of India in 1947, however, led to large number of Moslems leaving and an even larger number of Hindu refugees arriving, so that a population of 700,000 in 1941 (3.1) rose drastically to 1.44 million by 1951. Combined with the expansion of employment in the growing public sector, population increased further to 2.4 million by 1961 (3.2). Of this population approximately 70% were in-migrants (3.3).

It was at about this time that substantial growth occurred in the number of unauthorized settlements in and around the urban area. Surveys conducted by the Delhi Development Authority in 1959 show a rapid increase in the population of such housing to approximately 200,000 in 85 different settlements, (3.4). More recent

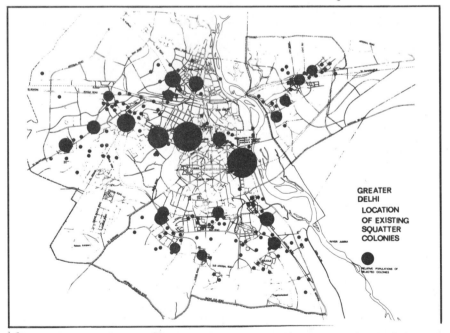

Figure 3.2     The distribution of squatter settlements and population in Delhi, 1968. The small circles represent the location of settlements, whereas large circles represent the relative population of selected sites. (After R. D. Gohav)

estimates (1968) indicate an even more rapid increase to 350,000, (3.5) the distribution of which is shown in fig. (3.2).

There can be little doubt that formal sector housing policies during this period contributed both directly and indirectly to an increase of such settlements. This was due to a range of factors which spring from a misconception about the *nature* of the housing problem and also of the reasons adopted to deal with it. It was assumed for example, that authorities had a responsibility to provide decent 'minimum' standard housing to the lower income groups despite the increasing international and Indian evidence (3.6) that people of *all* income levels had proved themselves perfectly capable of providing their own housing, and that what they need is access to resources and infrastructural supports. Secondly, the achievement of this assumed objective has been doomed to failure because of the incompatibility between high building standards (and unit costs) and extremely limited resources. As already discussed this has had two significant effects; it has meant that only a minute number of houses can be built compared to the number needed (3.7), and the cost of these was so high that it precluded the possibility of the low-income group benefitting (3.8).

*Figure 3.3    Typical example of official 'low-income' housing units, built to a cost of about Rs. 12 500. The form of this housing is often a scaled down version of the luxury housing.* (By courtesy of Delhi Development Corporation)

The sporadic application of 'slum clearance' programmes served only to exacerbate these policy contradictions still further and effected a reduction in the already low incomes of the families concerned, since they had to meet additional travel costs and often lost secondary domestic jobs (3.9), so that of the estimated 50,000 families affected, it is estimated that 25% sold their suburban plots and returned to squat in the city centre (3.10). Delhi is therefore

*Figure 3.4      Before . . . 'Stinking slums'*

*Figure 3.5      And after . . . 'replaced by a beautiful landscaped park'*

typical of many Third World cities in which conventional Western concepts have not only proved inappropriate to the realities of urban growth and limited resources, but have intensified the problems still further. As such they must be seen as an unsuccessful attempt to *control* rather than *resolve* the housing problems of the urban poor. These factors, and the polarities in income distribution which exist, have led to the formation of a wide range of unauthorized settlements. Studies of the social and spatial characteristics of these, therefore represent a means of exploring some of the housing processes involved and their relationship to the wider problems of urban growth. Any such evaluation must, however, clearly define the limits of enquiry and allow for the fact that the processes are dynamic and continuously changing.

## 3.2     The Case Studies — Method

It is essential at this stage to establish a simple typology of low-income settlements so that comparisons can be made between them and also of their changes. Rao and Desai (3.11) proposed a four-point classification of physical building types, whilst Ramachandran has used a similar framework for Bombay (3.12). Neither of these, however, includes an analysis of tenure status, an important indicator of the degree of security which housing provides. If this is included, the following typology can be proposed:

SETTLEMENT POPULATION:                    SETTLEMENT AREA:

| Dwelling type | % of type to total | Construction type | | | Tenure status | | | | | | | | | |
|---|---|---|---|---|---|---|---|---|---|---|---|---|---|---|
| | | Tempor-ary | Mixed | Perm-anent | 1 | 2 | 3 | 4 | 5 | 6 | 7 | 8 | 9 | * |
| exposed site | | | | | | | | | | | | | | |
| hutment | | | | | | | | | | | | | | |
| room in block | | | | | | | | | | | | | | |
| chawl/tenement | | | | | | | | | | | | | | |
| apartment/flat | | | | | | | | | | | | | | |
| linked house unit | | | | | | | | | | | | | | |
| detached house unit | | | | | | | | | | | | | | |

*1  =  freeholder
2  =  leaseholder
3  =  renter with contract
4  =  renter without contract
5  =  member of a co-operative

6  =  owner squatter — officially recognized
7  =  owner squatter — not officially
          recognized
8  =  squatter tenant
9  =  no regular accommodation

This classification method — if carried out regularly — would indicate:

1.   the range of housing types in an area and their relationship to those of the city at any one point in time, and

2.   the rate at which housing changed from one mode to another.

It does not, however, explain how housing is used or what roles it plays in the lives of its occupants. For example, in Peru it seems that the process of 'progressive development' operates, whereby a small hutment is constructed initially and is then improved by the same occupants over a period of time. Alternatively, however, the buildings themselves may be of a permanent or temporary nature which are not improved at all, but serve the temporary needs of a succession of occupants at various stages of their urban careers. These more complex and qualitative factors can only be assessed by more detailed analysis.

A further factor in the analysis of low-income unauthorized settlements is that of official intervention. It has already been observed that this is far from always being negative or hostile, yet the forms that it takes have rarely been evaluated in any systematic or comprehensive form. The policy in Delhi of 'regularizing' such settlements as have achieved a degree of permanence or political leverage, has led to substantial differences between such settlements and those still not regularized. (This policy does no more than acknowledge *de facto* occupation but generally involves the provision of services and facilities).

In their study of the integration of a Colombian squatter settlement into the officially approved planning, system Solaun, Flynn and Kronus (3.13), for example, assessed the policies of the authorities under five categories: legal, physical, economic, political and cultural. If administrative intervention is also included in this list, the following framework can be proposed:

1.   *Legal*
The granting of *de facto* or *de jure* recognition. The inclusion of settlements within the future urban planning context.

2.   *Administrative*
The coordination of policies for improvement, the granting of loans and leases, collection of taxes and rates, etc.

3. *Physical*
The provision of services such as water, sanitation, health services, electricity, street lighting and paving. Technical and material assistance for house improvement.

4. *Economic*
The provision of employment and/or training opportunities. The availability of 'seed' capital to help initiate a process of self-generated development through 'multiplier' effects.

5. *Political*
The inclusion of squatter and other unauthorized settlement households on voting registers on an equal basis to the remainder of the urban population and the freedom to establish local political pressure groups.

6. *Cultural/Social*
The provision of opportunities for the community to develop their own cultural patterns and to have right of access (and where necessary assisted access) to schools and community facilities).

In order to evaluate the more complex processes of the use of buildings and spaces, the relationship of individual units to the whole, and the role that such housing plays in the lives of its occupants, it is necessary to undertake a survey of both the spatial and the social structures of a settlement. In the case of the present study, a number of methods were adopted to achieve this: detailed physical surveys were conducted to ascertain the nature, location and condition of all services and facilities and the distribution of private and communal land; a random stratified social survey was conducted to obtain data on household structure, reasons for migration (if relevant), extent of progress within the city, present housing, employment and domestic circumstances and future needs and aspirations. Finally, a spatial/activity survey was made to assess the factors which facilitated or inhibited the ability of the settlement to support a stable domestic life. Two methods were used to analyze the intensification and nature of space utilization, as follows:

*Method A*
This consists of a statistical survey indicating the amounts of space used for all the activities observed. The method involves assessing the total areas of the spatial unit concerned, substracting all private areas and plotting the *effective* communal space relative to the

actual *physical* space. This is then used to formulate an 'efficiency ratio' which indicates the intensity of communal space utilization during the period of the survey.

*Method B*
This is a graphic technique. The private areas are again subtracted from the total area and the remaining communal areas are used to indicate visually the spatial distribution of activities. This is achieved by marking each activity and its spatial limits on a plan, so that a focal pattern is built up which is densest in the areas of greatest activity. In this way, the loss of statistical accuracy is compensated for by the increased utility of the material. Whilst this is a quicker technique and therefore easier to undertake, the essentially complementary nature of the methods increases their value if used together. Finally, to complete the study, a number of individual case histories were recorded to provide qualitative insights into the particular problems facing various families.

These methods were used to undertake a detailed survey and evaluation of two low-income settlements in the central area of Delhi (3.14). They both represent different settlement forms serving different types of community. The first, known as the Rouse Avenue settlement, is located in the heart of Delhi's commercial centre immediately behind Connaught Place and typifies the high density, low-income settlement evolved over a number of years. The second is known as the Maulana Azad Medical College settlement because of its position in the College grounds. This is a predominantly legal settlement for construction workers who provide the city's labour force, working on a semi-permanent basis for a labour contractor. Whilst the first settlement is one of the oldest and still exists, the second is now demolished and has been rebuilt elsewhere.

# 3.3     A Case Study of the Rouse Avenue Settlement

### 3.3.1   Location and Characteristics

Located within walking range of most of the city's employment areas and occupying an unobtrusive plot of land wedged between the main railway lines and some middle-income housing, the site

was ideal for migrants or refugees coming to the city. Some of the
first hutments were built well before Partition in 1947 and took the
form of temporary structures built against the high brick wall that
runs the length of the site and separates it from the railway property
immediately to the south (see Fig. 3.6).

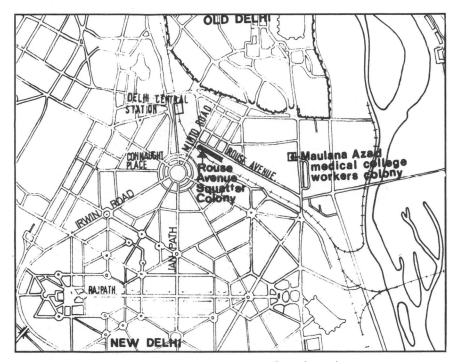

*Figure 3.6     Rouse Avenue settlement — location plan*

As the need for this type of housing increased and it became
apparent that the existing squatters would not be evicted, other
families moved in and building became more rapid, spreading out
from the initial alignments against the boundary wall in several
rows until the full width of the site was developed. The outer edges
were then filled in, leaving sufficient space between the huts and the
middle-income housing to provide a main thoroughfare from the
railway underpass, giving access to the city centre, down to the far
end of the settlement.

Today most of the site is built up and accommodates approximately 2150 people at a density of over 1000 per acre (2400 per hectare). What is even more remarkable is that this high concentration is achieved using only single storey dwelling units

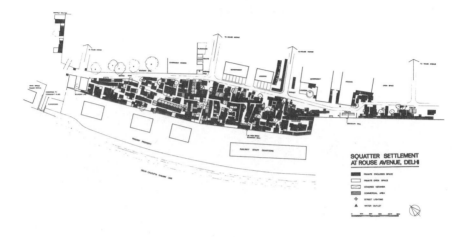

*Figure 3.7     Detailed layout of Rouse Avenue squatter settlement, showing open and enclosed private spaces, commercial areas and services.*

organized in such a way that several large open spaces have been retained adjoining the housing areas and these serve as recreation spaces for children and grazing plots for goats and buffaloes. Although it is obviously possible that further building may cover these areas also, it does appear that since this has not happened so far, the community regards them as essential. The saturation of available land by building ensures that there is no extension of the settlement and most building operations are limited to improvements or alterations. At present, there is a wide variety of construction methods employed and all three categories of 'katcha' (temporary), 'pucca'. (permanent or solid) and mixed are well represented. The vast majority of households are owner-squatters, though there are a number of tenants who share with the family and are usually distant relations.

*Figure 3.8     The location of the Rouse Avenue settlement showing the adjoining developments at Connaught Place.*

*Figure 3.9    A small communal space located directly outside the entrance to a hutment, does not disturb the sense of privacy and informality.*

*Figure 3.10    The main service road at the Rouse Avenue settlement — circulation is only one of its functions.*

*Figure 3.11     Charopy beds and domestic industry make the service road
an effective communal living space and work area.*

According to the proposed typology, the settlement can be
described in the following way:

SETTLEMENT POPULATION: 2150                    SETTLEMENT AREA: 1 acre (0.4 ha)

| Dwelling type | % of type to total | Construction type | | | Tenure status | | | | | | | | |
|---|---|---|---|---|---|---|---|---|---|---|---|---|---|
| | | Tempor-ary | Mixed | Perm-anent | 1 | 2 | 3 | 4 | 5 | 6 | 7 | 8 | 9 |
| exposed site | 0 | | | | | | | | | | | | |
| hutment | 100% | 25% | 55% | 20% | | | | | | 85% | | 15% | |
| room in block | 0 | | | | | | | | | | | | |
| chawl/tenement | 0 | | | | | | | | | | | | |
| apartment/flat | 0 | | | | | | | | | | | | |
| linked house unit | 0 | | | | | | | | | | | | |
| detached house unit | 0 | | | | | | | | | | | | |

3.3.2   **Official Intervention**

The settlement had achieved sufficient internal solidarity and external influence by the early 1960's for it to be 'regularized' by the housing authorities and for various programmes of rehabilitation and improvement to be initiated. Using the six-point classification previously outlined, we can assess this process as follows:

*Legal*
Although the settlement can now claim a quasi-legal status, it is still officially illegal and there is no long-term security for its occupants or any officially acknowledged expectancy of acquiring legal rights to the land. Since it and others like it, do not appear to have been incorporated into a Master Plan for the city, it must be doubtful whether its existence is being incorporated into the overall urban planning process. Action in this area can best be classified, therefore, as a holding operation which aims to prevent the worst excesses of environmental decay whilst obviating the need to rehouse the occupants or grant them a long term security of tenure.

*Administrative*
It appears that no charges are collected for ground rent or services provided in the area. There is little evidence that coordination of social welfare programmes regarding settlements of this type are being provided by the administration and a policy of *laissez faire* could be said to exist.

*Physical*
The emphasis of regularization policies is undoubtedly seen in spatial and physical terms, and it is here that the greatest effort has been made. The main thoroughfare through the site was surfaced in tarmac and secondary paths and *chowks* (communal urban spaces) provided with brick paving and open drains; taps were installed at approximately 50 m intervals through the site and street lighting was erected (but no domestic electricity supply). Facilities were also built for the laundry workers, or dhobies (see Fig. 3.27). This programme has done a great deal to improve the environmental condition of the settlement and has encouraged several households to improve their hutments. However, the lack of long term security still makes many of them unwilling to finance long term major improvements.

*Economic*
It is difficult to assess the impact of official intervention in these terms, apart from the example of the laundry facilities. There is arguably little that can be done to generate employment on a sufficiently large scale to effect a major change in the economic structure of the settlement, but by their tolerance of a settlement so close to the central business district, the authorities can claim to have at least maintained the possibilities for obtaining work in either the formal or informal sectors.

*Political*
The settlement has traditionally registered a block vote for the Congress (R) Party and it is as a result of their initiative that it was regularized. There is complete freedom to initiate other political organizations but the existing parties, which in any case cover a wide political spectrum, appear to hold sway. Internal political matters are organized on the *panchayat system* (this is a traditional decision making unit in Indian villages and towns, which consists of a council of elders whose job is to ensure the day to day administration and to arbitrate disputes). Local leaders are then elected into local committees.

*Cultural/Social*
There is no provision of social facilities such as schools or health centres within the settlement. Existing local facilities are, however, available for those able to afford their use, and this varies throughout the community. Several groups with good educational achievements appear to be able to obtain work as clerks or office staff and it does not appear that residence in the area in any way inhibits opportunities for job progress.

If official intervention can therefore be seen to have had a somewhat beneficial impact on the settlement, it is far from effecting a significant acknowledgement of the need for long term security and as such has been a somewhat superficial form.

### 3.3.3.  Physical Layout

### 3.3.3.i  Circulation
The circulation network consists of a hierarchy of paths organized in an informal way .and reflecting the pattern by which the settlement has grown. There is therefore an intimate relationship at

all points between the circulation areas and those of the hutment groups which ensures that all households have direct access to a space which they can use to extend into from their own plot, and which also serves to link them spatially to other parts of the site.

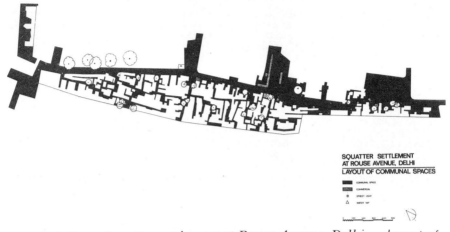

*Figure 3.12     Squatter settlement at Rouse Avenue, Delhi — layout of communal spaces.*

There are basically five types of circulatory space as shown in the photographs: 1. the main service road, which also serves as the central social, commercial and industrial area; 2. the secondary spine paths, which provide access from this road to the various hutment groups; 3. the narrow lanes which connect one housing group with another; 4. small chowks or open spaces which occur at the intersection of various paths and often exploit the existence of a small shading tree and 5. small cul-de-sacs which provide access to self-contained groups of huts.

The road which has an average width of between 4 m — 5 m and penetrates the entire site, not only provides space for a wide variety of social activities, but is also used for tethering water buffaloes and goats and as an emergency access to the settlement for ambulances or fire-fighting vehicles. Other types of circulation also fulfil a wide range of activities and this will be studied in greater detail later. The main point to make at this stage is that there is a complex and varied relationship between the various types of circulation mode which creates a rich structure of possible movement and activity patterns which is not normally considered to exist in what are assumed to th 'unplanned' settlements.

*Figure 3.13     Main pathways linking the service road to the various housing clusters.*

*Figure 3.14     A chowk used as the focal point of a housing cluster.*

Figure 3.15     *Chowks usually exploit whatever shade trees are available in the area.*

Figure 3.16     *Women and children meet in areas that are cool or quiet. Chowks are ideal spaces for the purpose and are an environmental form traditionally found in Old Delhi.*

*Figure 3.17    Narrow paths providing links between clusters of hutments. These are just wide enough to push a bicycle and accommodate a surface water drain.*

*Figure 3.18  Small culs-de-sac are used for communal purposes by adjoining households.*

### 3.3.3.ii  **Housing**

As can be seen from the layout plan, the housing consists of a large number of small house units grouped in a variety of ways along paths and around the small chowks. Whilst these vary a great deal in their standard of construction, size, number of inhabitants and facilities, there are certain characteristics which most have in common. They are, without exception, single storey and most consist of one or more rooms with a small covered verandah and an equally small private open space, (see photographs). The plot is usually defined by a low wall or the line of a drain and related to the adjoining houses and communal open spaces.

The inter-relationship between the house units and the group together with the circulation system provides the basic organizational framework of the settlement and provides a balance between them. In the hutments located along the service road, for example, a large number of people have built a screen wall between the road and the house proper in order to provide a high degree of visual privacy from passers-by; in the small cul-de-sacs, however, where there is less need for privacy, the paths themselves are regarded and used as extensions of the private open space. Such areas are commonly used for open air sleeping in summer and for cooking throughout the year.

*Figure 3.19     Example of typical, early housing, built against the boundary walls, or those of middle income government housing.*

*Figure 3.20     The standard of construction and comfort achieved in hutments is surprisingly high in view of the lack of inducement which insecurity of tenure engenders.*

*Figure 3.21     A good example of decent pucca housing and its relationship to communal spaces.*

*Figure 3.22     Decoration in the entrance to a private open space.*

Throughout, the function of the dwelling itself cannot be divorced from its relationship to the adjoining open space, both public and private, since even in wealthy families it is normal to spend a large part of the year living in the open, round a well-equipped private courtyard. The houses in the settlement often serve more as stores than living spaces, to which the occupants retreat in the cold winters or during the monsoon. It could even be argued that house structures as such, are less important than the size and nature of their adjacent open space (3.15).

The huts are built predominantly of brickwork of various qualities and types. Timber, due to its comparatively high cost, is used as sparingly as possible. Mortar is of the basic mud variety and is occasionally mixed with cow-dung. Although foundations are not normally used, the light weight of the buildings does not appear to cause excessive loading or structural deformation. Floors range from concrete screed with matted surfaces, to beaten earth, depending upon the income and priorities of the family. Roofs vary from pucca thatch lined with a waterproof membrane, to corrugated iron and tarpaulins held down by stones. No house has a private water tap or sanitary facilities and water is collected from outlets in the services road and occasionally stored in drums in the private open spaces. For those families who do not use the toilets provided by the local authorities, it is normal to use a portion of the private open spaces set aside for washing and bathing and to collect wastes early each

*Figure 3.23    Traditional brick oven built in a private open space*

*Figure 3.24    Using a bucket oven in one of the communal open spaces*

*Figure 3.25     Domestic chores during the monsoon*

morning and deposit them in the toilets. Young children frequently
use the open drains as toilets until they are old enough to go to the
pucca toilet blocks.

Cooking is normally carried out in mobile ovens made from
galvanized buckets, adapted to draw air in from the base through a
small metal grill near the top of the bucket, round which a mud
surround is packed to support the kettle or pans. The handle is
retained and the complete unit can then be positioned either in the
nearest open space or, in adverse weather, inside the house. A built-
in mud-brick oven is also usually incorporated in most hutments.

### 3.3.4.  Commerce and Industry

Although the settlement accommodates a large number of people,
many of whom have lived in the area for over twenty years, there is
very little industrial or commercial activity on the site itself. This is
no doubt due to the proximity of employment opportunities within
the formal sector in the city centre and outlets for service
employment that this provides.

A small market is held daily at which staple food items are sold.
This is intended primarily for the inhabitants of the settlement,
although its lower prices attract people from the higher income
housing colonies as well. The market is supplemented by several

small lock-up shops which sell a variety of domestic and general goods including cigarettes, clothes, transistor radios and lottery tickets. Informal employment for men consists of bicycle repairing and labouring jobs and for women, domestic employment in the surrounding areas, is easy to obtain on a part-time or full-time scale. The dhobies serve middle and upper income residential areas.

*Figure 3.26        A visiting locksmith displaying wares.*

*Figure 3.27        Laundry workers (dhobies) in the special area provided for them by the authorities.*

*Figure 3.28*
*Selling vegetables*
*in the market*

*Figure 3.29*
*Visiting services include*
*knife-sharpening*

### 3.3.5.  The Study Areas

### 3.3.5.i.  Introduction

It must be apparent, even after this cursory description of the settlement, that it is not a disordered development, even though it has evolved without an externally prepared plan, or according to any official definition of planned and balanced growth. The intensity of land use, and the intricate relationships between house unit, house group and communal space, that has been achieved within the constraints imposed by lack of capital, the need to maximize security and an optimum location against the threat of eviction, and the widespread acceptance of a small plot area and shared facilities, all indicate that the interaction of needs and constraints has resulted in a carefully evolved settlement type. This is not to say, of course, that it is an ideal type of housing, but it is far from being an unplanned blight upon the city, if considered as the functional expression of the environmental needs of a large number of people with extremely limited material resources.

It is therefore necessary to ask what underlying processes make it possible to achieve such high densities in single storey developments and how the relationships between the spatial and activity organization enable the settlement to support the wide range of necessary functions· at the high densities indicated.

Detailed observation of the settlement conducted over a period of several months, suggests that a symbiotic functional relationship exists both chronologically and spatially throughout the site, enabling the maximum use to be extracted from the limited amounts of available public open space, and compensating for many of the inadequacies of individual plot areas. In the case of the main service road, for example, it is normal for families whose huts are nearby and who have no adequate private open space, to do their cooking there in the mornings and evenings, whilst during the rest of the day, it is used for domestic industry such as making charpoy beds or repairing bicycles; by the old men for sitting and smoking their hookah pipes, and by children for playing. Over longer periods of time, there are seasonal changes as, for instance, when it used for open-air sleeping in summer. Spatial interdependence is achieved by allocating some areas to cattle where they can be supervised by their owners and their excreta used by the women to make dung-cakes for fuel.

In the case of small spaces, the communal areas are regarded as extensions of the private open space for certain functions such as working, sleeping, male meetings, children's play and domestic industry. At any one time, in any area, a wide range of such activities may be going on and this pattern changes according to the season and the time of day. In order to study how these activities were accommodated within the spatial structure, specific sections of the settlement were isolated and considered in greater depth. The criteria for this selection were: 1. observed boundaries in which activities congregated; 2. the need for a recognizable grouping of house units to each other and open spaces that served them, and 3. the area should be suitable for prolonged and detailed observation. As a result, selected areas were chosen as being representative of different layout types. One of these is a typical section of housing built alongside the service road; the second is a linear cluster in the centre of the site and stretching from the service road through the back boundary wall, whilst the third is an open court area. Since the settlement was originally built along the back wall and then spread away from it and finally along the service road, these groups can also be said to approximate to the three growth phases of the development. The study of spatial/activity organization within each cluster area is based upon the two methods outlined above.

### 3.3.5.ii  Study Area I — The Linear Cluster

This area is located adjacent to the main service road (see Fig. 3.30). It consists of a number of hutments built alongside the main service road and opening into it.

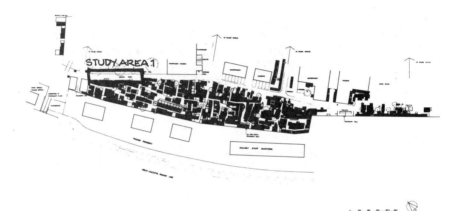

*Figure 3.30*     *Rouse Avenue — Study Area No. 1: The Linear cluster — location*

*Method A*

In this particular area, the following data were obtained:

| | |
|---|---|
| TOTAL AREA OF CLUSTER | 550.0 m² |
| PRIVATE SPACE AREAS: | |
| Private indoor space | 99.9 m² |
| Private covered verandah | 43.1 m² |
| Private open space | 23.9 m² |
| Total private areas | 166.9 m² |
| Therefore, | |
| Total Communal Open Space = 550.0—166.9 | = 373.1 m² |

COMMUNAL OPEN SPACES:

| | | |
|---|---|---|
| ⦿ | Circulation | 276.9 m² |
| ⊖ | Children's play area | 276.9 m² |
| ⊘ | Summer open air sleeping | 91.5 m² |
| ⊗ | Communal meeting space | 364.5 m² |
| ⦿ | Cottage industry/commercial areas | 209.1 m² |
| | | 08.0 m² |
| ⊖ | Open air cooking | 91.5 m² |
| ⊘ | Latrines and toilet areas | 00.0 m² |
| ⊗ | Water taps, washing and laundry areas | 73.5 m² |
| ⊗ | Cattle (grazing or tethered) | 87.6 m² |
| | Others | 00.0 m² |
| | Total Effective Public Space | 1479.5 m² |

The efficiency ratio of space in this situation is, therefore,

$$\frac{\text{EFFECTIVE SPACE}}{\text{ACTUAL SPACE}} = \frac{1479.5}{373.1} = 4.0$$

If we now assess these data in terms of the number of dwelling units which are directly served by this open space, we find

$$\frac{\text{EFFECTIVE SPACE}}{\text{NO. DWELLING UNITS}} = \frac{1479.5}{11} = 134.5 \text{ m}^2 \text{ per unit}$$

Since the average dwelling unit area is approximately 9.0 m² and average plot area $= \frac{166.9}{11} = 15.5$ m² (indicating a plot radio of 0.6)

we can see that the effective communal space per household unit is several times the area of their plot. It is this relationship which provides a clue to the ability to maintain a complex and coherent social organization, despite a minimal plot size and highly restricted communal space.

*Method B*
The graphic representation of the survey of this area is shown in Fig.
3.31.

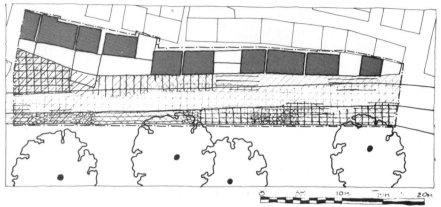

Figure 3.31     *Spatial activity organization — study area 1*

*Conclusions*
One of the main reasons why the effective communal space for each
dwelling unit is so high in the area, is that it is not only used by those
families adjacent to it, but also by many others, and is also
perpetually in use as the main thoroughfare for the whole.

3.3.5.iii.    **Study Area 2: The Chowk Cluster**
This area is located near the centre of the settlement as shown in Fig.
3.32. There is a greater range of house types and communal space

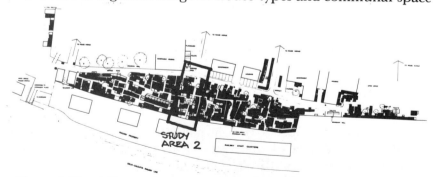

Figure 3.32     *Rouse Avenue — Study Area No. 2: The chowk cluster*
*— location*

here than was found in the previous example. This is partly because the area consists of a mixture of the earliest and latest constructions, and also because it links up areas of secluded cul-de-sacs with the main service road.

## Method A

Data for the area were collected on the same basis as for the first example, and are as follows:

| | |
|---|---|
| TOTAL AREA | 870.3 m² |
| PRIVATE SPACE AREAS: | |
| Private indoor space | 321.9 m² |
| Private covered verandah | 41.8 m² |
| Private open space | 168.1 m² |
| Total private areas | 531.8 m² |
| Therefore, | |
| Total Communal Open Space = 870.3—531.8 | = 338.5 m² |

COMMUNAL OPEN SPACES:

| | | |
|---|---|---|
| ⓫ | Circulation | 338.5 m² |
| ⊜ | Children's play areas | 132.1 m² |
| ⊘ | Summer open air sleeping | 250.0 m² |
| ⊗ | Communal meeting space | 98.5 m² |
| ⓫ | Cottage industry/Commercial areas | 93.4 m² |
| | | 00.0 m² |
| ⊜ | Open air cooking | 5.0 m² |
| ⊘ | Latrines and toilet areas | 00.0 m² |
| ⊗ | Water taps, washing and domestic areas | 5.0 m² |
| ⊕ | Cattle (grazing and tethered) | 0.0 m² |
| | Others | 0.0 m² |
| | Total Effective Public Space | 922.5 m² |

The efficiency ratio of this area is therefore

$$\frac{\text{EFFECTIVE SPACE}}{\text{ACTUAL SPACE}} = \frac{922.5}{338.5} = 2.73$$

E

The total number of dwelling units = 25, at an average plot area of

$$\frac{531.8}{25} = 21.3 \text{ m}^2$$

(and an average dwelling area of 12.8 m² indicating a plot ratio of

$$\frac{12.8}{21.3} = 0.6$$

The average effective communal space per dwelling unit is therefore

$$\frac{\text{EFFECTIVE SPACE}}{\text{NO. OF DWELLING UNITS}} = \frac{922.5}{25} = 36.9 \text{ m}^2$$

The effective space available to each family unit is therefore an average of almost double the actual area.

*Method B*
The graphic representation of the survey of this are is shown in Fig. 3.33

*Figure 3.33      Spatial activity organization — study area 2*

*Conclusions*

There is greatly reduced efficiency ratio for this area than for the previous example. It is possible that this can be explained by the fact that there is a much greater average plot size than in the linear cluster.

### 3.3.5.iv.   Study Area 3 — Open Court Cluster

This Cluster is located on the eastern end of the settlement as shown in Fig. 3.34. This area, which is probably typical of the early settlement patterns found in the settlement, is situated some distance away from the main access points, and is positioned adjacent to a large open space used by the tenants of the nearby middle income housing.

The regularization policy of the local authorities ensured that there would be no further expansion of the settlement by registering all hutments existing at the time and subsequently inspecting the area to remove any additions. This could possibly explain the lack of subsequent enclosure of this area by later building. The adjacent open space is, however, used occasionally for the purposes of grazing buffaloes and goats or for drying domestic laundry. As this use was not substantial however, it has not been included in the present analysis.

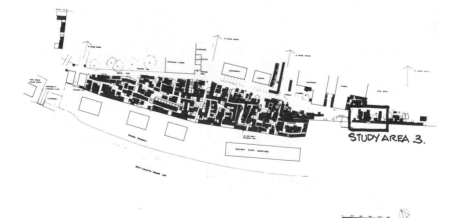

*Figure 3.34        Rouse Avenue — Study Area No. 3: The open court cluster — location*

*Method A*

| | |
|---|---|
| TOTAL AREA | 326.0 m² |
| PRIVATE SPACE AREAS: | |
| Private indoor space | 117.2 m² |
| Private covered verandah | 19.4 m² |
| Private open space | 24.2 m² |
| Total Private Areas | 160.8 m² |
| Therefore, | |
| Total Communal Open Space     = 326.0—1608 | = 155.2 m² |

COMMUNAL OPEN SPACES:

| | | |
|---|---|---|
| ⦿ | Circulation | 155.2 m² |
| ⊖ | Childrens' play areas | 155.2 m² |
| ⊘ | Summer open air sleeping | 155.2 m² |
| ⊗ | Communal meeting space | 109.0 m² |
| ⦿ | Cottage industry/Commercial areas | 37.4 m² |
| | | 00.0 m² |
| ⊖ | Open air cooking | 18.5 m² |
| ⊘ | Latrines and toilet areas | 00.0 m² |
| ⊖ | Water taps, washing and laundry areas | 18.5 m² |
| ⊗ | Cattle (grazing or tethered) | 00.0 m² |
| | Others | 00.0m² |
| | Total Effective Communal Space | 649.0 m² |

The efficiency ratio of this cluster is therefore

$$\frac{\text{EFFECTIVE SPACE}}{\text{ACTUAL SPACE}} = \frac{649.0}{155.2} = 4.2$$

The number of dwelling units in the cluster is 12, so that the average effective communal space per household unit is

$$\frac{\text{EFFECTIVE SPACE}}{\text{ACTUAL SPACE}} = \frac{649.0}{12} = 54 \text{ m}^2$$

The average dwelling unit area is 11.6 m² and the plot = 13.4 m² so that plot ratios in this cluster average.

*Method B*
The graphic representation of the survey of this area is shown in **Fig. 3.35.**

*Figure 3.35     Spatial activity organization — study area 3*

*Conclusions*
It will immediately be apparent that there is a high effective area in this cluster, even though the actual communal space is not relatively large. Since there is also little use of the space by people from other parts of the settlement, an explanation must be found elsewhere and it is possible that the high degree of enclosure of the central space and its suitability for use in a variety of ways (and its easy supervision by members of each household) make their relationship of plots to the spatial organization particularly successful.

One might be led to enquire why such characteristics, which no doubt existed in the phases of settlement which were laid out in the same way, should have been superceded by layouts with a reduced capability of sustaining such an intensity and variety of activities. Whilst no conclusive answer can be given to this, two factors appear to be relevant. The first is that the original settlers may have had a higher requirement for the security of their tenure and would be prepared to accept spatial restrictions in order to minimize their solidarity. The second reason has already been referred to, namely that there is little encouragement, since the settlement was regularized, to permit the building of any additional huts around the space.

These two examples of the influence of official intervention (or threat of it), indicate the impact of external factors upon changing criteria for spatial organization within the settlement.

### 3.3.6.  The Spatial/Activity Survey — Conclusions

Certain distinct characteristics emerge in comparing the spatial activity organizations of the various cluster groups surveyed. There is a clear grading of plot areas, for example, from 21.3 m² in the chowk cluster to 15.2 m² in the linear cluster and 13.4 m² in the open court cluster, which is inversely proportional to the efficiency ratios. In the chowk area, this ratio was 2.73, for linear cluster 4.0 and for open-court cluster 4.2.

It can be seen from this that where individual plots are small, there is a tendency for greater use to be made of the adjoining communal areas and that areas of high effective communal space are achieved using small courts surrounded by huts. In the chowk cluster, larger individual plot areas are associated with a reduced intensity in the utilization of communal areas, and in the linear type both the average plot size and the efficiency ratios are less extreme than in other areas.

The significance of these data are not, of course, that small plots are more efficient than large plots, but that there is a close inter-relationship between plots and their immediate spatial surroundings, which does indicate the ability of the communal areas to compensate spatially for the inadequacies of the private domain. Small, or especially poor families, or those with close kinship or class attachments to their neighbours, are therefore more readily accommodated in the small plot/high efficiency areas, whilst larger or more affluent families are less spatially dependent but require more private space. That both types exist and interact to their mutual benefit, is one of the major environmental achievements of the settlement.

The spatial structure of this apparently unplanned settlement has therefore revealed an ingenious and economical use of land which has proved able to sustain most domestic activities required by the residents, over a long period of time. This has been achieved without, until recently, any expense being incurred by the authorities. There can be, of course, little doubt that in most respects and by most standards, the settlement is environmentally substandard in that no dwelling has a private water tap or electricity supply, surface and sanitary drainage is inadequate and there are no community or welfare facilities that one would expect to find in an officially sponsored development. Nonetheless, the inhabitants appear to have done all that they can to make the settlement habitable and comfortable and it is noticeably  the facilities and services normally provided by local authorities which are the main inhibition to further improvement.

### 3.3.7. The Social Survey

Two questions dominated the analysis of this settlement throughout. The first was what sort of social structure it supported, whether there was evidence of group solidarity, or social mobility and how the inhabitants related to the urban context in which they found themselves; whether in fact they were socially integrated as a community and as a part of the wider urban context. The second question was what aspirations, needs and resources they had regarding the future, how realistic these were in the light of their economic prospects and also what means they were adopting to achieve them.

The survey method consisted of a random-stratified sample with a 10% coverage of households (of which there were approximately 440). The stratification was based upon a division of the settlement into coherent physical clusters similar to the types studied in the spatial/activity analysis, and random households were selected within these clusters. Wherever possible, interviews were held with the household head. The material and analysis follows the same general format as the original questionnaire, which is illustrated in the Appendix.

The settlement is organized on the panchayat system (3.16) and has two separate councils with close informal relations between them; one of these represents the eastern half and the other the western. It appears that the western section consists almost entirely of scheduled castes, whereas the eastern section described themselves as Rajputs. There do not appear to be any rigidly defined case boundaries, as one would expect to find in a village layout. There is a wide variety of castes ranging from the lowest scheduled caste (3.17) to a few Brahmins. Whilst it was not possible to provide concrete evidence, it did appear from observation that there was a full and free interaction between them; certainly one case was found where a Brahmin claimed to entertain lower castes and this was substantiated by the people referred to, but it was impossible to say exactly how representative this attitude was.

On the whole, economic and spatial constraints did not appear to enable the caste structure to survive in any complete sense. Several people referred to the frequent need to raise loans for various purposes, and stated that as the rates outside the settlement were usually excessive, loans were raised within it whenever possible. For this community, the situation had long since vanished when high caste was synonymous with wealth and social authority, and it was quite possible that such a family would need to borrow from a low caste one. In this way, the traditional restrictions were further weakened and did not appear to be a major factor in the social structure.

The need to increase security within the settlement in order to resist the continual fear of removal by the authorities no doubt helped to create a desire for a less formalized, but equally well developed sense of community. There is also evidence that this new basis of social relations is adapting to the wider urban social structure; the leader of the panchayat for the central part of the site, himself a committed Congress (R) member, boasted several enlarged photographs of himself being introduced to the Prime Minister and senior government officials, and the mere fact that the political influence wielded by the leaders was sufficient to secure official 'regularization' indicates the degree to which the inhabitants are aware of the means necessary to safeguard their position.

After being in existence for over twenty years the community, and the individuals in it, have passed through several major social changes. The trauma of Partition was, for many of them, the end of the old way of life, when traditional customs and attitudes in familiar locations suddenly gave way under their feet. They were forced to flee to the cities, and abandoned whatever wealth and influence they possessed to build a new life in strange and sometimes unsympathetic surroundings. Others had a less dramatic background and arrived in Delhi after being unable to continue on a subsistence agriculture which may have suddenly had a bad harvest; still others heard through relations of possible job opportunities which offered more hope of security and advancement than they were able to expect in their village. Few seemed to have been attracted to the city because of its glamour. The survey revealed that adult residents in the settlement originated from the following regions:

| | |
|---|---|
| Rajasthan | 19.4% |
| Madhya Pradesh | 19.4% |
| Uttar Pradesh | 16.1% |
| Haryana | 22.5% |
| Lahore (Pakistan) | 6.4% |
| Afghanistan | 8.2% |

Delhi                                                              6.2%
Others                                                             1.8%


This indicates that a large proportion of the migrants came from the regions directly adjoining Delhi and 6.2% actually moved from other areas of the city. The influx from Pakistan and Afghanistan, which is probably associated with Partition, is 14.6%. As regards the length of time spent on the site, 26.5% had in fact arrived before 1947, although a further 26.5% arrived during that year. Between 1947 and 1959 an additional 33.1% had arrived and by 1970 another 6.7%. It was also found that 6.7% were born within the settlement. If children and youths are included in the survey, however, a very different picture emerges. Virtually all children and the majority of youths were born here. Although specific questions relating to the age structure of the community were not asked in the questionnaire, it was apparent that a high proportion of the population is within the lower age bracket. It is therefore no longer feasible to think of the settlement as accommodating migrants, but rather a section of the indigenous urban poor. This should not be taken to mean that the social structure and life-style are the same as for other sections of the indigenous urban population, since the community is, in fact, only a second generation urban group, but the important change from rural to urban status has now been effected.

Three main reasons were given in reply to questions about people's motives for migrating:

1. poverty (or lack of land or an adequate job in the place of origin; 2. the after-effects of Partition in 1947; and, 3. the presence in Delhi of relations whom it was hoped would be able to assist in obtaining employment. Personal family reasons were also included in the last category. It was found that 52.4% came to Delhi out of reasons associated with poverty in their previous place of residence (lack of land, loss of job, starvation, etc.); 19% came because of the after-effects of Partition and 28.6% came because of relatives.

It was difficult to obtain data on existing kinship patterns, partly because of the problems of classification and also that of surveying. Since the situation was often fluid, it could not be assumed, for example, that households with a large number of people, implied the existence of an extended family structure. The following data were, however, obtained on family size:

| | |
|---|---|
| 1—2 members | 3.5% |
| 3—4 members | 10.8% |
| 5 members | 21.5% |
| 6 members | 10.7% |
| 7 members | 10.7% |
| 8 members | 17.2% |
| 9 members | 14.2% |
| 10 members + | 14.1% |

The predominant size grouping indicated by the survey was 5—9 members (inclusive), and this group accounted for 74.3% of all households. In view of the small size of the average indoor private space within dwelling units (12.75 m$^2$) the importance of close proximity to a relatively large effective communal open space can clearly be seen. Even so, there are severe limitations upon basic needs such as privacy; normal marital relations are impossible when a whole household has to share one room, and although the situation is a little easier in the summer when most people sleep out of doors and the hut is normally used for purposes of intimacy, the huts were too hot to permit comfort and during winter not even this degree of privacy is obtained. In less personal situations, there was an acknowledged lack of opportunity for the traditional village separation of the sexes into different parts of the house and there is no space for the women to cook or wash separately from the men. These aspects of the spatial organization are naturally a cause of frustration even to those who have adjusted to them, and many families stressed that they would like either a second room or a small courtyard attached to their present hut.

With regard to questions of shelter provision, it was apparent that most dwellings had been built at very little cost. It was found that 16.8% had, in fact, spent no money at all on their shelter, 5.5% spent up to Rs.100; 27.6% spent Rs.101-500; 39.0% spent Rs. 501-1000 and only 11.1% spent over Rs.1000. 75% of households built their hutments in at least two separate phases. Nearly all the hutments were erected at a total cost of less than Rs.1000, though several respondents did not include subsequent improvements or additions when making estimates. It was apparent, though, that materials were generally obtained either at a low cost through personal contacts or were simply waste-products from other sources, such as the widespread use of broken baked bricks collected from rubbish piles on building sites.

The low levels of financial investment were largely the result of rural claims on resources for food, clothing, travel and festivals (weddings, funerals and religious occasions). Even more important than this, however, was the feeling of insecurity that the settlement's illegality engendered, and few felt it worthwhile to invest in their house in case the local authorities decided to remove them.

Regarding the nature of their existing shelter, 45.3% of households lived in one room only, 37.5% occupied two rooms and 17.2% had three or more rooms. Without exception, those occupying the largest units were large extended kinship families and all the smaller households lived in one or two room hutments. The condition of the huts and the materials of their construction varied from substantial well-kept units to others which were built with a mixture of mud and baked brick, with mud and dung plaster rendering which was replaced annually. Roofs were generally corrugated iron (18%), tarpaulins (32%), thatch (22%), or rags (24%). None of the roofs were therefore structurally loadbearing or capable of supporting a further floor. There was a basic provision of home-made charpoy beds (3.18), (see Fig. 3.11), storage trunks and cooking utensils. Luxuries consisted of transistor radios and bicycles, both of which carry a high status value.

As was to be expected, there was a direct relationship between those inhabitants who had spent the longest time in the settlement and those with the lowest degree of mobility; conversely, those who had arrived more recently tended to have higher hopes of upward mobility.

There was also a noticeable change of situation regarding different generations; several families with young adult sons, who had achieved a degree of success in vocational promotion, hoped to move out of the settlement and purchase a site on the edge of the city and build a new house to which the older family members would then be invited.

Regarding education, it was found that 65.0% of respondents planned to send their children to school for as long as was economically possible and all of these placed a high importance on the qualifications education offered regarding hopes of better employment opportunities. There was an obvious conflict here between what was desired and what was feasible. The remainder did not seem to place any real importance on schooling. The overwhelming majority of families which had children at school or starting work hoped that if they were successful, that the family would stay together. Once again, economic motives are no doubt relevant, in that older members hoped that their children would look after them in their old age, but there was generally a high degree of emphasis laid on family unity in all matters, which could be considered more significant than purely economic motives.

Questioned about their interaction socially with the city as a whole, approximately one third of the respondents said they spent most of their lives in the settlement and had no real contacts outside it, whereas another third had friends outside and participated in social activities with them. The remainder were vague; nearly 20% expressed a dislike for the city and wished to return to their village when, or if, it was possible. Of those who had friends outside the area, the majority of these were a result of friendships made at their place of work or study. Regarding future plans, only 6.9% linked their hopes or plans with their jobs and stated that they would leave if jobs ended. This group held little hope of advancement economically and simply aspired to be able to maintain their present situation. The same attitude was confirmed by another 45% who had no plans, and a further 10.3% were awaiting the allocation of government quarters because they were classified as on the permanent staff.

Approximately 10% of respondents had definite intentions to improve their existing shelters. Usually, such plans were linked to a special event, such as the marriage of a son, in which case a separate room would be added if space permitted. If there was no opportunity for this, the covered verandah was occasionally walled in, or a roof was built over the private open space. In this way, a small degree of spatial flexibility was achieved despite the extreme restrictions of the plot area.

Several questions were asked in the survey in order to canvas opinions regarding environmental needs and aspirations. This was found, however, to present certain operational difficulties, since most respondents immediately assumed (or hoped) that the interviewing team would be in a position to put their views to a 'higher authority' and possibly even lead to their fulfilment. It was therefore necessary to ensure that comments made regarding shelter needs were related to socio-economic realities. A technique was evolved in which the respondents were allowed to think about their ideal solution, and if this was considered beyond their means, further questions were asked as to how they would finance this. Invariably the answer that 'the government would pay a subsidy' was offered, but this was dismissed and it was emphasized that needs were to be related to the ability to pay for them. After what was sometimes a prolonged discussion, an idea was obtained of optimum shelter needs approximating to the resources felt by the respondents to be within their means.

The most important single factor regarding future environmental needs was the desire to be located near the central area of the city and, if possible, adjacent to the existing settlement. This was mentioned by 69% of respondents, and a further 6% actually wished to remain in their existing settlement making a total of 75% seeking accommodation nearby; 12.5% were prepared to move to an area within two or three miles of the city centre providing adequate and cheap public transport was available, and the remaining 12.5% would accept a site within 5 miles of the centre, with the same proviso regarding transportation.

Equally significant was the way in which respondents sought to be re-housed: 62% wished to build their own house if given the opportunity, whilst only 38% wanted to move into government built accommodation. It was not ascertained whether this was felt to be because of a rejection of the type of housing offered by the official programmes, or the costs which it involved, especially as self-built houses were invariably cheaper and could be improved as funds became available. When questioned about the type of housing they would like, respondents' goals were found to be extremely modest and came within the following categories:

### Desired Housing Types — Rouse Avenue Survey

| | | |
|---|---|---|
| (i) | As existing | 24.0% |
| (ii) | One room and verandah/kitchen | 3.5% |
| (iii) | One room and verandah/kitchen and courtyard | 13.8% |
| (iv) | One room and verandah/kitchen and bath/w.c. and courtyard | 13.8% |
| (v) | Two rooms and verandah/kitchen and courtyard | 27.5% |
| (vi) | Two rooms and verandah/kitchen and bath/w.c. and courtyard | 17.3% |

Provided the location and price were both acceptable, all but 23% of respondents agreed to consider accommodation in tenement blocks, though 30% of these required a unit on the ground floor.

Priorities regarding environmental services were also surveyed, though answers were not conclusive. A good water supply was the greatest need, followed by electricity and sanitation; communal latrines were generally regarded as adequate, if only because the majority of respondents held out no hope of obtaining a private unit. Street lamps, refuse collection and the nearness of schools were also mentioned but with less frequency.

When asked for their views regarding desired plot area, respondents frequently listed large areas up to 100m², even when told this was not economically feasible in the suburban location, let alone on a site adjacent to their present one. This could well represent a desire to escape the present confines of the plots or to have an adequate area in which to invest in the future. It certainly indicated an awareness that the interview might provide a means of making claims upon the housing authorities which is a far cry from the apathy associated with the 'culture of poverty'! Not all respondents had such high targets, however, and approximately 30% considered that if they were given a plot of between 11-25 m² they would be satisfied. Existing financial resources and future estimated allocations for housing were also investigated. It was found that about 40% of households received between Rs.101-200 a month gross (including all earning members); 16% earned between Rs.201-300 and a further 20% earned Rs. 301-400 and the remaining 24% earned more than Rs. 400 a month. No household earned more than Rs. 700 a month and only 4% earned over Rs. 600.

When asked what resources would be available if the house types they had requested were granted to them, it was immediately apparent that the crucial factor was the tenure status which would be involved. In all cases the resources which respondents were willing to invest in a unit they were able to purchase were substantially higher than if the accommodation was to be rented. In the case of housing to rent, no family appeared able or willing to afford more than Rs.30 a month. If purchasing were possible, 17.9% of respondents were prepared to put down a deposit or full payment for a dwelling, provided again that it conformed to their needs. The amounts varied between Rs.500 and Rs.5000, and a further 7.1% were even prepared to pay Rs.7000. The vast majority of respondents however, preferred to pay by monthly installments without deposit, as follows:

**Amounts available for Purchase of desired Accommodation**

| Monthly installments | % of respondents |
|---|---|
| Rs.0-10 | 9.1 |
| Rs. 11-25 | 22.9 |
| Rs. 26-30 | 36.3 |
| Rs. 30-40 | 15.5 |
| Rs. 41-50 | 9.1 |
| Rs. 51 and above | 9.1 |

It can be seen from this that of 81.5% who wished to purchase but not to put down a deposit, approximately two-thirds, or 54.4% of the total sample, were unable or unwilling to pay more than Rs.30 per month. These data on potential resources give a clear indication of the extent of commitment which could be mobilized in the community given adequate and appropriate support.

At the end of each interview any points which had appeared to be of particular concern to the respondent, or about which there was a need for more information, were mentioned informally in order to provide a more qualitative basis for discussion. Most respondents considered that there was little point in hoping for any real change in their living situation and would be quite happy if it simply got no worse. In view of this, it would perhaps be unwise to attach too much significance to the opinions expressed regarding future needs, since it was apparent that only a few people had ever thought of them before being asked. Information on resources and dislikes, is however, more reliable. A general fear seemed to be that existing family arrangements would collapse as soon as one of the senior members died or retired and this was obviously a major cause of stress and fear of the future. In spite of such misgivings and the comparatively large proportion of respondents who had kinship ties with their place of origin, there was little evidence that many families hoped or expected to return to them; most appeared to be committed to the city and in the case of children and young adults the question never arose, since they were normally fully adjusted to urban life.

Related to family problems was the expressed need to marry off one's offspring and this featured in a number of interviews. In general respondents seemed much more concerned and positive when discussing subjects of this nature than when asked questions regarding environmental matters. Hopes of social and economic progress were largely centred on hopes for their offspring, and little ambition or hope of promotion existed among older respondents.

In summary, the survey revealed the following factors:

1. The preference of all respondents for a central location in Delhi.
2. A marked preference for owner-occupation.
3. Misgivings regarding the impending dislocation of family ties.
4. A greater concern for family and social problems than those of the environment.
5. Commitment to socio-economic improvement expressed in the high priority given to the education of their children.
6. A low-level of material investment in environmental improvements, due to a feeling of insecurity of tenure.

### 3.3.8. The Case Histories

The social and spatial surveys provide an indication of the underlying rationale of the settlement and its community. To fully appreciate the type of people who make up the larger group, however, it is necessary to describe briefly some examples (3.19). Three such families are presented here, all of whom represent contrasting aspects of the general pattern.

### 3.3.8.i Babalou

When his village job in Madhya Pradesh folded up in 1946, Babalou's relations in Delhi invited him to the city to try his luck. He worked for a while as a domestic servant and was able to live in the servants quarters of the large house in which he worked. When he was sacked, however, he also lost his accommodation and having cut his ties with the village, and not wanting to return as a failure, he looked for a place where he could build a shack away from prying eyes of the authorities and in a place where he stood a chance of getting work. The Rouse Avenue settlement was expanding and suited his needs, so he moved in and built a small hut where he and his wife and their six children now live.

The family live in the one-roomed house and some of the older children sleep in the small verandah/courtyard next to the hut. The layout of this arrangement is shown in Fig. 3.36. The hutment is built of mud-brick walls to a height of about 2m and the roof is a mixture of canvas and thatch held down by stones. The courtyard, which measures 3.0 m x 2.5 m, is partially roofed and enclosed on these sides. This is where cooking takes place (there is a small fixed oven, consisting of these bricks placed on edge and covered with puddled mud) and also where the family eat and Babalou entertains his friends over his hookah pipe, without disturbing the rest of the

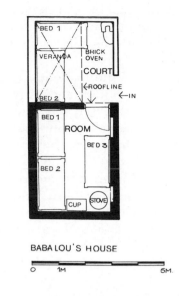

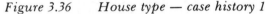

BABA LOU'S HOUSE

*Figure 3.36     House type — case history 1*

family. The poor insulation means that in winter the family, particularly the children in the courtyard, suffer badly from the cold.

The original house was built at a cost of Rs.10 but was demolished by the authorities shortly afterwards. Undeterred, he built another at a cost of Rs.200, and this is the one he occupies today. He has a brother in another part of the settlement but the rest of his relations are back in the village.

Babalou still has the same job that he obtained after leaving domestic service and he works as a peon or messenger at one of the big offices nearby. He has no hopes of promotion and expects to keep the same job until he retires. Whilst he cannot therefore claim economic or vocational mobility, he is proud of being a member of the panchayat council and all his children of school age are attending classes. As a family, they have kept much to themselves and only become involved with others during times of emergency or at festivals, whilst they have no contacts at all beyond the immediate neighbourhood.

Although he had no personal ambition, he hoped that if he could keep his children at school long enough, they would be able to look after themselves and get the sort of office clerical work which offers high status and could give them a chance to move out of the settlement and set themselves up in better surroundings. He sees very little future for the traditional form of extended kinship family and expects his own to split up when his sons marry. When that happens, he will retire with his wife to their village and leave the hutment to them.

The uncertainty of the future makes it impossible for him to think of improving his house and it was obvious that his expectations and needs were closely related to his limited resources. With his wife's approval he listed a one room unit together with a kitchen, bath and w.c. as his acceptable solution. This, of course, was more or less what he had at the time, with the exception of bath and w.c. Whilst he would accept a tenement flat, he insisted that it would have to be centrally located. In spite of the extreme difficulties he experienced in living within such a restricted space, Babalou was very happy with the efforts of the local authorities and cited the provision of latrines, paving and drains as reasons.

As the only earning member of the household and with an income in 1971 of Rs.200 a month, his scope for housing expenditure was naturally limited. However, he said that if given the opportunity to purchase, he could raise a loan of Rs.500 and pay up to Rs.30 a month, though for renting he would only pay Rs.15-20, since there would be nothing to show for the outlay.

### 3.3.8.ii  Saadi

This example is a very different type of family. They were interviewed over a long period of time, so that a detailed picture emerged which in turn threw light on other aspects of the study. The close contact was partly the result of the oldest son's fluency in English and he became a valuable guide and interpreter, though care was taken to ensure that this did not prejudice relations with the other families.

The household represents perhaps the best example of social and economic mobility within this settlement. It is an extended kinship structure consisting of the household head, his wife and their four sons. Two of these are married and live with their wives and children; the oldest son has five young children and the next has four, so that there is a total of eight adults and nine children spanning three generations. all within the same compound. Two other daughters, both of whom are married, live with their husbands' families in Haryana, from which the family migrated in 1940. They are members of the scheduled caste and an example of how this is now necessarily a barrier to socio-economic mobility.

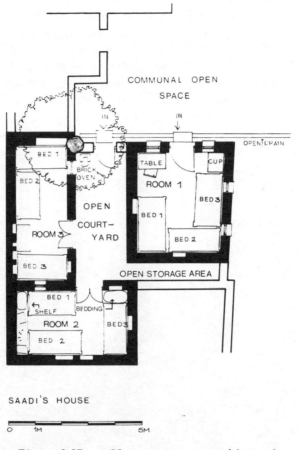

*Figure 3.37     House type — case history 2*

Their shelter arrangements are amongst the most sophisticated and comfortable. The compound is located in the centre of the settlement next to the panchayat leader, and at the entrance to the chowk cluster analyzed previously. It consists of three distinct units (see Fig. 3.37) together with a private, open courtyard situated between them. The largest house (the term 'hut' seems inappropriate), is entered directly from the social meeting area at the chowk entrance, and this house, measuring about 5.0 m x 3 m, is self-contained. The other two units are entered via the small courtyard which also has an entrance door on to the communal open space. These two rooms are also self-contained and each measures about 3.5 m x 2.5 m.

All the three houses are made of 'pucca' brick walls of good quality, rendered internally and externally and well painted and decorated. The roofs, which are showpieces, consist of extremely well cut thatch lined with waterproof membrane and built as a double pitch structure with two gables at a height which ensures thermal comfort, as well as space for high level storage. The floors throughout are of concrete screed and well carpeted. The court is used in the same manner as all others, for sleeping in the summer, (though the communal space in front of the house is also colonized for this purpose), cooking, and as a general purpose meeting place for the whole family.

*Figure 3.38      Saadi 'holding court'*

The household's head, whose name is Saadi, which name appears to have strong Muslim or even Persian associations and it is possible that the family have lineage or religious links in the past. They insisted, however, that they were Hindus and their own admission of a low-caste status can be held to confirm this. He has retired and lives a benignly paternal life smoking his hookah pipe outside the house where he holds court to other senior men in the area. He is highly respected and still rules his family, including the married sons, with a firm hand. This man, his wife and their two unmarried sons, live in the largest house opening into the chowk. The younger generation live in the remaining huts where the wives do all the cooking and other domestic duties. The women are kept busy throughout the day and only emerge from the seclusion of their rooms or the private courtyard to meet other young married women in the space just outside. Because there is a suitably large and quiet corner of the public space near their door, this has become a favourite rendezvous for many women.

The family are well endowed with equipment and furniture, including good quality cooking utensils, two bicycles and a radio and vast amounts of bedding and storage boxes. Saadi's wife has not retired, however, despite the status which is attached to being able to take one's wife out of employment. She works as a stray cleaner, which means that she has no regular employer but 'free-lances', doing a morning a week in one place and then moving on to others and earning a few rupees each month.

There is a marked difference between this type of employment and that of her sons. The eldest, who speaks English, is a clerk in the railways and is well educated. He goes to his office in a smart suit and carries his briefcase on his bicycle. His earnings of Rs.300 (which are due to go up soon), make him comparatively affluent, while the second son also has a permanent job as a bank guard and earns Rs.125 a month. The third son does not have a regular job, but is employed by one of the central government ministries on a daily basis, for which he receives Rs.7 a day; the youngest son is still at school. The total household income is therefore in the region of Rs.575 per month though this, of course, has to feed fifteen people.

The high social status enjoyed by the father is more than matched by that of the eldest son. Not only does his job and ability to speak English and act as a host to visitors, entitle him to respect, but he has worked for several years on a part-time basis to obtain a B.A. degree in law from a Delhi college and this, of all qualifications, makes him a person of influence and authority. With his knowledge of the workings of the housing situation and its legal complications, he has bought a plot of land on the edge of the city across the River Jumna, on which he intends to build a small pucca house. This construction will then form the basis for his intended law practice which he hopes will provide sufficient income to enable him (once the development seems to be secure) to erect further rooms, and eventually to accommodate the rest of his family. When asked what would happen to their existing house, there was a contrived vagueness, but it seems that it would either be sold or given over to another family relative in their Haryana village. Questions concerning desired housing were therefore somewhat irrelevant in this case, though the family stated that they would be able to afford Rs.60 per month to obtain the type of accommodation they wanted. Concern regarding services (which was extremely valid since most settlements of the type they were moving to often had to make do without them for several years), was explicit and included a desire for water and electricity, a septic tank for sewage treatment and a large unobstructed site. Location was a secondary problem since all earning members had, or would obtain, bicycles.

This is in many ways a classic example of upward social mobility in which the family have strong links within their community, informally as neighbours of the panchayat council leader and as senior and successful members of the community, and have also moved beyond this to integrate themselves socially and economically with the wider urban structure. At the same time they had not cut themselves off from their roots and still maintained close traditional caste and kinship ties, visiting Haryana approximately every three months. It also seems that they are not moving away from the traditional extended family structure as was happening to some of their less economically successful neighbours, and this might be held to indicate that the future of large families may be threatened more by economic than by social forms and that given the opportunity, family ties remain extremely strong and act as stabilizing influences in times of rapid social change.

### 3.3.8.iii  Shankar Lal

This last interview was with a young man whose family had originally migrated from a village in Madhya Pradesh because of starvation. His parents had since returned to the village, but he had stayed on for the opportunities available in the city, and he still lived in the same hut as his parents had occupied: Although only in his late twenties, he was a widower and had to look after his four young children himself, though he was helped by a brother-in-law and another friend who was at present unemployed.

The seven of them lived in a hutment located at the centre of the area and consisting of one pucca room measuring approximately 3.2 m x 2.5 m with a private yard of about the same size. Half of the yard was roofed over to provide a verandah and storage area within their compound. The layout is shown in Fig. 3.39.

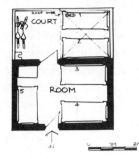

*Figure 3.39*        *Shanker Lal's dwelling*

The house is well-built in mud-brick with the usual mud and cow-dung rendering and finished in white paint. The floor is of weak concrete screed and windows and fittings are of good quality. The father and the youngest children sleep in the main room and the brother-in-law, friend and oldest child share the covered verandah. The rest of the yard is used for cooking and for open-air sleeping in summer. The whole house was built in one stage at a cost of approximately Rs.700-800.

The respondent has been in government service for fourteen years which represents the whole of his working life. Although he was therefore secure in his job and was likely to remain permanently based in the city, he had maintained continuous close links with his village, and his family were in the process of arranging for him to be married to a village girl of his own Chamar (scheduled) caste, and she was due to join him within three months. He had never met the girl but was happy with his family's choice and in any case urgently needed someone to look after his children.

Shankar Lal's social life was firmly linked to the area and he had not developed many contacts as a result of his work. In spite of this, he was not really happy in the settlement and considered that many of the people were lazy and unwilling to work. By living carefully and saving he had acquired a bicycle and radio but otherwise the equipment in the house was basic; another bicycle was owned by his brother-in-law. He was not satisfied with the efforts of the authorities, and felt that more hygienic standards should be set providing basic services and facilities; in particular the drains never worked and the pucca toilets stank in summer because there were so few of them and a large number of the cubicles were concentrated together. He was, however, very enthusiastic about staying in Delhi and valued the opportunity for jobs and better educational facilities than were provided in his village.

His work as a revisor for the government press gave him a wage of Rs.370 a month and of this he was prepared to spend up to Rs.40 if given the chance to buy a government built house. He would he happy to move a little way out of the centre of town if it meant he would have more space. His bicycle would make it possible for him to get to his present office and he would not need public transport.

When asked what accommodation he would hope to get for his Rs.40 a month, he thought he would need a unit of two rooms, kitchen, bath/w.c., and a yard of not less than 2.5x2.0 m. He would, however, reduce this to one room if necessary, but he would not want to be in a tenement block.

### 3.3.9  Conclusions

It would be wrong to assume that these three families are in any way representative of the community as a whole — two are members of the panchayat council and hardly likely, therefore, to give highly critical comments on the administration or the extent of rehabilitation programmes, while the third cannot represent all other families. However, it is true to say that their generally tolerant or passive views were expressed also by the majority of the population in the settlement, whose attitudes can perhaps be characterized as one of stoical resilience. In other aspects, such as attitudes and behaviour regarding housing, the families reflect the spectrum observed. It is important to note, however, that despite their differing situations, the housing which they have provided for themselves has been more than adequate in terms of their needs at the time and in the case of Babalou will be sufficient for many years.

With regard to the community as a whole, it can be seen that this settlement is a classic example of the value of urban marginal space. Its central location, unobtrusiveness and unsuitability for any other use, make it an ideal location for the growth and development of ultra-low cost, self-generating communities. The degrees of variety and intensity of activity within the site have been demonstrated to be the result of a symbiotic interaction of the social/activity and social/spatial structures both over time and at any one moment. To this extent the settlement can be regarded as a sophisticated exercise in unconscious urban planning, in which the needs of the builders are balanced against the restraints imposed upon them (hostility, lack of resources and limited space) and a solution arrived at which maximizes their own needs and minimizes the impact upon the urban community as a whole.

This basis of decision making (3.20) is the rule-structure within which decisions are made by the squatters in evolving the settlement; to any change in official planning or housing policies, there will inevitably be repercussions in the framework within which further decisions are made, but the actual rule structure will remain and adjust to the new situation. Within the settlement, the same detailed social/spatial interaction operates to create a dynamic and responsive environment in which changing needs or resources can, to a certain extent, result in changes to the physical and spatial structure. When the limits for any group are reached, people tend to move out to new areas and make way for others whose needs are more compatible. Both the social and spatial structures reflect this continuous process.

The settlement has been seen to have a strong core of residents who have lived in the same area for about twenty years and who are unlikely to move out unless external pressures force them. On the other hand, there is evidence of upward social mobility especially among the more recent migrants or the younger generation of the indigenous population. These are filtering through the community and using it to establish themselves within the wider urban socio-economic structure before moving on to other types of housing which they feel answer their new requirements. More often than not, these aspirations are land and long term security from eviction. The mixture of stable and mobile groups operates to the possible benefit of both; there is a strong sense of community and a coherent social structure to which new arrivals can relate themselves and also a healthy mixture of families who move through and prevent the community from becoming introverted or acquiring the characteristics of a ghetto. With the exception of limitations on privacy, deprivation is more closely associated with lack of normal urban services and facilities, such as adequate water and sanitary supplies or the availability and suitability of schools or health centres. The major constraints upon the degree of further progress are not within the competence of the community to provide for themselves, and there is a need for a major effort by urban planning agencies to ensure that the existing valuable contributions to the physical environment of the settlement are matched by equal efforts in the field of administrative, economic, social and legal programmes. Any estimate of resources for housing must, however, bear in mind that whatever their income, families have widely differing environmental priorities and need to be given adequate opportunities to reflect these. This factor could well account for the views of 62% of respondents to the effect that they would prefer to build their own homes.

## 3.4   A Case Study of The Maulana Azad Medical College Settlement

The housing and people described in the previous example represent the typical situation for the lowest income group in Delhi. It is not, however, the only type to be found and a number of other processes: official, unauthorized and semi-legal all serve various markets for various groups. Of these, one of the most interesting is that of the construction workers' settlements.

### 3.4.1.   The Construction Workers' Organization

In Delhi, the continuous programme of large-scale building projects (3.21), has created the need for a large reservoir of building labourers who can be organized according to the needs of the building project. Since a permanent arrangement would involve employing a large labour force who could not be reorganized easily, there was little call for local recruitment and a system has evolved whereby labour is recruited according to demand, accommodated on a temporary basis within or adjacent to the building site, and then either dismissed or moved into other projects as the need arises.

Such a system is unable to operate without a middle-man to co-ordinate the needs of the building contractors with those of safeguarding the basic interests of the labourers. This middle-man, called a Jamadar, is known as a labour contractor and is normally directly responsible to the main building contractor for the supply of the necessary size and type of labour. Accordingly, he needs to be in close touch with the building industry and the source of potential labour.

There has been a long tradition in Delhi for building labour to be recruited from the villages near Jaipur in Rajasthan where subsistence farming has always been exposed to the risk of crop failure and migration is therefore a recurrent possibility. A Jamadar is usually from these villages and maintains close links with them. When labour is required, he returns to Rajasthan and uses his network of contacts to recruit the necessary force. It is normal for him to pay their travelling expenses to the city, to advance any loans or other necessities they require and generally to act as a 'father-figure', in return for which he collects a proportion (normally Rs.0.5 or 20%), of each labourer's daily wage of Rs.2.50. Single men or young nuclear families are preferred, since women act as the unskilled labourers and carry the bricks and mortar around the site using small padded cushions placed on their heads; sometimes the youngest child is carried on one hip throughout the day, if there are no older family members at their new home to look after them. The men are employed to do the heavy unskilled work such as lifting steel reinforcement rods, or for more specialized tasks such as carpentry.

On arrival in Delhi, the groups move to their site and build their shelters. Because the need for such labour is officially acknowledged, there is legislation controlling the provision of housing and welfare facilities. (Legislation varies from one state to another; in Delhi, regulations are governed by Act of Parliament) Building contractors are required to provide sufficient materials to build a small hutment of 3 m x 2.5 m, a paved area in front of it, and toilet blocks for each group of hutments, and workers are entitled to two days with pay in order to build their shelters.

At the end of the project it is the responsibility of the Jamadar to obtain further labour contracts for his team. Failing that, a proportion or all the workers may have to leave the city and return to their villages, though this may also happen if there is a need for extra labour on the farms, for example to help get the harvest in. In this way, the required labour force is made instantly available for Delhi's large construction programmes and no unemployed surplus is created, though whether this is to the advantage of contractors who are freed from any responsibilities towards labour, more than to the labour force itself, is an open question. What it does, however, is to achieve additional surplus in rural areas, in which farming is far from easy or profitable, and the benefit of this form of rural-urban economic interaction is therefore to a large extent mutual.

Since the labourers have a legal entitlement to housing, and it is organized on a temporary rather than permanent basis, there are many differences in the context of their settlements when compared say, to those of Rouse Avenue. The actual layout and groupings, however exhibit a marked similarity and this also applies to patterns of social life. These differences are reduced still further by the existence in the settlement of an old mosque which attracted a small group of Moslem families, who built hutments adjoining those of the labourers, and a further group which consisted mainly of relations of the labourers — they also used the connection as an opportunity to build hutments in the area. Although most of these additional hutments are built separately, a great deal of interaction takes place between the groups.

### 3.4.2. Location and Characteristics

The Maulana Azad site was located on the main road linking the two areas of New and Old Delhi, near a rapidly expanding office area known as Indraprastha Estate. The building project for which the labourers were recruited consisted of extensions to the Medical College residential hostels and the settlement is built in an undeveloped part of the site to the south of the main buildings. (see location plan, Fig. 3.40).

In its early phases, the settlement was completely legal and it was only after it was completed, that a group of squatters moved in and built their own hutments alongside those of the building workers, thereby modifying the legal status. In order to increase their

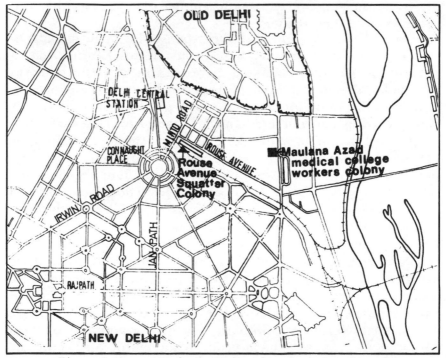

*Figure 3.40    Maulana Azad settlement — location plan*

security of tenure, the squatters built their huts in a similar style to the other groups and it is difficult to differentiate between the appearance of either section. The total of hutments was 124 and according to our typology, the settlement can be described as follows:

SETTLEMENT POPULATION: 1590                    SETTLEMENT AREA: 3435m$^2$

| Dwelling type | % of type to total | Construction type | | | Tenure status | | | | | | | | |
|---|---|---|---|---|---|---|---|---|---|---|---|---|---|
| | | Tempor-ary | Mixed | Perm-anent | 1 | 2 | 3 | 4 | 5 | 6 | 7 | 8 | 9 |
| exposed site | 0 | | | | | | | | | | | | |
| hutment | 100% | 87.5 | 8.5 | 4.0 | | | 79.8 | | | | 20.2 | | |
| room in block | 0 | | | | | | | | | | | | |
| chawl/tenement | 0 | | | | | | | | | | | | |
| apartment/flat | 0 | | | | | | | | | | | | |
| linked house unit | 0 | | | | | | | | | | | | |
| detached house unit | 0 | | | | | | | | | | | | |

The dwelling units were organized in five distinct groups. Three of them were for various construction labour teams, each under their own Jamadar; another group was for additional labourers who work with which ever team could absorb them, and the last group, near the mosque, was that of the squatters. Fig. 3.41 indicates the layout of the entire settlement, together with the location and extent of each sub-group.

Group 1 was the first to be built and was the largest. It was constructed in one phase and consisted of a large square, around which the workers' huts are erected. The large space in the centre was left to accommodate the Jamadar's house, together with those of other labourers who were expected to arrive at a later date. Several of these second stage huts were built and the originally simple layout was difficult to appreciate from the ground.

Similar planning processes were followed in the subsequent areas 2 and 3, though they were not completely enclosed or developed in the centre. The last two phases were less formally organized and reflected the process of individual addition by which they were created.

Taken as a whole, the groups partially enclose an area of open ground to the south-east of the main concentration. This was used in the traditional village manner, as an open defecation area to which people walked before dawn and after dusk, taking with them their brass water bowls. Along the western edge of the site was a path linking the main site access to the construction site further to the north. The hutments on this path accommodated the various communal activities such as the tea shop and grocery 'shops'; the only water tap was also positioned in this area.

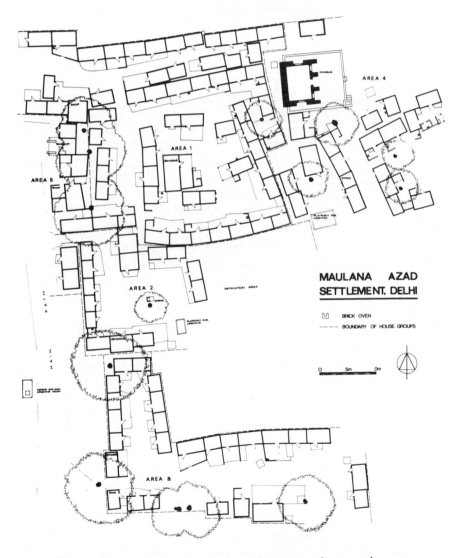

*Figure 3.41     Maulana Azad settlement — layout plan*

3.4.3   **Official Intervention**

*Legal*
The settlement was deficient in many of the environmental standards laid down as minimal by local legislation. This varies for public and private sector construction projects. For the former, contractual obligations are included within the Central Public Works Department Regulations entitled 'Contract Conditions'. Private projects are controlled under various Contract Labour Acts, which vary slightly from one state to another and are under the responsibility of a labour commissioner. Generally speaking, it is required that workers be provided with adequate materials to build a hutment with a floor at least 300 mm above external ground level with a roof 2.0 m high and a floor area of 3 m² for cooking. Bathing and washing facilities are required in the ratio of one unit per every 25 residents, and toilets and latrines are required to a rate of 4 per 100 residents. A minimum of 2 gallons of drinking water per person plus 3 gallons per person for washing is normally required. All these basic standards are to be met by the building contractor to the satisfaction of the engineer-in-charge (3.22). Not only were the huts small and their roofs often not waterproof, but until the survey was being completed, there were no toilets or latrines of any type and the semi-enclosed space at the south-eastern end of the site was used for defecation. There was also only one tap for the whole population of 590 people.

Intervention in the form of legal status is granted to all construction workers' settlements. Long term security was still, however, difficult to develop because of the job uncertainty which dominates their lives even more than in the case of the Rouse Avenue groups, where employment was usually fairly regular, even if marginal in its returns.

*Physical and Social*
The degree of positive physical intervention was therefore extremely poor and did not in any way reflect the minimum standards required. There was also no assistance given to those families with children of school age to attend local schools and most young children sat and played in the building site or remained in the settlement, although a few managed to attend classes locally. Even with the full co-operation of the employers, it was difficult for such children to be registered, since the families often moved from one

area to another too quickly to enable continuity of education to be achieved and it was in any case a luxury many could not afford. Attempts are being made to improve this situation,however, and a privately organized group known as 'Mobile Creches for Working Mothers' Children' have been taking education to the workers by building temporary school huts with play spaces where ayahs (nannies) look after babies and the older children are taught by recently qualified university graduates, who spend several months on the project while seeking more permanent careers. Basic classes in literacy, nutrition, and hygiene are taught and children are often raised to the level where they can go on to further their studies at a higher level. Evening classes are also given for workers when they finish on the site and the accent here is on literacy, domestic management and job skills, (to try and make them into skilled craftsmen rather than labourers). The organizers, who met with severe hostility when they first opened, are rapidly winning support from the public and from many official institutions and hope to co-operate in the future with the authorities responsible for the welfare and shelter needs of construction workers, in order to improve their conditions.

Health programmes were also lacking generally, but doctors received patients at virtually no charge, under the auspices of the Mobile Creches project. It was stated by one doctor that over 60% of children in all construction workers' settlements he had visited suffered from worms of one type or another, and he attributed this to the lack of toilet provision or, in some cases, the reluctance of the workers to use them. This follows on from the common rural habit of using fields adjacent to the village for sanitary purposes. The villagers carry their small brass bowls with them to the fields before dawn and clean themselves with water rather than paper, so that the deposit is immediately absorbed by the soil.

While this is sound ecological practice in a rural setting, it has obvious limitations in an urban area. The difficulties arise in the period of adjustment required, especially if the workers are returning occasionally to their village and thereby reinforcing traditional habits.

*Administrative*

Administrative integration was not involved in these settlements since they were organized independently of the overall urban structure and their needs were in any case largely attended to by the Jamadar who negotiated directly with the building contractor. There were no formal links between contractors or Jamadars engaged in different projects, and to some extent this may explain the difficulties experienced by the workers in generating any degree of solidarity necessary to guarantee their advancement. This function, again, has to some extent been taken over by the leaders of the Mobile Creches project.

*Economic*

Economic intervention on behalf of the building contractor cannot be said to have existed in any other form than the payment of the minimum daily wage rate as required by law. There was no provision for long term economic security and the nature of the work ensured that those who do not acquire specialist skills would be unable to maintain employment much beyond their youth. The only form of welfare provision which helped the workers to adjust to the situation, was that provided by their Jamadar and the knowledge that they could always return to work on the farms in their village when younger relatives replace them. Only a small nucleus of workers acquired sufficient skills to be able to hold down a permanent job, and only a few of these, who also possessed talents for organization or leadership, could themselves become Jamadars when they became older.

*Political*

Political intervention was not a major factor with these settlements, since all eligible voters are normally registered in their villages rather than in the city and do not become involved in urban politics. There was little opportunity, or encouragement, for the workers to modify this situation.

### 3.4.4  Physical Layout

There was no clearly defined network of pathways providing access or internal circulation for the settlement. Each group of housing units had been located adjacent to the others and the only consideration of movement had been the route between the site access to the south, and the building site itself to the north, within the main college complex. Other routes were diffused and informal and movement was generally within the central open spaces around which the house groups were built. Since the settlement occupied far

F

more land than it required for its accommodation, there was little pressure to intensify the usage of circulatory space and it was this factor which explained its lack of definition.

*Figure 3.42    The simple layout pattern of the settlement is not apparent from the ground because of periodic infilling of additional huts in a more informal manner.*

*Figure 3.43    The large open space of area 1 has gradually been filled in by a number of hutments, leaving spaces in between for both domestic and cottage industry activity.*

*Figure 3.44        Women chatting outside one of the hutments.*

When the housing was first built, the basis of settlement was that each Jamadar was allocated an area of land in proportion to the number of workers under his control. In order to maximize this amount, it was usually marked off as a square and the Jamadar then organized the layout of house units so that they were dispersed evenly around the boundary. In this way it was then impossible for the area to be encroached upon by outsiders and the settlement was turned in on itself rather than dispersed at low density over the land. All housing therefore focused on to courtyards of various sizes. If the initial settlement was small, the area would not be totally enclosed but would form a 'U' or 'L' shape in which the boundary was indicated by paving or a low wall. Space was therefore maximized in the centre of each group and the Jamadar, together with any later arrivals, could be accommodated within the central space, as happened with Group 1.

The hutments themselves exhibited a standard form and were built of materials given by the building contractor (see photograph). Only the houses of the Jamadar differed and these were not only larger, but boasted better quality roofs, and additional equipment, such as private water storage. Outside each house was a small paved area which was used for cooking and sleeping out in the summer. Some hutments had a low brick wall around part of this area, which was then used for washing and bathing and sometimes as a night toilet. If this was so, the solid wastes were taken early in the morning to the open area and deposited. Roofs were generally of rushes tied together with string and laid directly on the tops of the walls and on to a central ridge pole. No insulation was provided and when the first rains came the roof was incapable of preventing water entering the huts. This early rain did, however, swell the material so that it was subsequently able to resist continuous downpours. In order to alleviate this initial hardship roofs were often removed before the monsoon, soaked in water and then replaced. No damp-proof course was incorporated however, and all floor levels were the same internally as externally, so that in the event of heavy rain, there was nothing to prevent a hutment being completely flooded, unless the door was partially blocked.

*Figure 3.45      Building a typical hutment. Stage 1: No foundations are required. Broken bricks are used to lay out the plan.*

*Figure 3.46      Stage 2: Gable walls are completed and space left for a door (but no windows) and a built-in shelf.*

*Figure 3.47    Stage 3: The rush matting roof is added; in this case, it has been supplemented with a tarpaulin and plastic sheet membrane. Mud plaster is then added to increase the weather protection of the hutment.*

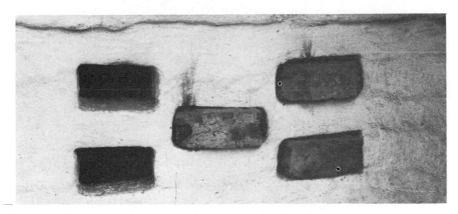

*Figure 3.48    Removable brick air-vents built into the walls*

The size of the houses was generally similar and was based on two factors; the need to position one charpoy or string bed on each side of the central entrance door, and the structural need to limit the width of the huts to a dimension which can be spanned by the roofing material. Average dimensions were therefore in the region of 3.0 m x 2.0 m and the height of the walls was often only 2 m at the ridge and 1.5 m at the side walls. Windows were not normally

*Figure 3.49     Typical hutment of construction workers, showing wall decoration.*

provided except in the form of removal brick air vents.

Cooking normally took place out of doors unless it was too cold or wet, in which case small ovens made of three bricks placed on their side and covered with mud plaster, were erected inside the huts. There was little need for storage, partly because most families have only basic possessions and partly because they kept most valuables such as jewellery on their persons and more bulky items remained in their village. The house therefore only had to fulfill the most basic needs of shelter and it was not regarded as a home which would need to be improved when possible. Uniformity was therefore natural. It was difficult usually to distinguish between the houses of either construction workers or the squatters near the mosque. Those of the latter were however, sometimes a little larger.

The only commercial activity in any sense, consisted of a small tea-shop which was located at the western end of the site on the way to work. This was operated by the relative of a labourer and served as the main meeting place for men of different Jamadar groups. The barber attended to his customers whilst they had their tea and orders were taken for snacks such as samosas or dosas.

Two or three families in the same area were responsible for most of the shopping required by the community. Usually this was done

*Figure 3.50     Squatter hutment built next to the mosque.*

*Figure 3.51     Semi-legal hutment; one of the construction workers'
clusters.*

*Figure 3.52      Cleaning rice*

*Figure 3.53      Preparing the evening meal indoors*

by one of the women, or a man would take time off work to purchase heavy bulk items. Visits were made early each morning to the city's main food markets and flour for poppadams and chappatis was purchased together with lentils and other provisions (tobacco or lottery tickets). In this way, the majority of workers had their basic needs satisfied within the settlement and rarely needed to use facilities provided in the city proper.

*Figure 3.54      Small private open spaces are used for sleeping:  screened toilet areas are ritually cleaned by women every day.*

*Figure 3.55      Maulana Azad settlement: typical squatter hutment.*

## 3.4.5  The Study Areas

### 3.4.5.i  Introduction

The close interaction that was found to exist, in the Rouse Avenue settlement, between the house groups and the spaces which related to them can also be found here. Similarly the spatial/activity organization was a central factor in the maintenance of the social structure. This settlement was different from that of Rouse Avenue, however, in one major respect. Whereas Rouse Avenue was organized socially on a cluster basis and politically as a whole community, these two aspects were integrated in this settlement, so that the Jamadar group was the primary source of spatial, social and political unit. It is also important to note that this site was not built under the same constraints of hostility, insecurity and the resulting need for maximizing solidarity through increasing the population and its density. Even so, there is a remarkable degree of similarity between the two settlements.

In order to assess the particular characteristics of the spatial/activity organization operating in this settlement, the same methods will be used as for the previous example. In this case, the socio-spatial and activity boundaries are identical to each other and it is therefore appropriate to analyze the areas in terms of the various sub-groups.

### 3.4.5.ii  Study Area I

As can be seen from the layout plan (Fig. 3.56), this was the largest and most developed of the various groups. Its area of 1120 m² containing 60 units accommodating 250 people, and organized around a large central space which was totally enclosed and almost fully built up in the centre. In this space was the detached house belonging to the Jamadar. There were two "overflow" areas along two sides of the square which consisted of two parallel rows of huts.

Using the same methods of analysis as for the previous settlement we can see that the 'efficiency' of the spatial/activity organization is as follows:

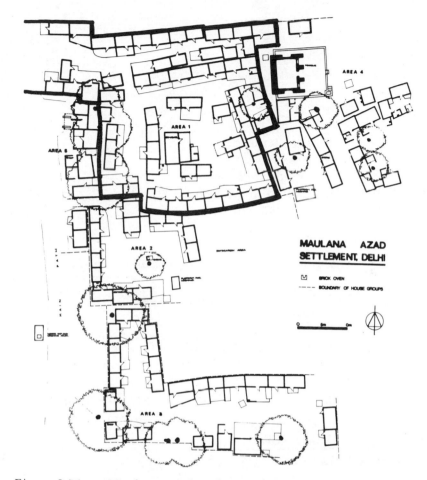

*Figure 3.56     Maulana Azad settlement: study area 1 — location*

## Method A

| | |
|---|---|
| TOTAL AREA | 1120 m² |
| PRIVATE SPACE AREAS: | |
| Indoor space | 477.0 m² |
| Covered verandah | 3.0 m² |
| Open space | <u>286.0 m²</u> |
| Total Private Areas | <u>766.0 m²</u> |
| Therefore, | |
| The Total Communal Open Space   =1120.0—766.0 | = 354 m² |

COMMUNAL OPEN SPACES:

| | | |
|---|---|---|
| ⓪ | Circulation | 354.0 m² |
| ⊖ | Childrens' play areas | 175.0 m² |
| ⊘ | Communal meeting space | 175.0 m² |
| ⊖ | Open air cooking | 00.0 m² |
| ⊘ | Summer open air sleeping | 65.0 m² |
| ⊘ | Latrines and toilet areas | 00.0 m² |
| ⊗ | Cattle (grazing or tethered) | 00.0 m² |
| ⓪ | Commercial areas | 00.0 m² |
| ⓪ | Domestic or cottage industry | 142.0 m² |
| ⊖ | Water taps, washing and domestic laundry areas | 00.0 m² |
| | Others | 00.0 m² |
| | Total Effective Public Space | 911.0 m² |

The efficiency ratio of this area was therefore as follows:

$$\frac{\text{EFFECTIVE SPACE}}{\text{ACTUAL SPACE}} = \frac{911.0}{354} = 2.58$$

Since the number of individual plots = 60, and the total plot area = 776 m² the average plot area = 12.0 m² of which approximately 8.0 m² (0.66 of the total area) was occupied by the huts themselves.

The average effective communal space per dwelling unit was therefore:

$$\frac{\text{EFFECTIVE SPACE}}{\text{NO. OF DWELLING UNITS}} = \frac{911}{60} = 15.1 \text{ m}^2$$

On this basis, the effective space per household was more than twice the actual space.

*Method B*
The graphic representation of the survey of this area is shown in Fig. 3.57.

*Conclusions*
For purposes of analysis, this group had the limitation that there were two secondary spatial forms appended to the main group layout which had to be analyzed at the same time. The main space itself was also broken up into unequal parts because of recent additions and data for the group are not therefore easy to interpret.

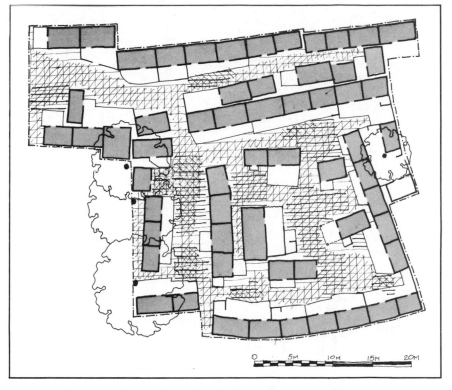

*Figure 3.57     Spatial activity organization: study area 1*

The group enclosed a larger area than that found in any other cluster or group so far analysed. As such, the activity pattern was dispersed and later additions had been channelled into more restricted locations; for example, there were specific areas which were used for all mens' and womens' meeting spaces.

Marginal spaces had also been evolved (perhaps unconsciously), which enabled the layout to incorporate more activities without producing undue strain upon the spatial or social structures. The large and functionally undefined central space facilitated the generation of such spaces from the original low density simple layout, to the high-density and more differentiated plan of the later stages.

### 3.4.5.iii  Study Area 2

This group was located to the south of Area 1 (see Fig. 3.58) and was much smaller in area, being only 460 m². It consisted of 14 hutment units occupying a total area of 155 m² at an average of 11.0 m² and

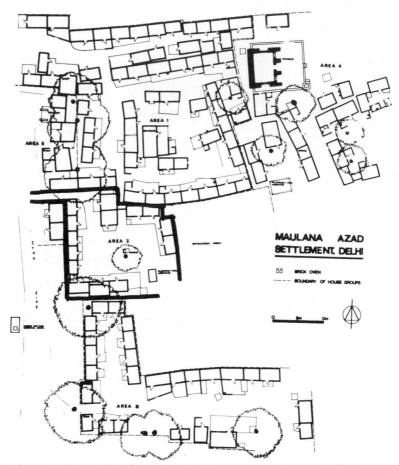

*Figure 3.58     Maulana Azad settlement: study area 2: location*

accommodating altogether 70 people. It was not totally enclosed, but had a quarter of its periphery still open, leaving a gap which provided access to the open defecation area. Unlike the previous group, it had a tree in its central space and at the foot of this there was a small portable shrine. The Jamadar's house reflected the fact that he only had a small work force under his command and it was incorporated into the main row of houses. Its only distinctive feature was that it was slightly larger and higher than its neighbours and boasted a corrugated iron roof.

The space enclosed was naturally much smaller relative to the number of housing units than in the previous group and this not only indicated that the Jamadar expected his team to remain at the same size but that there was less potential for the space to be able to accommodate new activities.

*Method A:*

| | |
|---|---:|
| TOTAL SITE AREA | 460 m² |
| PRIVATE SPACE AREAS: | |
| Indoor space | 95.0 m² |
| Covered verandah | 00.0 m² |
| Open space | 60.0 m² |
| | |
| Total | 155.0 m² |

Therefore,
The total Communal Open Space = 460.0–155.0 = 305.0 m²

| COMMUNAL OPEN SPACES: | |
|---|---:|
| ⦾ Circulation | 305.0 m² |
| ⊜ Children's play areas | 145.0 m² |
| ⊘ Communal meeting space | 145.0 m² |
| ⊜ Open air cooking | 00.0 m² |
| ⊘ Summer open-air sleeping | 30.0 m² |
| ⊘ Latrines and toilet areas | 00.0 m² |
| ⊛ Cattle (grazing or tethered) | 00.0 m² |
| Commercial activities | 00.0 m² |
| ⦾ Domestic or cottage industry | 115.0 m² |
| ⊜ Water taps, washing and domestic laundry areas | 10.0 m² |
| Others | 00.0 m² |
| | |
| Total Effective Communal Space | 750.0 m² |

The efficiency ratio of this area was therefore as follows:

$$\frac{\text{EFFECTIVE SPACE}}{\text{ACTUAL SPACE}} = \frac{750}{305} = 2.46$$

As the number of dwelling units in the group is 14, the average effective communal space per household was:

$$\frac{\text{EFFECTIVE SPACE}}{\text{No. of HUTMENTS}} = \frac{750}{14} = 53.5\,\text{m}^2$$

*Method B:*
It can be seen that in this area the central space permitted a diffusion of activities over the whole area, so that it could be used to the greatest effect. The lack of additional building within this area did not reduce this characteristic as it had done in the previous group (see Fig. 3.59).

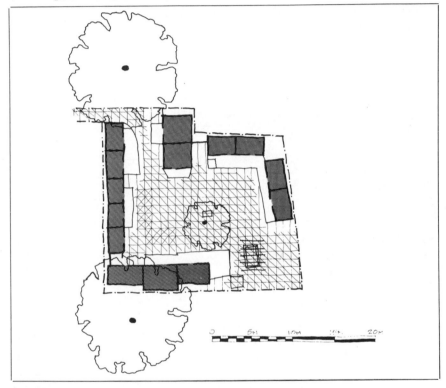

*Figure 3.59     Spatial activity organization — study area 2*

*Conclusions*
This area had two major similarities with Area I, in that the average plot areas were 11.05 m² (compared to 12.0 m²) and the efficiency ratio was 2.46 (compared with 2.58), however when the average effective communal space figures per household unit are compared. In Area 1, the effective communal space was 15.0 m² against an actual area of 5.6 m² (a ratio of almost 300%). In Area 2, the effective communal space was 53.5 m² against an actual area of 21.8 m² (a ratio of 240%).

The minimal size of plots of Area 1 can therefore be seen to have created a slightly greater dependency upon the communal areas than in Area 2, though the actual amount which was effectively available is still much less. The space standards of Area 2 were, therefore, substantially higher both in terms of actual plot area and the relationship of the plots to the available communal space. Area 2 had the additional advantage in that all house units had an equal access to this communal space and its size obviated the possibility of further building in the centre reducing its value. Since the square was not entirely enclosed it was possible to absorb necessary additions around its proximity or even by extending the area itself.

### 3.4.5.iv    Study Area 3:

This area took the form of an 'L' shaped layout and was built in two phases (see Fig. 3.60). The initial development was the group located

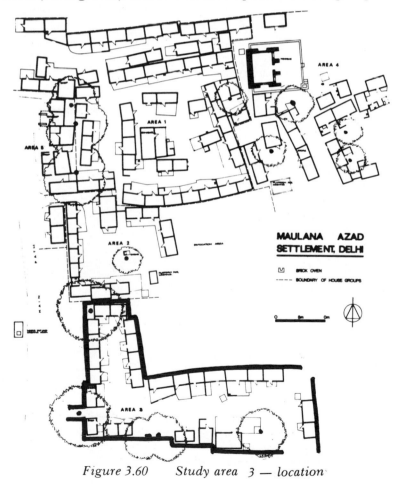

*Figure 3.60        Study area   3 — location*

adjacent to Area 2 and consisted of a small row of huts laid out on either side of a central path open at the south end. To this had been added another double row, orientated on an east-west axis and containing several hutments belonging to squatters, some of whom were relatives of the construction workers. One or two of these claimed to have had the unofficial permission of the Jamadar to permit them to build their huts, so that their presence was, in fact, semi-official. Several houses exploited the shade from large trees.

*Method A*

| | |
|---|---|
| TOTAL AREA | 790.0 m² |
| TOTAL PRIVATE SPACES: | |
| Indoor space | 203.0 m² |
| Covered verandah | 00.0 m² |
| Open space | 131.0 m² |
| Total | 334.0 m² |

Therefore,

Total Communal Open Space  $= 790.0 — 334.0 = 456.0$ m²

COMMUNAL OPEN SPACES:

| | | |
|---|---|---|
| ① | Circulation | 456.0 m² |
| ⊜ | Childrens' play area | 105.0 m² |
| ⊗ | Communal meeting places | 55.0 m² |
| ⊜ | Open air cooking | 00.0 m² |
| ⊘ | Summer open air sleeping | 41.0 m² |
| ⊘ | Latrines and toilet areas | 00.0 m² |
| ⊛ | Cattle (grazing or tethered) | 00.0 m² |
| ① | Commercial areas | 00.0 m² |
| ① | Domestic or cottage industry | 114.0 m² |
| ⊜ | Water taps, washing and domestic laundry areas. | 00.0 m² |
| | Total Effective Communal Space | 771.0 m² |

The efficiency ratio for this area is therefore:

$$\frac{\text{EFFECTIVE SPACE}}{\text{ACTUAL SPACE}} = \frac{771.0}{456.0} = 1.69$$

Since the number of dwellings in the group was 26, the effective communal space per household is:

$$\frac{\text{EFFECTIVE SPACE}}{\text{NO. OF DWELLINGS}} = \frac{771}{26} = 29.7^2$$

The average actual plot area 12.8 m² of which 0.61 (7.8 m²) was occupied by the hutment itself.

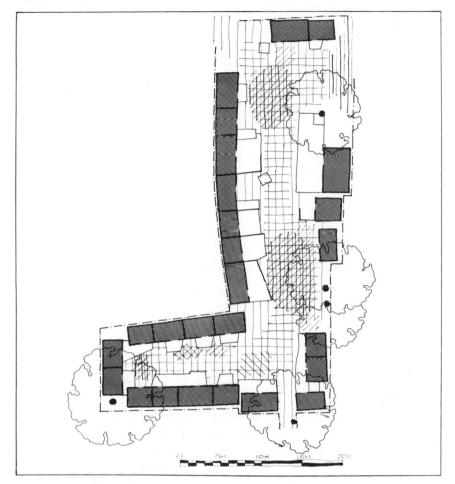

*Figure 3.61      Spatial activity organization — study area 3*

*Method B*
The graphic representation of the survey of this area is shown in Fig. 3.61.

*Conclusions*
It can be seen in this area that the effeciency ratio was lower than that of the previous two groups. It was also apparent that the individual plot area was larger, even if the hut area itself was approximately the

same. This corresponded closely to the material obtained for the linear cluster in the Rouse Avenue settlement, where it was noticed that those activities which could not be incorporated within the communal space led to an enlarged private plot area as a compensation.

The public open space in this area was more prone to being colonized by individual households because of the long corridor form and the lack of movement along it. In fact, colonization did appear in the form of paved areas in front of each house and the pressure put on the communal space was inevitably reduced to those specific functions such as circulation. The individual needs normally carried over into the communal area had therefore been formally incorporated into the private domain. Such a process did not tend to occur in areas with a greater focal character. The implication of these data and comparison with the linear cluster at Rouse Avenue would suggest that the linear areas were more successful when used as major thoroughfares surrounded by relatively large plots, and that when this 'extra-territorial' function was absent and an area was self-contained, a more focal space was more successful.

### 3.4.5.v  Study Area 4

This area was located to the east of Area 1 and was built around the mosque (see Fig. 3.62). It consisted of 21 hutments accommodating 100 people, all of whom were officially squatters. These families were mostly Moslems and had moved into the site in order to be near the old mosque which they had restored and re-opened.

The layout of the area revealed the process of piecemeal addition by which it had grown. It had much more in common with Rouse Avenue in this respect, although land had not been a constraint of any importance on this site, so that densities were low and there was little attempt to create a coherent or intense spatial/activity organization. The residents were aware that they would be forced to move at the same time as the construction workers and this may well indicate the lack of any form of spatial elaboration. The mosque provided virtually the only organizing factor in the layout of the group and huts were laid out approximately on a line around the mosque and from it towards the open defecation area and the site entrance. The area was visually isolated from the other groups in the site and was only linked spatially by a small gap between hutments in Area 1.

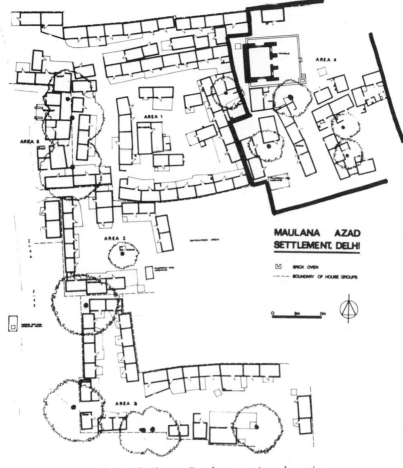

*Figure 3.62        Study area 4 — location*

## Method A

| | |
|---|---:|
| TOTAL AREA | 740.0 m² |
| PRIVATE SPACE AREAS: | |
| Indoor space | 189.0 m² |
| Covered verandah | 00.0 m² |
| Open space | 81.0 m² |
| Total | 270.0 m² |

Therefore,
Total Communal Open space        = 740.0—270.0 = 470.0 m²

COMMUNAL OPEN SPACES:

| | | |
|---|---|---|
| ⦾ | Circulation | 470.0 m² |
| ⊖ | Children's play areas | 90.0 m² |
| ⦸ | Communal meeting places | 80.0 m² |
| ⊖ | Open air cooking | 20.0 m² |
| ⦶ | Summer open air sleeping | 62.0 m² |
| ⦸ | Latrines and toilet areas | 00.0 m² |
| ⊛ | Cattle (grazing or tethered) | 00.0 m² |
| ⦾ | Commercial areas | 00.0 m² |
| ⦾ | Domestic or cottage industry | 92.0 m² |
| ⊖ | Water taps, washing and domestic laundry areas | 10.0 m² |
| | Others | 00.0 m² |
| | Total Effective Communal Space | = 824.0 m² |

The efficiency ratio of this area was therefore:

$$\frac{\text{EFFECTIVE SPACE}}{\text{ACTUAL SPACE}} = \frac{825}{470} = 1.75$$

The number of dwelling units in the group was 21 so that the average effective communal space per household was:

$$\frac{\text{EFFECTIVE SPACE}}{\text{NO. OF DWELLING UNITS}} = \frac{824}{21} = 39.2 \text{ m}^2$$

*Method B*

The graphic representation of the survey of this area is shown in Fig. 3.63.

*Conclusions*

The actual communal space per household is 22.4 m², so that this was a relatively low-density development. The average plot area was 13.0 m² (the largest of all the areas) and the average dwelling area 9.0 m², which was again much larger than in the other groups. It is apparent therefore, that the squatters had built their settlement independently of the more rigid constraints imposed upon the construction workers. Whilst their area had the lowest efficiency ratio of all the groups, it also had the lowest density and the largest huts and plots, so that spatial standards were much higher and they were relatively less dependent spatially than any of the groups in Rouse Avenue, or among the construction workers. The similarities between the two are therefore limited to visual appearance and building methods.

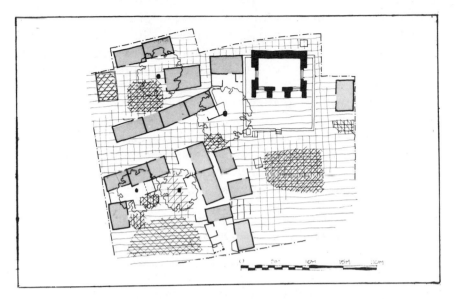

*Figure 3.63      Spatial activity organization — study area 4*

### 3.4.5.vi   Study Area 5

This area, which was located along the western part of the site, consisted of a group of hutments which belong both to squatters and to construction workers. Since they did not possess any spatial features which had not been previously observed in other areas and since the activities with the exception of the tea house were similar to other parts of the settlement, this area will not be analyzed in terms of its spatial/activity organization.

### 3.4.6   The Spatial/Activity Survey:
### Conclusions and Comparisons with the Rouse Avenue Settlement.

The study of spatial/activity organization in these two settlements provides the opportunity to make comparisons between them and to evaluate the performance of various spatial types relative to the groups of hutments surrounding them.

It has been noted that the Rouse Avenue settlement evolved over a long period in a pragmatic and piecemeal manner in which individual additions maximized their own security and thereby increased the solidarity of the group. The construction workers' settlement however, operated within very different criteria. The workers arrived in the city with a clearly developed social structure, which was reinforced by the organization of their work pattern. Their housing was planned at the outset by the Jamadar and space was provided into which any additional workers might build later hutments. As far as the squatters, who moved into the construction workers' settlement, were concerned, there was no possibility of the land being available permanently and their huts were scattered around the site, since there was an abundance of space.

The spatial form of the settlements however, provides a basis upon which comparative studies of the settlements can be made, and the table below indicates the relevant data obtained from the various spatial groupings analysed in each example.

## Rouse Avenue and Maulana Azad Settlements
## Spatial Activity/Organization

*Rouse Avenue*

| Area | No. of hutments | Average plot area in m² | Efficiency ratio | Effective communal space per hutment in m² | Actual communal space per hutment in m² |
|---|---|---|---|---|---|
| linear cluster | 11 | 15.2 | 4.0 | 132.7 | 33.2 |
| chowk cluster | 25 | 21.3 | 2.7 | 36.9 | 13.5 |
| court cluster | 12 | 13.4 | 4.2 | 56.0 | 13.3 |

*Maulana Azad Settlement*

| Area | No. of hutments | Average plot area in m² | Efficiency ratio | Effective communal space per hutment in m² | Actual communal space per hutment in m² |
|---|---|---|---|---|---|
| 1 | 60 | 12.0 | 2.58 | 15.0 | 5.9 |
| 2 | 14 | 11.05 | 2.46 | 53.5 | 20.9 |
| 3 | 26 | 12.8 | 1.69 | 29.7 | 17.5 |
| 4 | 21 | 13.0 | 1.75 | 39.2 | 22.4 |

From these data, certain important characteristics become evident. Those areas in both settlements which possess a high rate of effective to actual communal space (a high 'efficiency ratio'), were the areas that put the available space to the most intense use. Generally speaking, the Rouse Avenue settlement maximizes the use of its area more than that of the Maulana Azad settlement, and yet it has still managed to obtain a higher average plot area for each hutment than was the case with the construction workers: individual plot sizes and the 'efficiency ratios' at Rouse Avenue are higher throughout than in the Maulana Azad settlement, even though building densities are also higher.

Within the Maulana Azad example, the areas with the highest ratios of effective/actual communal space, were the two court plans in which the central spaces were surrounded by the small hutments, accommodating small households. The same spatial characteristic exists in the Rouse Avenue site where the court cluster has the highest 'efficiency ratio' of those studied, and is again mainly surrounded by smaller families. The next most 'efficient' area at Rouse Avenue, the linear cluster, serves larger plots in which a high proportion of the families are also much larger and generally consist of extended kinship units.

A clear pattern can therefore be seen to exist in both areas in which courtyard plans, of a focal rather than linear form, represent the most efficient use of limited land to accommodate groups of small families. Linear groupings appear to be more efficient for the larger family units providing that their plots are large enough to accommodate the necessary domestic activities. Even then, such areas are only really efficient if they incorporate a high degree of general through traffic serving other parts of the site, as at Rouse Avenue. If this extra-territorial activity is lacking, as in Area 3 at the Maulana Azad settlement, then the land tends to be less efficiently used.

One more characteristic which can be observed from these data is that the smaller groups of hutments, and their associated spaces, generally have a higher efficiency in using land than is the case with larger groups. This is mainly because each hutment can obtain direct access to communal areas and they can therefore be a natural extension of the domestic living space for each family, whereas in areas where the spatial scale is larger and the close relationship between the individual plot and the communal space is broken, fragmentation of the activity pattern results and the symbiotic use of space is impossible.

In conclusion, it can, therefore, be said that the most successful areas are those in which small spaces relate directly to their appropriate housing groups. For small families, courtyards appear to be most efficient and for the larger ones, the relatively larger plots are most suitably located on the main thoroughfare through a site. The manner in which the people in these settlements have achieved this balance must be regarded as a sophisticated, if unconscious, exercise in settlement planning under extremely difficult constraints.

### 3.4.7　The Social Survey

The same pre-occupations determined the form of the social survey for this site as for that at Rouse Avenue. It was intended to find out the degree of social cohesion that existed together with any examples of upward social or economic mobility and interaction with the wider urban context. The second consideration was the nature of the residents'interactions with their environment and their aspirations for the future. The survey method was also the same as for Rouse Avenue but, because of the differences in the migration pattern, minor adjustments were made to the questionnaires to avoid redundancy. A sample of the amended questionnaire is included in the Appendix.

The settlement was composed of two groups, the largest of which was the construction workers, who were legal settlers and occupied the majority of Areas 1-3. These groups were all low-caste Hindus from various villages in Rajasthan. The small group of squatters in Area 4 were mainly Moslems who occupied the area adjacent to the mosque. There were also a few other squatters who claimed kinship links with the construction workers and had the approval of the Jamadars to settle in the same area as their relatives. Of all the residents interviewed the majority came from Rajasthan, including 100% of the construction workers. This latter group, which will be discussed separately from the squatters, had generally not been in Delhi for more than a year or two and the longest period of residence was from 1967. Several of the Jamadars, however, had been in the city for fifteen years or so.

The inadequacy of land in their village was the most common reason for migration, though one worker stated that he was trying to raise enough money to offset the costs of a wedding. Crop failure was the other factor which had led people to move to Delhi. All had obtained their jobs (and therefore their houses), as a result of being recruited by their Jamadar. Their recent departure from village homes, the anticipated temporary nature of their work, and the fact that their lives were still linked with their village neighbours, all reinforced the traditional values, customs and aspirations of the workers. Since Jaipur was within easy reach by train, it was normal for them to pay frequent visits to their homes for religious or social festivals, or for the more practical purpose of helping with the harvest. Strong social ties therefore existed between the rural and urban areas and the long hours worked on the building site, together with the general cohesion of the group, provided little incentive for individuals to use the social facilities provided in the city.

Most workers had been members of extended kinship families in their villages and had found that the size of hutments in the city did not easily permit this to continue, even if they had migrated with brothers or brothers-in-law and their families. However, it was often possible to exchange hutments with other families and this enabled them to live closely together. It was quite common, for instance, to find examples of women who cooked for their young single relatives who lived in the next hut. In this way, it was possible to maintain some of the traditional social patterns. When asked about their interaction with their neighbours, it was apparent that the respondents were so closely integrated because of common ties and the nature of their work, that they had little conception of being independent. Several families specifically stated that they liked their Moslem neighbours (the squatters) because 'poverty united them more than religion separated them'.

The existing accommodation provided a clear indication of the temporary nature of their settlement. Although great care was taken to clean and maintain the huts, and paintings often adorned their entrances, the provision of equipment or private space was so rudimentary that little scope was offered for comfort, or the development of emotional ties to their house. Furniture was limited to the basic essentials of charpoy beds, blankets, cooking utensils and small brick ovens, either inside or outside the hut. It appeared that the contractor had not been forthcoming in providing sufficient materials, or the required two paid working days to permit their construction, and that the workers had therefore been forced to build smaller huts to a lower environmental standard than that required by legislation. Some workers had even been forced to buy additional materials for their roofs, to supplement inadequate ones given to them. Most were, understandably, not interested in spending their limited wages on housing and preferred to save, or post money back to their families.

Privacy, (or the lack of it), did not appear to be a major problem. The large proportion of young single men explains this to some extent, and the fact that the remaining households consisted of small families of young parents and very small children, whom it was not considered had to be isolated from their parents. When families started to grow up and the parents became too old to undertake the manual labour, they normally returned to their larger family homes in their village and were replaced by younger members.

The social structure of the community was closely geared to the requirements of the work process and prospects for social mobility were therefore geared to the possibility of job promotion. In such cases, the workers entered the group and were under the direct authority of the Jamadar, both vocationally and socially. They remained in this situation until they were normally dismissed or decided to return to their village, in which case they were often replaced by other family members. However, some workers were occasionally promoted to semi-skilled or even fully skilled jobs such as carpenters, and achieved both social and economic progress as a result. Skilled workers normally remained in the same hut as they occupied before their promotion and some indicated their new status by building a more durable roof of corrugated iron, which was then taken with them when they moved. They remained under the nominal authority of their Jamadar, with whom they had developed close personal ties by the time they were promoted. Most of their neighbours, who then became their social inferiors, were still bound to them by ties of caste or kinship, so that there was little reason for them to move away.

The skilled workers were often able to get work independently and there was therefore a strong incentive for the Jamadar to ensure that his valuable team members did not feel the need to complain. The bonds changed from dependence to inter-dependence through to independence, according to the skill of the worker and his ambition. Successful workers often graduated to become Jamadars in their own right, if they had the talent and opportunity. To achieve this, it was necessary to maintain close ties with their village of origin where they would have to obtain their own recruits, so that they were also subject to the constraints upon their freedom of action as were imposed upon less mobile members. No individual in the social structure could afford to give offence, whatever his position, since to do so would have been to cut himself off from the village-based networks on which the urban work groups depended.

The question of mobility can therefore be seen to provide a means of enabling determined and talented individuals to improve their socio-economic status and also to reinforce the normative values of the group as a whole. Such activity can therefore be regarded as one of competition rather than conflict and the latter only arose if there was a breach of the code or an incompatability amongst individuals. The increased social cohesion provided by mobile individuals did, however, involve a change in their social base. From being primarily located in the village, workers who graduated to positions as Jamadar became increasingly based in the city and were more closely involved in the wider context of urban development programmes. In this way individuals were gradually urbanized, in that they learnt to operate within a wider sphere of choices and absorb new criteria for action on top of the more traditional modes. In short, they were both more urban and urbane.

When asked about their future plans, the majority of construction workers made it clear that they would prefer to return to their village if given the opportunity. The factors which made this impossible in the short run were the lack of jobs or land which had made them leave in the first place. None saw the situation in their village changing enough to make some form of urban migration unnecessary. Questions concerning their shelter needs in the city were therefore somewhat artificial, in view of the popular preference for returning to their villages. Most were clearly influenced by their present standard and style of life and were not generally aware of the standards of the official housing programmes, such as the 25 m² plot allocations. Accordingly, they stated a preference for a plot a little larger than their existing average of 12.0 m². No clear pattern emerged regarding desired housing preferences and it was apparent that they had not considered the problem real enough to be worth considering; most stated, therefore, that they would accept whatever was offered, providing it was centrally located and inexpensive. Their low wage of Rs.2.50 per day, made it impossible for any of them to afford more than Rs.20 per month towards housing, though one worker was prepared to spend Rs.30 each month if he had the opportunity to purchase. Environmental services such as water, toilets and electricity were mentioned by almost everyone as being high priorities. Most had possessed such facilities within their village, and were conscious of their increased availability within the city generally, (especially since they were helping to construct the most modern and sophisticated buildings in Delhi!). They did not mention schools, health centres or other social services however, although it was understood that other areas in which Mobile Creche projects had started, had become more conscious of their value.

As previously stated, the majority of the squatters in Area 4 were Moslems, and had moved into the site since the settlement was founded. The survey indicated that about 60% of these were from Uttar Pradesh and others were from Kashmir, Nepal or other parts of Delhi. All had been in the city for at least nine years and one had married a girl born in Delhi.

The reasons for migration were similar to those of people of Rouse Avenue, in that lack of land or work had forced them from their village. They had come to this settlement when evicted from their previous houses or because they wished to be near the mosque. All the families operated as nuclear units, varying in size between one and seven members, with over half of them consisting of four to six members.

The settlement reflected a lack of social cohesion between the families apart from that provided by religion. Although the huts and plots were generally larger than those of the construction workers, they were not well built or maintained and their temporary nature was noticeable. Only a small minority could be excluded from this assessment. Hutments were generally of one room, with a small patio of beaten earth in front of the entrance. Little money was spent on these and several of the huts appeared to have been made from the same materials as used by the construction workers. This low investment in shelter is presumably a result of insecurity and reluctance to waste valuable capital.

A remarkable feature of all families was that each had a secure job, one being a mechanic and others peons (messengers), guards or plumbers; one woman even possessed a sewing machine and made clothes for more wealthy families. Average per capita incomes were in the region of Rs.100-150 per month. When questioned about their future plans, the majority wished to remain in the city and would welcome the chance of legal pucca housing, in fact it became apparent that the lack of housing was the major obstacle to their future progress. The squatters were aware of the government's housing and squatter relocation programmes and said they would accept any house or plot available providing it was centrally located. General requirements were for one room and kitchen and verandah and, if possible, a bathroom and w.c. for which they were prepared to pay up to Rs.30 per month (especially if purchasing).

The families inverviewed in this area had several characteristics in common with the squatters of Rouse Avenue, in that they were committed to the city and had managed to make a reasonable degree of economic progress in securing permanent, moderately paid jobs. They were not, however, earning enough to be eligible for any of the official housing offered to the low-income group and had been unsuccessful in their attempts to secure permanent housing elsewhere. As such they were effectively outcasts within the city and were unlikely to be considered eligible for either the government housing which they cannot afford, or the squatter relocation housing because they did not have sufficient political strength to claim the interests of the authorities.

### 3.4.8   A Case History: Hari Shankar

Only one of the construction workers was sufficiently forthcoming to justify a personal history. This was Hari Shankar, a married man in his mid-thirties who shared a hut in Area 3. He had migrated to Delhi after trying to obtain work in Jaipur and Jodhpur, where he had found employment opportunities limited.

In 1967, the crop on his farm in Rajasthan had failed because of freak snow storms in the winter and he had moved to Jaipur for a few months, leaving his wife and family in their village. When this proved unsuccessful he moved back to his farm, but the following year there was a drought and with three other brothers also farming the same 1.5 acre (0.6 ha) plot, he was forced to move out again and obtained a job with the Delhi Jamadar who brought him to this site. One of his brothers had come at the same time and brought his wife and they had all managed to obtain adjacent huts, so that the wife cooked for the two brothers. He shared his hut with another single man and their only furniture is a charpoy bed each and these were positioned either side of the entrance, as shown in Fig. 3.64.

The hut measured 2.0 m x 2.6 m (internally) and had no windows; the floor consisted of beaten earth at the same height as the ground outside, so that there was no prevention against flooding. The door was of beaten tin fixed to a timber frame and the roof was of

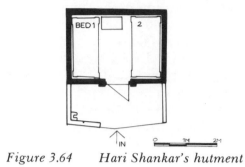

*Figure 3.64     Hari Shankar's hutment*

the usual rush-matting, resting on a wall plate about 1.4 m above floor level rising up to a height of 2.0 m in the centre, so that there was clear headroom for only a small proportion of the whole area. Hari Shankar stated that the roof was inadequate and did not swell up sufficiently to prevent rain penetrating. Because of the help given by his brother's wife in cooking his meals (she also worked as a labourer), he was free to spend his spare time earning a little extra cash and supplemented their joint income by making charpoy beds, which he sold either to other construction workers or in the markets.

He hoped to return to Jaipur for the harvest season and other festivals and was happy to become either a migrant farm worker or a permanent construction worker. He had not, however, developed any particular skill. If he stayed in the city he would not be willing to build his own house; as he claimed, he had quite enough work to do building them for the government! His wage of Rs.80-90 per month did not permit much expenditure on housing, since Rs.50 was required for food alone and he had to forward some of the remainder to his family. Rs.10 was the absolute maximum he could afford.

### 3.4.9   The Social Survey — Conclusions and Comparison with the Rouse Avenue Settlement

It has been shown in previous pages that the processes by which this settlement formed and developed were essentially different from those of Rouse Avenue, and this is reflected clearly in the spatial organization. There are, however, also points in common, especially with regard to the relationship of static and mobile groups within each settlement. In Rouse Avenue, there is a core of long-standing residents who have not achieved any degree of increased economic or social status, and other groups of more recent migrants, or second generation squatters, who are progressing in both respects. Similar patterns can be seen amongst the construction workers; there were some who had become skilled craftsmen and made a secure position for themselves with an increased wage as a result, and a few had the opportunity to become Jamadars and achieve a small measure of real wealth and even more social status. There are, therefore, mobile and static groups within each community, so that they retain their group solidarity and cohesion and at the same time provide opportunities for their more talented, determined or fortunate members to rise socially and economically.

Of the two settlements, that of Rouse Avenue can be considered more fully urbanized. Its occupants have made a more definite (though by no means complete), break with their place of origin and are more fully committed to their urban jobs and their settlements than was the case with the construction workers. Each can, therefore, be seen as related stages in the urbanization process of the individual or the family. At all of these stages it has been seen that there is strong evidence of coherent social structure, which is adapting to the opportunities available to it, and each community has been shown to act rationally in order to maximize its own social and economic interests without any liability to the wider urban community; in fact, the services which they provide make them an essential part of the city's economic and social life.

In neither of these examples is there any significant evidence of social disorganization, cultural or social alienation, or any of the other characteristics one has come to expect of inner-city housing areas. Despite the extreme poverty and restrictions of services, etc., there is strong evidence of social cohesion and economic dynamism. More significantly, the limitations of housing and planning as they exist, reflect more accurately the lack of adequate public sector assistance, and the layout of the settlements and the way they are used have created a far richer and socially acceptable spatial structure than any architect or planner could achieve.

In this respect there is no reason to suppose that the Rouse Avenue settlement is untypical of other similar housing areas built and planned by their occupants. A further example of the complexity and symbiotic organization of space at the level of the domestic environment which is achieved in high density, self-generated settlements can be seen in Vestbro's study of housing in Dar-Es-Salaam (Fig. 3.23). The Tondo area of Manila is another

G

example, and many such settlements widely assumed to be 'slums' and 'unplanned blight', in fact, manifest extremely stable and complex structures which do not reveal themselves to easy analysis by outsiders.

*Figure 3.65     High-density, self-generated settlements have achieved a rich spatial form in many Third World cities. In the northern central area of Manla, these fishermens' settlements display an order as rational and ingenious as anything created by professional planners or architects.* (By courtesy of Patrick Crooke)

Unauthorized housing settlements, as they manifest themselves in Indian and other cities may not be an ideal answer to the shelter needs of the urban poor, but on this evidence they have proved themselves able to come much nearer to providing shelter than the attempts of professionally trained architects, planners and public administrators. The people have therefore assumed these professional roles, and their efforts can be seen not only to compensate for the inadequacies of official programmes, but to be profitable to them.

Within the present social and political structure there is, however, a limit to the achievements of such actions unless additional assistance is made available. Since the responsibility for promoting a more comprehensive strategy rests inevitably with the public sector, policies for widening the range of opportunities and increasing the resources and services available to the urban poor, need to be urgently formulated. Housing may not be the most crucial factor in this respect, but it is of major significance and the problems of social justice and the long-term economic growth of the cities must remain unsolved until such questions have been resolved.

This raises perhaps the central question posed by such settlements. In view of the proven rationale and perhaps unconscious but real planning that they involve, what lessons do they offer in attempting to formulate alternative housing and planning frameworks which are based upon realistic assessments of available resources. It would seem that if appropriate means could be found for investing material, financial and other resources into such communities, that they would then be capable of resolving their own housing problems in a way which could also help them in their attempts at development. The next section will attempt to indicate some of these possibilities.

PART FOUR
# Possible Urban Futures

# PART FOUR
# Possible Urban Futures

## 4.1    The Need for New Concepts

In this final section, an attempt will be made to synthesize the material on urban growth and low-income housing presented earlier and to assess its significance for future planning and housing policies. It is, of course, highly dangerous to generalize from the evidence of a particular place at one point in time, or to prepare alternative approaches on the basis of a study of existing processes. However, the housing problems of rapidly expanding cities are sufficiently daunting to permit the accommodation of ideas from a wide variety of sources and to justify the attempt.

The raw demographic material is perhaps an unreliable basis upon which to formulate future urban development or housing proposals. Part 1 attempted to indicate the futility of applying historical precedents to contemporary processes, or present trends to the future, and this can be further appreciated by the estimate that if the proportion of people living in cities of 100000 or more continues to increase at the scale observed during 1950-1970, the entire population of the planet will be urbanized in such cities by the year 2045 (4.1). There is, however, less dispute over the projection that the high population growth rates of cities of the Third World will continue and that they may even increase their share of expanding total populations. Even allowing for possible reductions due to rural development programmes, it seems clear that the urban populations of developing countries in the forty years from 1960-2000 will increase by over one billion, four times the increase in the previous forty years and about three times the total urban population of the developed world in 1960 (4.2). If medium-sized cities accept an additional proportion of this growth, as seems possible, it remains a fact that these numbers, together with existing urban populations, will somehow have to be employed and accommodated in situations of extremely limited resources.

These processes are already well advanced and have transformed the face of large cities and their socio-economic structures as migrants and the indigenous urban poor increase in absolute numbers, and as a proportion of urban populations. Competition for access to scarce resources and places of employment is steadily becoming more intense and the environmental consequences are now becoming clear.

Under such conditions, it is vital that concepts which form the basis of development should be appropriate to the socio-economic realities in which they operate. From the evidence of Parts 1 and 2, however, it would seem that this is not always the case. There is still a widespread acceptance of inherited or imported concepts, despite the increasing realization that few countries will be able to follow the patterns of development that were taken by the industrialized West. The advantages that were available to such countries during the 19th century included guaranteed sources of raw materials and market outlets which no longer exist, whilst the contemporary population levels are higher and resources lower.

Nowhere are these problems more visibly evident than in the cities. Concepts of housing and of urbanism which were evolved in the West continue to be widely regarded as valid frameworks for the successful pursuit of development strategies, even though their effect when translated into policies is often counter-productive. The example of slum clearance was cited in part 2 to illustrate how certain unstated and unquestioned concepts of adequate housing served to justify the removal of dwellings which were considered 'inadequate'. Yet the process of slum clearance was shown to use up scarce resources and to actually *increase* the number of people needing shelter, thereby intensifying the problems such policies were intended to relieve.

Equally inappropriate concepts linking economic growth with specific types of urban growth are still widely accepted. Thus, the 'over-urbanization' thesis was shown to have evolved as the basis of an assumed relationship between the ability of the 19th century industrialized cities to provide productive employment for the surplus agricultural labour and the inability of currently expanding cities to do the same. This inability has been held to prevent cities from realizing their economic growth potential because of 'excessive' migration, despite the fact that urban income and employment levels are still higher than those of the rural areas. Consequently, policies which restrict accessibility to urban employment, or shelter, by low-income migrant groups only serve to encourage self-generated, informal alternatives which are even further removed from the types of urban growth intended. Similarly, policies of decentralization, which originate from the desire to restrict or control the form of urban growth, were shown to have concentrated on decentralization of labour rather than capital or other resources. Yet by maintaining investment in the cities, the already large gap between them and their rural hinterlands only increases still further and leaves the rural poor with no alternative but migration. If it is really considered necessary to disperse population, it must be acknowledged that an equal dispersal of economic activity would also be required and this may well necessitate a re-appraisal of the relationship between public and private sectors. Failing that, it is obviously unreasonable to expect the rural and urban poor to remain in areas of low productivity and low per capita incomes.

These, and other examples previously discussed, serve to demonstrate how the urban poor have frequently become the scapegoat for the failure of planners to fully evaluate the socio-economic context within which their policies operate. At all levels of policy formulation, it is the unstated assumptions underlying policies which need to be examined for their relevance. By failing to evolve concepts which are based upon social needs and economic capabilities, the likelihood of development strategies achieving their objectives can only recede. In the intensifying competition for resources urban planning and settlement policies must therefore increasingly address themselves to the major issues of who pays, who benefits and who suffers.

## 4.2   The Distinction Between Housing and Settlement Problems

Of all the major urban problems, housing must rank as less critical then employment generation. It need not, however, be considered separately since housing could, with appropriate support, provide a valuable source of productive employment on a large scale and realize tangible benefits to development programmes. This need not necessarily involve proportionally increased budgets, so much as a reorientation away from conventional mass housing towards policies which utilize existing resources and skills to enable people to help themselves.

Just as the informal bazaar economy has proved, in most situations, highly efficient in absorbing minimal capital resources and putting them to uses which generate considerable 'multiplier effects' and employment absorption capability, so similar approaches to housing might well be tried with success. To be effective, however, such approaches require an adequate framework. It has already been demonstrated that the vast majority of low-income groups have been capable of providing their own shelter, however modest, and doing this in a way which reflects their immediate needs and resources. This was certainly the case at the settlements studied in Delhi, where some families gradually improved their dwellings and others used them to serve short-term needs before passing on to other areas. In this respect the major cities do not, in fact, have a housing problem; what they *do* have, however, is a vast settlement problem. It is this latter area of action that the poor cannot solve for themselves, since individual or group initiative is restricted by the external constraints of access to land and services. It is at this level, also, that existing approaches of 'self-help' as discussed in Part 2 become inadequate, since they are primarily concerned with *housing* and not its urban dimension *settlement*. As the majority of residents in the Rouse Avenue settlement stated, a major feature of their shelter needs was a location which enabled them to gain access to employment areas. This may be considered equally representative of many of the lowest-income groups in other expanding cities, yet it is land in prime, central locations which generally has the highest value, so that there is a conflict between demand and supply which illustrates this central issue. Within the context of a land market system, therefore, low-income groups can only gain access by exerting political influence or by accepting the possible threat of violent eviction. Some, who are less locationally dependent, may be able to accept areas which offer greater security but higher transport costs, yet for all these groups, the ability to use shelter to help them benefit from and contribute to development programmes, rests upon the issues of land and land use.

Under conditions of rapid urban growth, it must be considered doubtful if land market mechanisms will facilitate, or even permit, the resolution of settlement problems on anything except an occasional, small-scale basis. As was shown in the case of the Delhi programme of land purchase, (4.3) even public sector initiatives have major limitations since they can only modify the market to a limited, and not always positive, extent. In most cases, it is likely that the core of urban housing and settlement problems can only be resolved by central agencies controlling the distribution of essential resources. The political and economic implications of such an approach are inevitably far-reaching, but until this issue is faced it is doubtful whether any improvements in the prospects of the poor; or the cities themselves, will be possible. It is conceivable that less extreme measures may be adequate in some situations, such as those where land speculation can be effectively taxed and spatial activity controlled, but the administrative capability and legislative powers are not always available. Certainly those cities which have achieved a measure of success in their housing and planning programmes by enabling a substantial proportion of their population to obtain appropriate housing, have all been able to provide land in locations where it is most needed: Turkey, for example, has only experienced private land ownership in recent times and although speculation is now increasing, there is still a large amount of land in and around Ankara in which it is possible for people to settle with the toleration of the authorities and without having to invade privately owned land. This has produced mass popular housing of extremely good quality, seen in terms of the income of residents. In Lima, the

*Figure 4.1      The urban dimension of low-income housing settlements is clearly shown in this view of Ankara, Turkey, where two-thirds of the entire population live in various types of unauthorized 'Gecekondu' housing.* (Photo by courtesy of Mehmet Darie)

*Figure 4.2    The availability of land has resulted in the creation of human environments of an arguably better quality than that achieved by the middle-income apartment blocks built by architects (background), now being built.*

*Figure 4.3    Housing standards are remarkably high, considering the income levels of their inhabitants.*

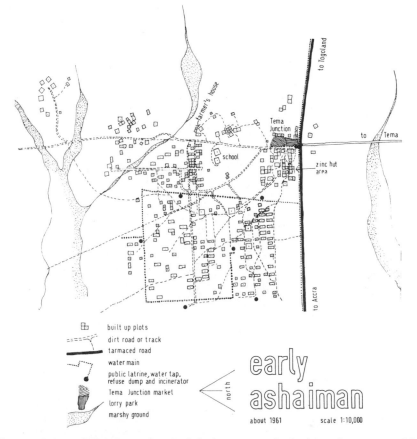

*Figure 4.4      The growth of Ashaiman resulted from its favourable position at the junction of major roads to Acera and Tema. Based upon an existing agricultural settlement, it grew in an informal way round the local services.* (By courtesy of Maurice Mitchell)

authorities have legalized the land tenure for many of the 'pueblos jovenes' (or young towns) (4.4), yet in areas where even committed attempts have been made to provide housing for the poor on a large-scale, as in the case of the National Housing Bank's programme in Brazil, major problems have arisen when the question of land was ignored. Thus, Wilsher and Righter report that despite the expansion of the house building programmes to the point where they were providing 500,000 new jobs a year, problems of location arose since the majority of such housing was on cheap land at the periphery of the city. As a result, the high cost of public transport (one teacher was reported to be spending her *entire* salary on bus fares), made it impossible for residents to keep up their mortgage

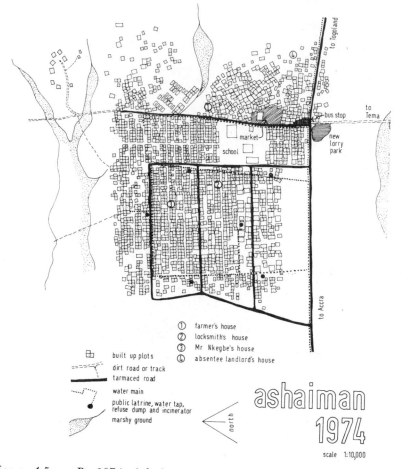

<br />

① farmer's house
② locksmith's house
③ Mr Nkegbe's house
④ absentee landlord's house

built up plots
dirt road or track
tarmaced road
water main
public latrine, water tap,
refuse dump and incinerator
marshy ground

north

ashaiman
1974

scale  1:10,000

*Figure 4.5     By 1974, Ashaiman was densely settled and incorporated a wide variety of economic activities integrated with the housing.* (By courtesy of Maurice Mitchell)

payments and many gave up altogether whilst more than half are three months or more behind (4.5).

In order to effect the change of priorities that can lead to alternative policies and programmes, a great number of existing assumptions regarding the functions and forms of cities will need to be revised. Housing is a good example of an issue where this is required, yet because it is a primary need, it is one of the most difficult about which to be objective. It is therefore all the more valid to assess the aspirations, needs and resources of the various groups needing housing, before attempting to create policies and programmes concerning them.

## 4.3     Alternative Frameworks

If questions regarding the provision of land and other resources can
be resolved, the issues of settlement planning become clear and it is
possible to consider alternative frameworks. As the numbers of
people in the low-income sectors increase, for example, it can be
predicted that there will be an even greater demand for housing
adjacent to employment areas. Just as the dispersal of economic
activities is essential to encourage programmes of regional
development, so there is a strong case, therefore, for the dispersal of
commercial, industrial and other employment generating activities
*within* the cities. Such policies would serve to alleviate the
concentration of activity in limited central areas and provide a
suitable basis for future growth.

It is likely, however, that even allowing for such approaches,
the demand will necessitate substantially higher densities than are
normally considered acceptable; yet high density settlements have
until recently been the rule rather than the exception. There are
numerous examples within both developed and developing
countries of settlement structures which have evolved to
accommodate intensive use of land, reducing the time and cost of
transportation and providing equitable access to services by all
sections of their population. In Part 2, the examples of Old Delhi,
Old Ankara and Old Baghdad were cited and in Part 3, the complex
and symbiotic use of space was shown to have permitted the Rouse
Avenue settlement to achieve a stable domestic life at densities of
over 1000 per acre (2470 per ha). What is more remarkable is that in
most of these examples, the control which individuals or groups
could have exercised over the location, type and cost of dwellings,
was often significantly greater than is possible in most commercial
settlements built to higher standards and lower densities.

If land is therefore a primary resource, its intensive and efficient
utilization is an essential requirement of any appropriate planning
framework. As Legates observed in the case of Santiago, there is a
strong argument in favour of redensification, especially in the
central areas (4.6). Similarly, in Delhi, the existence of mixed-dense
jungle on land adjoining the city centre (4.7) must be considered
anachronistic within the context of rapid urban growth. Within
most countries, there are examples of urban settlements which were

the product of indigenous social and economic systems and which offered climatically appropriate and technically sophisticated solutions to urban planning problems. It is now fashionable to discuss such areas as symbols of a backward state or traditional way of life that has now to be replaced in order to 'modernize'. Yet such cities, or areas of cities, were often, in fact, built as the expression of the last period of local independence before the impact of Western influences became pervasive and as such they are more to be admired and respected than despised and demolished. The other current fashion is, of course, to retain such areas as open-air museums, as a conservation area in the middle of urban redevelopment schemes, yet both attitudes equally serve to separate such structures from any meaningful relevance to contemporary urban development and prevents them serving as a basis for future schemes.

This is not to advocate that the specific spatial and physical *forms* which have been evolved within traditional indigenous or contemporary self-generated settlements should be duplicated on a wider scale. What it does indicate, however, is that such solutions do contain elements which are as valid today as they have ever been. These elements may be considered as follows:

1.  *High density:* To ensure that no land is wasted and that extensive and costly transportation systems are minimized. This also increases the accessibility to resources and services for all residents and reduces the infrastructure necessary to provide them.

2.  *Mixed land use:* This permits the interaction of activities as required and also reduces transportation requirements. The symbiotic use of space, that was found to exist at the Rouse Avenue settlement, can be encouraged and secondary economic activities developed.

3.  *Variety of plot size:* This permits the integration of socio-economic groups and enables buildings to meet diverse needs.

*4.  Local control over housing provision:* As seen in terms of location, type and cost.

The flexibility and economy of planning frameworks which exploit these elements and their ability to achieve socially acceptable housing is the very essence of most self-generated settlements built by the poor. Their judicious application would therefore form the basis for equitable and realistic measures which use urban land to its full potential within economic constraints. It is more than likely that such apparatus would encounter strong resistance from those who continue to hope that the wider application of conventional approaches to urban housing could somehow prevail. In this respect, the clash between the 'classcentric' *concepts* of housing, could well become a direct clash of *interests* which could jeopardize the possibility of an easy transition to alternatives. However, as the scale of social and economic deprivation which existing programmes generate becomes more apparent such alternatives may appear less dramatic.

## 4.4    The Role of Planning and Housing Agencies

If it is accepted that people living in most parts of the world and at all income levels are capable of building, or providing their own housing as all the evidence implies, then the role of public sector agencies should be conceived as providing those elements which people *cannot* provide for themselves. In a city, the central elements are the adequate availability of land in the places where it is needed, the provision of infrastructural services such as water-supply, sanitation, electricity, etc., and social services and facilities. With regard to social services, health clinics of a locally available and inexpensive nature together with schools are important, whilst other assistance in the form of low-interest loans and credits are also essential, even though they are often only available to the upper strata of the urban poor. It will be noticed that none of these aspects involves the actual provision of housing, so much as the frameworks or parameters within which housing can be conceived and constructed. This conclusion, which has also been reached by John Turner (4.8), and a number of other writers, characterizes the nature of a viable role which the public sector alone can play and distinguishes it from those areas in which outside help is destructive and counter-productive. The central issues of urban development and housing can now be stated more clearly. How, for example, within a socially just and economically viable framework is it possible for external investments (of a material, human, financial, or technological variety), to be injected into a specific community or settlement so as to generate self-sustained, internally controlled development?

If the parameters or framework as outlined above can be established, then a number of possibilities emerge. An example of limited external assistance generating a variety of 'multiplier' effects can be seen in two projects undertaken in Tema near Accra in Ghana. Here, a survey by Mitchell (4.9), indicated that a great deal of small scale enterpreneurial activity existed which could maximize the limited surplus of the local residents and any external in-puts. In the Ashaiman area of Tema, Mitchell found a mass of local cottage industries and other activities which recycled and multiplied inputs to the benefit of the community as a whole. Inevitably some of the more resourceful individuals were more successful than others, but by remaining in the area, they served a function which outsiders would have been unable to fulfil. In the field of housing, the locally generated schemes were found to be far more appropriate than the 'minimum cost' solutions proposed by the Tema Development Corporation. Mitchell describes how the Corporation sought ways of saving on costs and proposed a system of building using 'landcrete' blocks (a mixture of soil and cement), which would be adequate for low-storey buildings. The lack of experience in this system by the large contractors involved, however, made it difficult to implement the project and it is at this point that the problem of external inputs to local structures becomes relevant. A team at Kumasi University designed and built a simple block-making machine which they sold, on credit, to a local tradesman. This small operation was capable of producing the required blocks at such a reduced price that before long the tradesman was able to supply all the contractors with blocks, pay for the machine, build a house for himself and generate ten extra jobs. Whilst the officially sponsored scheme floundered because of organizational problems and failed to generate any 'multiplier' effects within the community, this block-making scheme used a nominal investment, in this case technological one, to great benefit. Mitchell concluded that the lessons of such a venture are that to make the best use of the limited resources, cash flow should be encouraged by concentrating on small contractors rather than monopolies and that research agencies are in a good position to encourage such developments, by proposing alternative methods and policies and offering technical advice (4.10).

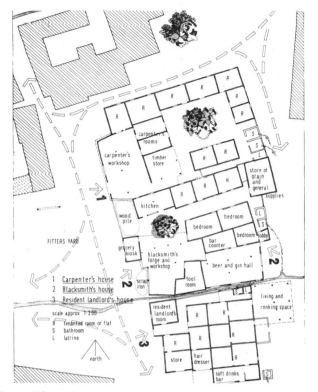

*Figure 4.6     The mixture of residential and economic uses can be seen in this plan of a group of typical buildings.* (By courtesy of Maurice Mitchell)

*Figure 4.7     Living and working in Ashaiman — the 'multiplier' effects of external inputs account for the vitality of the area despite its obvious handicaps.* (By courtesy of Maurice Mitchell)

In another project in the same area, Mitchell described the work of local co-operatives in financing, designing and building housing for the local communities. Under a government sponsored 'crash programme', a grant was made to the housing and builders co-operatives to construct 21 'core-houses' and to use the capital as the basis for a revolving fund which could then finance further building. Although this was therefore a small project, and was restricted for credit reasons to those with stable employment, it provided a participatory structure which insured that the benefits of central investment accrued to the intended occupants and enabled them to increase it still further by generating employment, security and houses (4.11). Naturally, to extend such proposals to a more general level, in which they could form the basis of an alternative approach to urban planning and housing programmes, would require changes in urban policy which have already been discussed. The point here is that the means for implementing such alternatives already exist.

With regard to the more general problems of urban resource allocation, one of the most promising approaches can be seen in the case of Ankara, where the methods of incorporating unauthorized settlements into the formal structure of urban administration has been evolved over several years into a pragmatic but highly effective process. As new areas are developed gradually, either by piecemeal invasion of public land or by the expansion of existing areas, local people can petition for their areas to become officially recognized. If settlements satisfy various criteria of population and density and exhibit a natural boundary, they are eventually recognized as *Mahalles* or wards of the city (4.12). Naturally, as this process continues, mahalles are subdivided, perhaps several times. When recognition is achieved, the community leaders are entitled to apply for services and facilities and these are normally available in a relatively short time. The authorities have been quick to recognize the positive achievement of the Gecekondus (the term literally means mushroom housing, or housing which grows overnight); only limited programmes of government-built housing are implimented and this, of course, leaves more resources available for wider distribution in the form of services. Even these are not always provided in the conventional, centrally administered manner however and in some cases, as for example the provision of electricity, the municipality provides the materials and technical advice, while all the local able-bodied men dig the trenches. Using such methods it is often possible to provide electricity and water supplies, roads and sewage much more quickly and at less cost than the available resources would permit using any other approach.

The relationship between central and local decision-making structures is therefore vital for any successful project  and if 'multiplier' effects are to be generated, it is essential that small-scale local groups are able to participate actively. This point explains why some of the more progressive policies such as sites and service schemes, do not always work in practice as they were expected to in theory. Apart from being located too far from the employment areas, they are often conceived simply as low cost housing estates, in which no provision is made to generate additional employment and the savings take the form simply of using the labour provided by the users themselves. Whilst these savings are often passed onto the users themselves, it is not always in their own interest; if control over the type of housing and the finances remain completely with the central authorities and as LeGates has demonstrated, it depends to a large extent in how labour is organised; in his case, in Chile, the essential point was whether labour costs should be deployed in a syndicate form (as in the case of Tema), or individually (4.13). There can be little doubt that the former is more beneficial, though in the Chilean case the opposite applied. The principal of serviced settlements however, offers a great deal of potential and as Crooke has observed, they enable an authority to differentiate the components of urban settlement from each other and allow each servicing agency to act with real responsibility in its own component field (4.14).

If the various factors outlined above are accepted as influencing the success or failure of individual projects, and if it is also accepted that to be implemented at the scale required in the expanding Third World city structural change of priorities is essential, then the following points can be considered as relevant to the formulation of alternative settlement policies.

## 4.5    The Basic Elements of Housing Policy

Whilst the very nature of housing problems ensures that no single approach can offer an optional basis for future policies in the varying contexts of Third World cities, a certain direction does appear to be indicated by the evidence. Even then, of course, it is difficult to conceive of a 'solution' or 'solutions', since housing is an expression of dynamic processes and it is inevitable that the problem to be tackled will change continuously, especially as a result of rising expectations. Existing priorities, however, are concerned with the adequate provision of serviced settlements as part of a socially just urban strategy, even if these may later be replaced by less basic requirements.

### 4.5.1   The Need for Administrative Reform

In order to increase the effectiveness of planning and to prepare the basis for alternative models, major organizational changes would appear to be indicated in the framework within which planning operates. At present, administrative structures tend to insulate planners and policymakers from the consequences of their actions, and the separation of policy and implementation agencies serves to reduce the element of accountability to the public as a whole. The applications of dogmatic approaches within a rigid professional hierarchy completes this process and discourages any attempt to challenge the conventional wisdom or to generate new approaches.

If planning is to become more responsive, it is vital that it be based upon existing socio-economic and environmental realities. Several means are available to achieve this purpose; departmental isolation could be reduced by integrating policy and implementation departments and establishing high-level coordination of various areas of urban policy; regional offices could be opened by local authorities in order to serve various urban communities and to implement planning programmes at local-level; special 'action groups' could be established to make surveys of particular planning problems and to prepare policy proposals. Perhaps even more importantly the dependence upon statutory 'master plans' with all the opportunities that they provide for avoiding critical re-assessments, could be replaced by more flexible methods. The more pragmatic approach which this implies should not, however, be interpreted as a sign of weakness in the operational capabilities of planning, since it would result in the eventual policies being more likely to achieve successful implementation than at present. The mere existence of unauthorized settlements in such large numbers bears ample witness to present failures and any reform which integrates policies with social and economic realities and serves to reduce rather than increase disparities will naturally be held in higher regard. As mentioned in a recent report by the United

Nations, 'The legality of squatting and slum dwelling should be determined in the light of the capacity of squatters and slum-dwellers to comply with legal measures' (4.15).

The report goes on to state that 'such an effort would act towards closing the gap between legal structures formed at an early stage of urbanization, and current reality and objectives. This is particularly critical in connection with the formulation of municipal regulations and standards . . . such basic needs as water, education and sanitation should be provided to everyone'. Finally, it is claimed that 'the important question is not whether squatting or slum dwelling is legal but why they occur and what factors led to the laws being broken in the first place' (4.16) and the report concludes that 'since the processes will continue to operate despite the law or opposition of the authorities, it is essential that policies be formulated which will lead to the integration of such families or communities into national and local development strategies and social policies' (4.17).

At the operational level, it is essential that housing processes be prepared in close coordination with other aspects of urban planning and social services provision, especially with regard to such elements as hospitals, clinics, schools, industrial/commercial development and transportation policies. Public transport in particular can reduce the dependence of low-income groups on locational proximity to resources, and subsidies in this area might prove more beneficial than in the field of housing. However, these also embody major limitations; for one thing, a transport subsidy requires a charge on public funds and secondly, it is generally necessary to subsidize the whole transport network, since any restriction to selective routes or modes of transport would be subject to intense political difficulties.

As a result, there is no means of ensuring that the subsidy would be received by those groups for whom it was intended. A combination of policies is therefore relevant in every specific situation and this will vary according to need; the unchanging factor is the need for coordination and the opening of decision-making processes on planning and housing to public influence.

### 4.5.2 The Redefinition of Building Regulations
Planning restrictions building codes and other regulations in many Third World countries are only infrequently geared to the needs and resources of either builders of users, in general they reflect the

standards achieved in more affluent, industrial countries and on some points may even be higher. '(The requirement of a recent Delhi low-income housing competition stipulated separate bathrooms and W.C.s, something that is not required of official housing in Great Britain.) In part, this may be due to an understandable reluctance to accept lower standards for ones own society than were originally imposed upon it by a foreign one. However, when the gap between so-called 'minimum' standards and economic and demographic realities has reached the level that is commonly already existing throughout the Third World, then the case for more modest and appropriate standards is undeniable, especially since it is apparent that the provision of high standards for some, reduces them for others. If, as is commonly the case, the majority of urban populations live in one-room tenements or unauthorized hutments, almost anything is bound to be an improvement above present *actual* standards.

Such an approach could achieve dramatic results in enabling local builders and user-groups to provide their own housing to simple and modest official standards and effect great cost savings. Subsidies would not be required and the additional funds made available could be used to spread more thinly over a wider range of projects and to provide the essential supply of land.

### 4.5.3 The Replacement of Slum Clearance Programmes With Those of Rehabilitation

The self-defeating nature of slum clearance projects has already been noted in Part 2 and leading observers such as Charles Abrams have catalogued not only these disadvantages but also the difficulties of making public authorities acknowledge them. Summarizing the situation, it appears that the myopic approaches of middle class interests are particularly influential in continuing such policies. A glance at the literature reveals that 'slum' housing is assessed primarily in aesthetic and hygienic terms, linked with traditional fears of crime and social disorganization, which the evidence does not appear to justify. These factors remain, however, one of the strong motives behind most slum clearance projects, and it is therefore difficult for rational arguments to prevail. One can only hope that by reiterating Abrams' arguments to the effect that slum clearance actually encourages the growth of new slums, planners will eventually be influenced into curtailing such policies and instead implement projects based upon rehabilitation.

This alternative, which has been initiated on a large scale in Calcutta, was in fact advocated many years ago in India by the sociologist and town planner, Patrick Geddes. His many reports between 1915 and 1919 were major landmarks in the evolution of a unified social and physical environmental approach. It is an approach which still has many lessons for contemporary urban planners and administrators: Geddes was a strong advocate of undertaking detailed social and environmental surveys before preparing plans for an area and he believed in learning from the achievements of local people rather than imposing arbitrary solutions (4.18).

As a result, he was able to identify the major environmental problems of a community and indicate what was necessary to remove inhibitions to its efficient functioning. It was unthinkable for him to advocate wholesale demolition and rebuilding, for he realized that this could destroy the entire community in an area and create the alienation that planning was attempting to prevent. Accordingly, he evolved his well known approach of 'conservative surgery' (4.19), which aimed at removing the worst excesses of the local environment and using the space left over to either construct new buildings of a slightly higher standard using a similar technique, or to provide community facilities and services. Both these solutions, therefore, retained the existing community and its environment and provided an incentive for improvement. Geddes emphasized that orderly growth was more important than order at the expense of growth (4.20) and he recognized the distinction between visual order and social order.

Such a holistic approach to urban social and physical planning, as Geddes advocated, received widespread recognition during his lifetime. However, since then, the relationship between the two has ceased to be the basis for planning proposals, so that arbitrary and socially inappropriate projects invariably result. Slum clearance projects are a clear expression of the separation of social need and public funds and represent nothing less than the squandering of scarce resources. The abandonment of these policies and the rehabilitation of slums, and the communities which occupy them, would form a more appropriate framework for urban programmes which aim to increase and improve the existing housing stock.

As a temporary measure, and one that will apply until the demand for housing has been reduced, it would appear essential that all slum clearance projects be suspended. The regularization of existing settlements would go a long way towards reducing demand and provide new scope for introducing planning programmes for new settlements.

Such proposals are, of course, tantamount to recommending what may be considered as 'planned slums'. However, as Abrams has eloquently stated, 'it may be conceded that in the formative years of industrialization the slum would be the inevitable by-product of urban development. When this occurs, it should be planned rather than denounced . . . (since) unplanned slums may defy government correction for ever. The term 'planned slums' may raise the reformer's eyebrows, but enable him better to see. If slum building shatters Utopian dreams, it may soften the rudeness of the awakening' (4.21). The evidence of the case studies in Part 3 also confirms Abrams' implied comment to the effect that 'slums' are a relative concept and for their inhabitants they are, in fact, home.

### 4.5.4   The Role of Self-Help

The case studies also revealed that even when the poor were excluded from official housing programmes, they evolved a positive, imaginative and coherent form of urban settlement, which was only constrained from further improvement by the lack of communal services and facilities. It can be imagined that if housing and planning agencies worked with, and for, these groups instead of in opposition to them there would be increased scope for the future of such groups at costs as low as existing unauthorised settlements. To achieve this, however, it is necessary for planners to accept that there is a great deal to learn from squatters and other self-generated communities regarding the efficient development of urban land at high density. Almost all those interviewed in the Rouse Avenue settlement for example, showed themselves fully capable of developing their own housing and local environment. The potential for self-help which this suggests, reinforces the conviction already expressed that housing as such is not required for  large sections of the low income groups, but that serviced settlements, integrated within a comprehensive social policy, would be more appropriate.

It is somewhat ironic that many governments and agencies have in fact already initiated such projects, but abandoned them after an initial period (4.22). Perhaps such solutions appeared as a compromise with the aspirations of the planners, though it would be hard to believe that they clashed with those of the poor. Any project experimenting in self-help does, of course, involve a great deal of administrative coordination and possibly requires a higher degree of supervision than conventional projects and this admittedly puts great stress upon governmental resources. It would seem to be unreasonable to discontinue them for this reason, however, and more worthwhile to recruit and train staff with the necessary competence; certainly manpower represents one of the Third World's greatest resources.

### 4.5.5 The Role of Technology

Recent developments in this field now make it unnecessary (and undesirable), to continue applying capital intensive, inappropriate and expensive techniques in the field of housing construction or settlement servicing. Such technologies are not only beyond the resources of most developing countries, but frequently represent a source of environmental pollution and a high degree of energy waste.

Some of the most common examples of the success of low level technologies are methods of producing power from natural resources, (sunlight, wind, water, etc.) or ecologically efficient methods of recycling used energy or materials. An indication of possibilities in this report and their application in the field of housing has been explored by the team of Ortega, Rybczynski, Ayad, Ali and Acheson at McGill University in Canada (4.24). Although their solutions have been developed within the context of a society with an advanced technology, (the sulphur blocks which they use extensively are made from the by-products of various technologically advanced industries), their approach of exploiting whatever resources are at hand and applying basic ingenuity to exploiting their potential, can be considered valid in any situation.

The extensive work of architects like Hassan Fathy in developing existing or traditional mud-brick technologies in a contemporary architectural context, together with the work of the Intermediate Technology Group and other similar groups (4.25) all reflect the increasing relevance of intermediate, alternative or adapted traditional technologies to current housing problems. In energy generation, a number of projects are being carried out to exploit solar energy (4.25), and all these examples illustrate the point that intermediate technology need not be any less sophisticated than other types; it simply needs to be appropriate.

## 4.5.6   The Role of Public Health Programmes

The application of serviced settlement programmes could provide sufficient incentive for the poor to help themselves instead of remaining dependent upon charity in the form of subsidized rent for conventional housing. Unfortunately, little research has been conducted as yet by any of the national or international agencies responsible for public health on the minimum standards which such projects should satisfy. This represents a large gap in our knowledge of urban hygiene and it is impossible to recommend appropriate standards until more empirical knowledge is available. It is also possible that many authorities hesitate to enshrine in official edicts any standards which are generally considered below the level society would wish to be able to set for itself, and this may well explain the lack of such research. It is often preferred to maintain an ambiguous position on the grounds that certain standards are officially required, but since it is impossible to implement them, unofficial action at a lower level can be rendered acceptable because of the extent of the shortage. However, this does not justify ignorance of the economic, physiological and sociological aspects concerning appropriate provision of services and facilities, and it is perhaps surprising that in most countries decisions on these basic questions are still a matter for arbitrary or intuitive solutions. Existing studies on 'minimum standards' (even accepting that definitions on this question are themselves arbitrary) are often more concerned in fact with *optimum* standards (4.27), and do not equate the nature or extent of services, densities of housing, or climatic factors to the observed incidence of various diseases. Consequently, it is difficult for any authority to make realistic assessments of what is an appropriate level of servicing for a community according to resources available. Van Huyck (4.28) even goes so far as to say that there are no minimal physical standards which are relevant for all sites and services programmes, or for all cities or countries, and that standards should be predicated upon the ability of residents to pay for them (4.29). His study, which represents the most authoritative statement of site and service programmes to date, stresses the need to plan settlements in such a way that they can be easily improved, both in individual constructional terms and also in the extent of public services provision, leading up to water outlets and other elements being available for each plot.

For similar reasons, Van Huyck refrains from specifying recommended plot sizes, and instead suggests that analysis of existing low-income settlements in a city created by self-generated communities and reflecting their standards, provides a more accurate and realistic basis for formulating detailed proposals. The high costs of modifying or increasing the capacity of public service infrastructure elements relative to their initial cost, however, make it desirable to instal all services to as high a standard as possible. This has two advantages; if initial settlement densities are as high as the economic use of land suggests they should be, then high capacities will be needed immediately; if, however, densities eventually drop as other areas are settled, then the existing services will automatically result in an increased standard being available to residents remaining, without any cost increase being involved.

It may well be that sanitary services cannot be supplied to every plot on an individual basis because of costs, but studies of relocated squatters in Singapore have indicated that habits of public hygiene endured for some time after re-housing had been completed (4.30), so that rapid transition from one method of sanitary provision to another may not, in fact, be socially, or even physically, necessary. It is possible that grouped services may be adequate, with the possibility that solid wastes can more easily be collected and at cheaper costs than for individually served units.

It is of course conceivable that technological innovations in the form of self-sufficient processing of wastes, can enable even inner-city, high-density settlements to become independent of centralized supply and disposal systems for energy and wastes. If these advances have yet to reach a stage where they are operational for settlement planning on a wide basis, they certainly offer attractive and viable means of reducing costs and may even result in the eventually processed wastes being capable of recycling for use in such forms as hydroponic urban horticulture, or as fuel for cooking or heating.

### 4.5.7 The Role of Housing Management

One of the most difficult and yet essential requirements of an appropriate responsive and efficient housing programme is the need for good management. The high degree of coordination required between the various agencies involved in urban planning and between agencies and the population which they serve, depends primarily upon how this coordination is developed and maintained. Ideally, staff responsible for such work should be able not only to implement policies, but to initiate research work on behalf of policy and planning agencies. The formulation of social programmes is another area of interest in which housing management could be usefully involved.

### 4.5.8  The Role of Research and Development

The survey carried out at the Rouse Avenue and Maulana Azad settlements yielded valuable information on what priorities residents had regarding their housing and their wider socio-economic needs. Other surveys have also indicated many of the needs and aspirations of the residents and led to the formulation of policy recommendations. Such projects provide an invaluable basis for new policies, although there is a need to use caution in interpreting the stated needs of residents and to ensure that they realize the economic costs of satisfying them. Continuous research programmes, however, serve as a vital element in the formulation of policies and can indicate not only the housing processes at any one time, but also the rate at which they are changing. In order to maximize the potential contribution of such research, it should ideally be integrated with pilot projects for the testing of alternative approaches and their evaluation. In this way, research and development projects can serve to monitor on-going programmes and explore alternatives without committing large investments of scarce resources and successful projects could then be incorporated into the mainstream of local authority programmes. As such, research performs a critical function in housing and planning programmes, as well as an economic method of generating improved solutions.

## 4.6     The Application of Alternative Programmes

It is not within the terms of this study to consider possible urban planning frameworks for specific urban areas, beyond stressing the need for a revision of existing planning methodologies. In the field of housing settlements, however, various possibilities offer themselves as illustrations as to how alternative programmes could fundamentally improve the situation of the poorer sections of the population.

Since existing attempts to provide completed housing units on a scale sufficient to accommodate the large numbers of the lowest income groups have been shown to be misconceived, it is more relevant to look to the environmental solutions adopted by squatters as providing a more realistic basis for new housing settlements. Analysis of the existing unauthorized housing settlements indicates that one of the most vital factors regarding housing for the poor is that of easy accessibility to places of work. This can be confirmed as a result of the social survey in both Rouse Avenue and Maulana Azad settlements and any proposals intended to meet the basic needs of these communities, must therefore be able to provide equally good access to areas of possible employment as exists at present. This can either be provided by allocating plots in the areas adjoining such centres, or alternatively, by providing heavily subsidized public transport of a standard sufficiently capable of off-setting the increased distance to work places which a non-central location would involve. In view of the limitations of transport subsidies mentioned, however, it is difficult to see how this could compensate for the loss of a suitably located site. A further possible alternative is that of providing more dispersed employment locations within cities, so that potential sites for low-income settlements would be increased.

### 4.6.1  Methods of Settlement Planning

How could such new settlements be organized and developed? This question, which has to be faced immediately by all authorities who acknowledge the need to reorientate their existing policies is, of course, less easy to answer. The crucial problem is that existing settlements have been self-generated within economic and spatial constraints by groups who have now become sophisticated at creating habitable settlements by operating the rule structures to their advantage. Any change in these rule structures will inevitably have a corresponding impact upon settlement patterns; in short, it is easier to analyse a settlement which has evolved through spontaneous and unconscious processes into a community, than it is to plan such a situation in advance.

However, if the planning process is made more responsive to the needs of urban populations, it should be possible to bring the representatives of existing settlements into a central position in the decision-making process at an early stage. In this way, related kinship or interest groups could be recruited for new settlements and lay the basis for coherent new communities.

One way in which this could be achieved might be to establish permanent councils consisting of community leaders drawn from the existing settlements, who can negotiate the terms of specific projects and be responsible for the implementation of details. Such a body might eventually assume some of the existing duties of the local authorities, and problems of arranging special assistance for individual families, or resolving detailed problems of plot layout and house construction, would all appear to be within the competence of such a community organisation. Thus, not only would authorities be relieved of many detailed problems, leaving them free to concentrate on those aspects which are within their wider terms of reference, but the increased responsibility of community leaders should assist in creating wider public support. Within this framework, applications for plots in the new settlements could then be invited from residents for their relations and friends living in existing settlements. This would also serve to discourage the formation of new areas of unauthorized housing and stabilise the situation until new programmes can get underway. Recruitment methods, therefore, offer an opportunity to maintain and increase the degree of self-sufficiency developed by the poor regarding their shelter needs as well as their rate of integration with the wider urban community. At the same time, the administrative problems of local government in implementing programmes can be reduced.

In order to achieve an organized movement of population into new settlements, it would be necessary to ensure that only those families that wish to move do so, since any element of coercion would immediately prejudice the future of a new settlement and increase the sense of insecurity which would reduce investment. Accordingly, security of tenure should be available to existing squatters and leave them free to stay where they are and possibly improve their existing shelter, or move into a new plot. Security of tenure would also be required for those moving into new settlements and in order to equate this with some form of public control over land use, the possibility of long term leases may be applicable, though in Ankara, projects are being prepared which provide legal tenure of dwellings, but not for the land upon which they are built. In these ways the authorities have the power to repossess sites at some future date, providing compensation and an alternative plot are provided.

Discussions between housing and planning agencies and local leaders could then establish specific priorities for new settlements and indicate the appropriate nature and extent of intervention required of the authorities. It may well be, for example, that educational or health facilities occupy a higher priority for residents than other services, or that space is required for cottage industries in order to provide a basis for gradual savings and economic progress. Broadly speaking, we have already observed that intervention can be categorized under six headings; social, economic, legal, administrative, political and physical. This should provide an adequately broad context for any given settlement project.

### 4.6.2   Site Organization — Maximizing the Modes of Aggregation

Within new sites designated for low-income housing, one of the most difficult but important factors in the creation of a physical and spatial framework within which the individuals or groups intending to build can be given the greatest freedom of location and of aggregation with other plots and building units. The somewhat rigid grid forms which characterize many of the larger unauthorized settlements, as, for example, at Pampa de Curvas in Lima, or in another example surveyed by Romanos in Athens (4.31), do have the major advantage of providing easy access for motor vehicles and also for the layout of public services. They do not, however, facilitate the

*Figure 4.8     A peri-urban settlement in Lusaka, Zambia, dating from the mid 1960s and photographed in 1970. The rich use of space appears to be based upon rural patterns but nonetheless uses land in a rational and ingenious way to suit local needs.* (By courtesy of Patrick Crooke)

richer, more intense use of urban space observed in the settlements of Old Delhi of those illustrated from Ashaiman, Ghana, or of others surveyed for example, by Christie, Andrews and Martin in Lusaka (4.32), and this more symbiotic use of space has been shown to permit varied and informal use of space even at the highest densities, a feature which is also common to the more sophisticated of traditional urban settlements.

*Figure 4.9    An excellent compromise between the needs for providing planning flexibility together with a simple layout of services can be seen in this photograph of Guayaquil's suburbios. Although access to the houses still in the swamp is by catwalk (see bottom left), roads are gradually consolidated by truckloads of fill (see centre top) and eventually the whole settlement is ready to recieve sewers (top right). The informal grid plan of the settlement is determined by local authorities, and willingly followed by builders seeking essential services. The intense use of land is still, however, achieved.* (By courtesy of Patrick Crooke)

It is therefore at this community or settlement planning level that the job of the central planners or housing agencies ceases and local action takes over. But if this is the case, the interaction between the two can hardly have a clear boundary, since by determining the outline form of the services infrastructure and the disposition of major communal elements (schools, bus-stops, etc.) the possible forms of aggregation will be increased or reduced.

To take the Delhi example, on which the case studies were based, it was observed, for example, that the house units were frequently grouped in clusters of between 10-25 units, each of which related to a communal space similar to those found in rural areas. Allowing for the range of household sizes observed, it would appear that such clusters approximately accommodate 100 people at densities of about 2400 per ha (1000 per acre). If this material is used as the basis of planning new settlements in the Delhi context, it should be possible to facilitate the formation of similar aggregation modes by organizing an appropriate distribution of services infrastructure. In transferring existing data into future projects it should, however, be noted that household sizes may well vary from their present levels and that they will require somewhat larger plots than at present. In the Rouse Avenue settlement there was a preponderance of large extended families in linear clusters adjacent to paths and thoroughfares, whilst smaller households were grouped around courts or chowks. If the layout of infrastructure provided the possibility of clusters in which each household had direct access to both a thoroughfare *and* a courtyard, high densities could be achieved which could improve still further upon existing layouts. If similar principles of settlement planning, based upon an understanding of existing local priorities were followed in other areas where new low-income settlements were required, the possibility of residents controlling the full extent of their housing needs would be greatly increased and the demands upon central authorities reduced to those areas which were appropriate.

For those reasons and in order to reduce their own overheads, public authorities should desist from providing any form of house units for the lowest income groups. Instead, every facility should be available to assist small builders to design and construct decent and imaginative units, of whatever cost standard or layout is required by the residents. Based upon the evidence of the case studies, it can be assumed that this will be done in a manner which encourages the possibilities of subsequent gradual improvement. Only two forms of assistance should be required in this direction — first, loans may be necessary to establish small builders for their initial projects, and secondly, advice aimed at creating an appropriate technology and providing a source of low cost materials. Experiments conducted on mud-brick and stabilized soil blocks, for example, indicate that it may be possible to establish low-technology sources of structural materials within new and existing settlements which should be able to encourage small scale industry. Other means of providing low-cost materials for house construction which obviate existing market shortages, (especially in the fields of cement, steel and aluminium) also need to be explored and exploited. In these ways, the initiative for housing can be maintained by the poor, so that they have a real stake in their own future and can even use the process of housing to generate a source of new wealth.

## 4.7  Conclusions

It must be apparent by now, that the possibilities for the majority of Third World countries being able to repeat the path to development — and the forms of urbanization and urbanism associated with it — that characterized the 19th century experience in Europe and North America, are relatively remote. The limitations upon export opportunities, the problems involved in import substitution policies and the great disparities in demographic, technological and economic factors, all act as a weight to inhibit attempts at development. The social and economic problems that these factors have created within countries, can be seen to manifest themselves in a spatial form at both the regional and urban levels. Amid a context of rapid rural population growth, the agricultural labour surplus has turned increasingly to the cities as the only hope for the future. Population planning policies have so far only made a limited impact on this process and there is a good deal of truth in the view that 'the rich get richer whilst the poor get family planning advice'. Such proposals do not, for example, resolve the basic problems of underdevelopment and in the short term, they are in any case irrelevant, since the majority of migrants who will move to the cities of the Third World by the end of the century, (together with the indigenous urban population seeking employment) are already alive today.

The scale of urban growth is therefore not likely to be stopped by wishful thinking and in the vast majority of  cases it can be expected to continue at its present rate or even increase further; this is particularly possible in areas of Africa, where urbanization started comparatively recently. Neither is urban growth likely to be restricted by policies which attempt to decentralize labour whilst keeping all the economic resources and the surplus they create, within the cities; if the jobs will not go to the people, the people will inevitably come to the jobs. In mixed or free-enterprise economies, the scope for dispersing economic activity — or even its desirability

— is open to serious doubt and in such cases, urban growth must be accepted for at least the near future. For those countries which decide to follow strategies of more dispersed growth, it is likely to require increasing public sector control or initiative, with obviously enormous political and social implications.

Whichever path is followed, the major cities of the Third World are here to stay. If this is the case, then the major problem of how they should be planned (or at least regulated), and how their increasing populations can be employed and housed within the limited resources available present planners, and others involved in housing and urban development, with one of the greatest problems of the present period. The scale of the processes involved, their complexity and rate of increase, all make it vital that urgent attention be given to the criteria by which planning and housing policies are formulated and the priorities which need most urgent action. Whilst job provision must rank as the most urgent issue, it has been shown in the previous pages that urban spatial structures can restrict or assist people to get work and to get *to* work. Furthermore, housing is itself a major area in which productive use can be made of labour and in which savings can be generated to serve valuable economic functions. Such a role is dependent, however, upon suitable frameworks being formulated which make it feasible for those with limited resources — that is, the bulk of the urban populations — to invest their labour and savings in a manner which will help them to fulfil such wider economic potential. The increasing evidence regarding the individually marginal, but collectively substantial, contribution made by urban migrants and the indigenous poor, is an indication of the human and economic possibilities which wait to be harnessed, yet which at the present time are subject to a wide range of restrictions.

If the recent and contemporary experiences are a valid guide, it must be seriously doubted if systems depending upon market mechanisms will ever enable the majority of the poor to obtain either jobs or housing. This is partly because private sector activity in the Third World is generally capital-intensive and geared to the maintenance of economic growth rates rather than the distribution of such growth. The shelter needs of the poor cannot be met within the constraints of such mechanisms, since their lack of credit-worthiness makes it difficult for them to afford conventional housing and uses up valuable savings even when it can be obtained. The need for increased public sector initiative within cities and for control over land use in order to ensure an adequate supply of new development, would appear to be an essential prerequisite of any comprehensive attempt to resolve urban settlement and housing problems.

The first section of this study attempted to show how dependent the Third World had become not only economically but also in terms of planning concepts and methods upon those of other countries and how self-defeating these were. Ample evidence exists therefore, not only of the need for alternative approaches, but also of the material which can be used to formulate them. This has been alleged to exist in understanding the rule-structures which have generated traditional urban settlements and contemporary unauthorised housing development. If such alternatives are developed within a planning context which can generate the supply of basic requirements such as land, services and security, the possibilities are immense. It has already been demonstrated that even the poorest type of settlement in one of the Third World's largest and least affluent countries, has exhibited a marked degree of rational and resourceful planning under difficult circumstances. With more favourable conditions, these qualities could achieve economic and socially acceptable environments which could make a significant contribution to development programmes. As many observers now agree, the Third World does not in fact have a housing problem at all, since the mass of the people have always housed themselves and are perfectly capable of still doing so, even in the changed environment of large cities. What does exist is a problem of land use and resource planning — in short a settlement problem. Given a willingness to take the necessary measures and to use approaches based upon tried and tested local solutions, adapting them where necessary to future needs, it is still possible that cities will be able to accommodate their present and future populations. The alternatives do not bear contemplation.

# Appendix

## APPENDIX

A sample questionnaire used in the social survey of the Rouse Avenue settlement is included below. This is designed to reveal information covering the background of respondents, their present situation, and their future aspirations and resources within the context of the settlement type.

| Site          Interviewee: | Dwelling No:       Date: |
|---|---|
| 1.0 Background | Respondent:     Other Adults: |
| 1.1 Place of origin of respondent and other adults in household. <br> Date of migration <br><br> 1.2 Reasons for migrating: <br> Why Delhi: <br> Why this site: | |
| 2.0 Present Situation | |
| 2.1 Kinship structure within settlement <br> 2.2 Relationship with kin at place of origin: <br> 2.3 Male/Female role relationships: <br><br> 2.4 Caste situation: <br><br> 2.5 Existing environmental situation; house type and area; materials used; allocation of space within household. (Sketch layout): <br><br> 2.6 Cost of existing shelter and process of its construction and development: <br><br> 2.7 Equipment and personal effects: | |

| 3.0 Socio-economic Mobility | Respondent | Other Adults in Household |
|---|---|---|
| 3.1 First and present job in city: hopes and expectations for future: | | |
| 3.2 Social integration within settlement and beyond it; attitudes and behaviour regarding education, life in the city; changes in attitudes of different generations: | | |
| 3.3 Changes in settlement pattern since arrival. Hopes and expectations: | | |

| 4.0 Future Plans and Aspirations | Respondent |
|---|---|
| 4.1 For respondent and remainder of household: | |
| 4.2 Employment and economic possibilities: | |
| 4.3 Changes envisaged or aspired to in housing situation: | |
| 4.4 Type of accommodation desired within existing or anticipated financial restraints; location:<br><br>Hutment as existing:<br>Hutment pucca construction and larger area:<br>Tenement or house:<br>Plot area required:<br>Layout pattern required: | |

| 4.0 Future Plans and Aspirations | Respondent |
|---|---|
| Services:  Water, <br>           Electricity, <br>           Toilets, <br>           Street Lighting, <br>           Schools <br>           etc. <br> Purchase or renting desired: <br> Govt. or self-build required: | |
| 5.0 Resources Available | |
| 5.1 Income per head and total <br>     for household: <br><br> 5.2 Amount available for housing: <br>     a. if for purchase <br>     b. if for rent <br><br> 5.3 Terms: <br>           Deposit <br>           Cash <br>           Monthly instalments | |
| 6.0 Any Other Remarks | |
| (Elaborate on any subjects of <br> personal concern; explore under- <br> lying socio-economic or other <br> aspects which cannot be covered <br> by previous questions). | |

A sample questionnaire in the social survey of the Maulana Azad settlement is also included below. The main differences between this form and that used at Rouse Avenue is due to the known variations in legality and function of the two communities. It must be admitted that these questionnaires are therefore of extremely limited general applicability and were in fact only arrived at after a certain amount of field experiment with each community had been achieved.

| Site: | Interviewee: | Hut No: | Date |
|---|---|---|---|

| 1.0 Background | Respondent | Other Adults |
|---|---|---|
| 1.1 Place of origin of respondent and other adults in household | | |
| 1.2 Reason for migrating Why Delhi: Why this site: | | |
| 1.3 How this job was obtained: | | |
| 2.0 Present situation | | |
| 2.1 Family here and in village: | | |
| 2.2 Relationship to neighbours: | | |
| 2.3 Existing house: (Sketch layout): Area, No. of rooms, Plot size, materials: | | |
| 2.4 Village house: Area, size, No. of rooms, plot size, materials: | | |
| 2.5 How are communal areas used: Water source: Washing Toilets Sleeping Entertainment Privacy | | |
| 2.6 Reasons for present layout: | | |

| | |
|---|---|
| 3.0 Future Needs and Aspirations: | |
| 3.1 What improvements planned:<br>    To existing<br>        site layout:<br>        house:<br>        open areas:<br><br>3.2 Service requirements | |

# References

1.1    STEDMAN JONES G., *Outcast London*, Oxford University Press, 1971.

1.2    See, for example, DWYER, D.J., (Ed.), *The City in the Third World*, Macmillan, 1974; MCGEE, T.G., *The Urbanization Process in the Third World — Explorations in Search of a Theory*, Bell, 1971. (Many other examples will be referred to later).

1.3    See, for example, JACOBS, J., *The Economy of Cities*, Jonathan Cape, 1969; the essence of the arguments advanced by writers such as HOSELITZ, B., 'The Role of Cities in the Economic Growth of Underdeveloped Countries', *Journal of Political Economy*, Vol. 61, 1953, pp.195-208, reprinted in BREESE, G. (Ed.), *The City in Newly Developing Countries*, Prentice-Hall, 1972, pp. 232-284, follow similar lines.

1.4    One of the best descriptions of this process can be seen in BRIGGS, A., *Victorian Cities*, Odhams, 1963; Pelican, 1968.

1.5    PAHL, R., 'Urban Processes and Social Structure', paper read at an open lecture at the University of Berlin, 1972, at the Seminar of the Research Committee on Urban and Regional Development of the International Sociological Association, Berlin, 1972, mimeo.

1.6    The urgency of the need for new approaches at the global level has been discussed in a number of recent works. For an up-to-date analysis see, for example, MESAROVIC, M. and PESTEL, E., *Mankind at the Turning Point — the Second Report to the Club of Rome*, Hutchinson, 1975.

1.7    This literature is well represented, for example by BERNSTEIN, H., (Ed.), *Underdevelopment and Development — the Third World Today*. Penguin, 1973. Diametrically opposed to this approach and seeking to use the experience of developed countries is the work of writers such as ROBINSON, R., (Ed.), *Developing the Third World*, Cambridge University Press, 1971.

1.8    Kingsley Davis, in evaluating the historical growth of an urban population has stated that, "The growth in urbanization during the three post medieval centuries in Europe was barely perceptible . . . if the growth of Europe's population between 1650-1800 works out at slightly more than 0.4% . . . the average rate of growth of towns was less than 0.6%. Only 1.6% of the population lived in cities of 100,000 or more".
       DAVIS, K., 'The Urbanization of the Human Population, *Scientific American No. 213*, September 1965, pp. 40-53; also in BREESE, G., (Ed.), *op.cit.*, pp.9-11.

1.9    SJOBERG, G., *The Pre-Industrial City: Past and Present*, Free Press of Glencoe, New York, 1960. This is reviewed by the same author see, SJOBERG, G., 'Cities in Developing and Industrial Societies', in HAUSER, P. and SCHNORE, L., (Eds.), *The Study of Urbanization*, John Wiley, 1965, pp. 213-263.

1.10   WEEKS, J., 'Employment and the Growth of Towns', paper presented to the British African Studies Association, September, 1972, mimeo, p.2.

1.11   MABOGUNJE, A.L., 'The Pre-Colonial Development of Yoruba Towns', in DWYER, D.J., (Ed.), op. cit., pp.26-33, originally published in MABOGUNJE, A.L., *Yoruba Towns*, Ibadan University Press, 1962, pp.3-10.

1.12   WEEKS, J., *op.cit.*, p.3. This distinction is also made by a number of other writers concerned with development studies; see, for example, O'CONNOR, J., 'The Meaning of Economic Imperialism', in RHODES, R., (Ed.), *Imperialism and Underdevelopment*, Monthly Review Press, 1970, pp.101-150.

1.13    DOBB, M., 'Political Economy and Capitalism', London, 1937; quoted by
        O'CONNOR, J., op-cit., p.111.
1.14    FURTADO, C., 'Elements of a Theory of Underdeveloped Structures', in
        BERNSTEIN, H., (Ed.), op.cit., p.34.
1.15    Ibid., p.35. This point is also made on p.42.
1.16    FRANK, A.G., Lumpenbourgeoisie and Lumpendevelopment —
        Dependence, Class and Politics in Latin America, Monthly Review Press,
        1972, p.19.
1.17    WEEKS, J., op.cit., p.2.
1.18    HOPKINS, A.G., 'The Lagos Strike of 1897, an Exploration in Nigerian
        Labour History', Past and Present, XXXV, 1966.
1.19    WEEKS, J., op.cit., pp.3–5.
1.20    MARX, K., The First Indian War of Independence,Foreign Language
        Publishing House, Moscow, 1959. The reports contained in this book were
        originally published in The New York Daily Tribune on receipt of the news
        in London in 1857. It is interesting to note that Marx considered the Indian
        Mutiny as one of the first revolutionary situations in which a popular
        insurgence movement would lead to the overthrow of colonialism and the
        establishment of socialist nation states. The dates of the reports make them
        clearly well in advance of possible events in Russia. The failure of the
        mutiny left Marx still optimistic — hence the title, 'The First Indian War of
        Independence'!
1.21    MALIK, S.C., 100 Years of Pakistan Railways, Government of Pakistan Press,
        Karachi, 1962.
1.22    BERNSTEIN, H., op.cit. Introduction, p.27.
1.23    DOS SANTOS, T., 'The Crisis of Development Theory and the Problem of
        Dependence in Latin America', in BERNSTEIN, H., op.cit., p.75.
1.24    DOS SANTOS, T., Ibid, p.76.
1.25    FRANK, A.G., op.cit., p.1.
1.26    DAVIS, K., 'Colonial Expansion and Urban Diffusion in the Americas', in
        DWYER, D.J., (Ed.) op.cit., p.39.
1.27    RODNEY, W., How Europe Underdeveloped Africa, Tanzania Publishing
        House, 1972; Bogle-L'Ouverture, 1972.
1.28    Two of the most widely read introductions to this subject make only limited
        reference to the impact of colonialism or other means by which
        underdevelopment originated. In BREESE, G., Urbanization in the Newly
        Developing Countries, Prentice-Hall, 1966, brief mention is made of
        colonialism (pp.32–41) but this indicates it to be a specific phase which is
        now over. In a later source by the same author (BREESE, G., (Ed.). The City
        in Newly Developing Countries, op.cit.), the analysis is demographic and
        little historical evidence is offered to explain the distinctions between
        developed and underdeveloped patterns of urbanization and urban growth.
1.29    SJOBERG, G., 'Cities in Developing Industrial Societies', in HAUSER, P. and
        SCHNORE, L., op.cit. pp. 213–263.
1.30    WEEKS, J., op.cit., p.5.
1.31    Ibid., p.6.
1.32    NILSSON, S., The New Capitals of India, Pakistan and Bangladesh,
        Scandinavian Institute of Asian Studies Monograph Series, No. 12; Student
        Literature, Lund, 1973, p.13.
1.33    KING, A., 'Cultural Pluralism and Urban Form: the Colonial City as
        Laboratory for Cross-Cultural Research in Man-Environment Interaction',
        paper presented at the International Congress of Anthropological and
        Ethnological Sciences, Chicago, 1973.

1.34    *Ibid.*, p.3.
1.35    See, for example, KING, A., 'The Colonial Bungalow-Compound Complex — a Study in the Cultural Use of Space', *Indian Anthropologist*, 1973/4; also 'The Language of Colonial Urbanization', *Sociology*, vol. No 8, No. 1, Clarendon Press, 1974, pp.81–110.
1.36    For a detailed case study of the negative aspects of aid see, for example, ALAVI, H., and KHUSRO, A., 'Pakistan: The Burden of U.S. Aid', in RHODES, R., *op.cit.*, pp.62–78.
1.37    FRANK, A.G., *op.cit.*
1.38    COALE, A., 'The History of Human Population', *Scientific American*, September, 1974, p.51.
1.39    DEMENY, P., 'The Population of Underdeveloped Countries', *Scientific American*, September, 1974, pp.150-155.
1.40    DAVIS, K., 'The Scale and Pace of Urbanization', in BREESE, G., *The City in Newly Developing Countries*, *op.cit.*, p.16.
1.41    DAVIS, K., *World Urbanization, 1950-70*, Vol. 1, University of California, 1969. Reproduced in World Bank Sector Paper, International Bank for Reconstruction and Development, Annex 1, Table 3, 1972, pp.76-79.
1.42    World Bank Sector Paper, *Ibid.*, p.11.
1.43    DWYER D. J., (Ed.), *The City in the Third World op.cit.*, p.9. Davis also argues that although the world is not yet fully urbanized, it soon will be. DAVIS, K., 'The Urbanization of the Human Population', *op.cit.*, BREESE, G., (Ed.), *The City in Newly Developing Countries*, *op.cit.*, p.6 Meier has even projected a total population of India in 2050 as 1500 million, of which 90% are considered to have become urbanized. See MEIER, R., *Resource-Conserving Urbanism for South Asia*, Regional Development Studies VII, Ann Arbour, 1969.
1.44    World Bank Sector Paper, 'Urbanization', *op.cit.*, p.12 and Annex 1, Table 1, p.74.
1.45    These data also conceal the fact that an increasing proportion of this total population is living in the largest cities (100 000+) which now accommodate 52.41% of India's entire urban population and are growing at the fastest rates. Census of India, Provisional Population Totals, paper 1, supplement, published by Census Commissioner, Government of India, 1971, pp.6–9, statement 5, 'Distribution of Population by Size of Town', Table C, p.55.
1.46    World Bank Sector Paper, 'Urbanization', *op.cit.*, Annex 1, Table 2, p.75.
1.47    *Ibid.*, p.75.
1.48    WILSHER, P., and RIGHTER, R. *The Exploding Cities*, Deutsch, 1975. pp.32–33.
1.49    U.N. 'The Growth of the World's Urban and Rural Population, 1920-2000', U.N., 1969, table 32; quoted in World Bank Sector Paper, *op.cit.*, Table 2, p.12.
1.50    World Bank Sector Paper, *op.cit.*, p.13.
1.51    *Ibid.*, p.77.
1.52    *Ibid.*, p.13.
1.54    See, for example, ANDREWS, P., CHRISTIE, M. and MARTIN, R., 'Squatters and the Evolution of a Life-Style', *Architectural Design*, January, 1973, pp.16-25.
1.55    MCGEE, T.G., 'The Cultural Role of Cities: the Case of Kuala Lumpur', in MCGEE, T.G., *The Urbanization Process in the Third World*, *op.cit.*, pp.121–147.
1.56    DWYER, D.J., *The City as a Centre of Change in Asia*, University of Hong Kong, 1972.

1.57    For a good introduction to the complexities of caste see SEGAL, R., *The Crisis of India*, Penguin, 1965, pp.35–41, and WISER, C., and W., *Behind Mud Walls*, University of California Press, 1963, pp.14-20.

1.58    WISER, C. and W., *op.cit.*

1.59    LIPTON, M., 'Strategies of Security — A Game against Nature', *The Listener*, April 4th, 1968.

1.60    For example, WEEKS, J., 'Factors in Determining the Growth of Output and Employment in Poor Countries', mimeo, 1972; and MCGEE, T.G., *The Urbanization Process in the Third World, op.cit.*

1.61    MCGEE, T.G., *op.cit.*, pp.84–5.

1.62    WILSHER, P. and RIGHTER, R., *op.cit.*, pp.152–165.

1.63    A notable study of the dynamism of this sector can be seen in a study by HART, K., 'Informal Income Opportunities and the Structure of Urban Employment in Ghana', paper presented to the Conference on Urban Unemployment in Africa, Institute of Development Studies, University of Sussex, mimeo, 1971.

1.64    SOVANI, N.V., *Urbanization and Urban India*, Asia Publishing House, 1966, pp.112–115.

1.65    National Sample Survey, 1963–4, Indian Statistical Institute, Government of India.

1.66    The first translation of this work was by PETERSON, published as *A Treatise, Concerning the Causes of the Magnificencie and Greatness of Cities*, London, 1606.

1.67    HOSELITZ, B., 'The Role of Cities in the Economic Growth of Underdeveloped Countries', *op.cit.*, BREESE, G. (Ed.), p.240.

1.68    SJOBERG, G., 'Rural — Urban Balance and Models of Development', in SMELSER, N. and LIPSET, S., (Eds.), *Social Structure and Mobility in Economic Development*, London, 1966, p.237.

1.69    MCGEE, T.G., *The Urbanization Process in the Third World, op.cit.*, pp.20–21.

1.70    *Ibid.*, p.21.

1.71    See, BRIGGS, A., *Victorian Cities, op.cit.*, and ENGELS, F., *The Condition of the Working Class in England, 1892*, Granada, 1969.

1.72    HARVEY, D., *Social Justice and the City*, Arnold, 1972.

1.73    DAVIS, K., 'The Urbanization of the Human Population', *op.cit.*, p.11.

1.74    This concept was partly based upon surveys made in the 1950s, see DAVIS, K. and GOLDEN, H., 'Urbanization and the Development of Pre-Industrial Areas', *Economic Development and Cultural Change*, vol. III, 1, October, 1954. This is reviewed in SOVANI, N.V., *op.cit.* pp.1–7.

1.75    Unesco Seminar Report, 'Urbanization in Azia and the Far East', Unesco, Bangkok, 1957, p.133.

1.76    SOVANI, N.V., *op.cit.*, p.5.

1.77    Unesco Seminar Report, *op.cit.*, p.133.

1.78    WILSHER, P. and RIGHTER, R., *op.cit.*, pp.44–45.

1.79    SOVANI, N.V., *op.cit.*, p.5.

1.80    World Bank Sector Paper, *op.cit.*, p.10.

1.81    SOVANI, N.V., 'Notes on In-Migrants to Indian Cities, in SOVANI, N.V., *op.cit.*, pp.112–153. Bose states that in urban India, the unemployment rate was 8.2% amongst the resident (non-migrant) population, whilst it was 6.5% among the migrants. BOSE, A., *Urbanization in India*, Academic Books, India, 1970, pp.60–80.

1.82    RAO, V.K.R.V. and DESAI, P.B., *Greater Delhi — a Study of Urbanization 1940-57*, Institute of Economic Growth, Delhi, 1965.

1.83 ZACHARIAH, K.C., 'Historical Study of Internal Migration in the Indian-Sub-Continent', Bombay Demographic Training and Research Centre, 1965.

1.84 World Bank Sector Paper, *op.cit.*, p.10.

1.85 According to Mitra, substantial sums of money are sent from Calcutta to Delhi and the surrounding rural areas in the form of small postal orders. In the case of Calcutta, Rs.276 million with an average value of Rs.46.1 are sent in this way each year, whilst in Delhi the figure is Rs.133.6 million, with an average value of Rs.56.1 for the year 1965-6. MITRA, A., *Calcutta — India's City*, New Age Publishers, Delhi, 1963, p.22. MITRA, A., *Delhi — Capital City*, Thomson Press, New Delhi, 1970.

1.86 WILSHER, P. and RIGHTER, R., *op.cit.*, p.49. See also, DWYER, D.J., *People and Housing in Third World Cities*, Longman, 1975, pp.69-71.

1.87 KAPIL, I. and GENCAGA, H., 'Migration and Urban Aocial Structures', Discussion Paper No. 1, Economic Staff Papers, Usaid, Turkey, mimeo.

1.88 For a thorough description and analysis of the ideas of Owen and their reception by later critics see, THOMPSON, E.P., *The Making of the English Working Class*, Gollancz, 1963; Pelican, 1968, pp.859-866.

1.89 Hauser has listed these examples, together with that of Redfield much later, and shown how they were classified. See, HAUSER, P. and SCHNORE, L., (Eds.), *op.cit.*, pp.503-504.

1.90 A good review of the evolution of these concepts can be found in BELL, C. and NEWBY, H., *Community Studies*, Allen and Unwin, 1971.

1.91 DURKHEIM, E., *The Division of Labour*, Macmillan, 1933, Free Press, 1964.

1.92 REDFIELD, R., 'The Folk Society', *American Journal of Sociology*, No. 57, January, 1947, p.293.

1.93 REDFIELD, R., *The Folk Culture of Yucatan*, Chicago University Press, 1941, p.112.

1.94 *Ibid.*

1.95 WIRTH, L., 'Urbanization as a Way of Life', *American Journal of Sociology*, XL, IV, July 1938, pp.60-83; also in REISS, A., (Ed.), *Louis Wirth on Cities and Social Life*, University of Chicago Press, 1964, p.100.

1.96 *Ibid*, p.66.

1.97 DURKHEIM, E., *op.cit.*, p.72.

1.98 *Ibid.*, p.75.

1.99 PAHL, R., 'The Rural — Urban Continuum', *Sociologia Ruralis*, IV, 1966; also in PAHL, R., *Readings in Urban Sociology*, Pergammon, 1968; pp.163-297.

1.100 WIRTH, M.E., 'Louis Wirth — a Biographical Memorandum', in REISS, A., *op.cit.*, p.334.

1.101 WIRTH, L., 'Social Disorganization', in REISS, A., *op.cit.*, p.48.

1.102 BENET, F., 'Sociology Uncertain — the Ideology of the Rural-Urban Continuum', *Comparative Studies in Society and History*, 6, 1963, pp.1-23.

1.103 HAUSER, P., quoted from the posthumous collection of Wirth's writings in proceedings of the Unesco Seminar 'Urbanization in Asia and the Far East', *op.cit.*, p.93.

1.104 BANNISTER, J., 'Urban Development and Housing the Urban Poor — the Case of India', US Aid, 1971, mimeo, p.4.

1.105 ZORBAUGH, H., *The Gold Coast and the Slum*, Chicago University Press, 1929, pp.11-12.

1.106 PAHL, R., 'Urban Processes and Social Structure', *op.cit.*, pp.1-5.

1.107 HARVEY, D., *Social Justice and the City*, *op.cit.*, p.133.

1.108 For a general discussion of class attitudes towards this problem, see, DESAI, A.R. and PILLAI, S.D., 'Slums and Urbanization', Popular Prakashand,

Bombay, 1970, p.3. Similar attitudes can be found in a large number of press reports throughout the Third World.

1.109   BOSE, N.K., *Culture and Society in India*, Asia Publishing House, London, 1967. Bose's claim, in particular, that regional ties were weakened by the effect of urban growth seems to contradict his own evidence of increased interaction with adjoining urban centres and therefore an increase in regional interaction. Apparently, he considers regions as being rural-based and as excluding any form of urban development.

1.110   AVILA, M., *Tradition and Growth*, University of Chicago Press, 1969, p.165.

1.111   *Ibid.*, p.167.

1.112   DAHL, R., *Who Governs*, Yale University Press, 1963.

1.113   BETEILLE, A., 'Closed and Open Social Stratification', *European Journal of Sociology*, Vol. 7, 1966.

1.114   GUSFIELD, J., 'Tradition and Modernity; Misplaced Polarities in the Study of Social Change', *American Journal of Sociology*, Vol. 72, 1967.

1.115   LEWIS, O., 'Folk-Urban Ideal Types', in HAUSER, P. and SCHNORE, L., *op.cit.*

1.116   LEWIS, O., *Life in a Mexican Village, Tepoztlan Restudied*, University of Illinois Press, 1951, p.434.

1.117   LEWIS, O., *Children of Sanchez*, Penguin, 1964, p.xxiv.

1.118   *Ibid.*, p.xxv.

1.119   For example, LEACOCK, E.B., (Ed.), *The Culture of Poverty*, Simon and Schuster, 1971, see especially LEEDS, A., 'The Concept of the Culture of Poverty-Conceptual Logic and Empirical Problems with Perspectives from Brazil and Peru', for a critical analysis of the comparative and theoretical implications of Lewis' concept.

1.120   MANGIN, W., (Ed.), *Peasants in Cities — Readings in the Anthropology of Urbanization*, Houghton Mifflin, 1970, p.xxiii.

1.121   CHANA, T.S. and MORRISON, H., 'Detail Analysis and Evaluation of Housing Subsystems in the Low-Income Housing Systems of a Particular Context', a Case Study of Mathare Valley, Nairobi, MIT Thesis, 1972, mimeo.

1.122   ANDREWS, P., CHRISTIE, M. and MARTIN, R., 'Squatters and the Evolution of a Life Style', *op.cit.*

1.123   ASAD, T., (Ed.), *Anthropology and the Colonial Encounter*, Ithaca Press, 1973. See, for example, his discussion of structural-functionalism.

1.124   This is an approach supported by many planners and administrators, particularly those in the major cities. For a typical example, see, *Jagmohan*, 'Failure of Will Responsible for Slums', *The States*, September, 1970, pp.–20.

1.125   WILSHER, P., and RIGHTER, R., *op.cit.*, p.98.

1.126   Government of India, 'Fourth Five Year Plan, 1969–74', Planning Commission, 1970, Ch.14, para. 11, p.302. The report states that dispersed industrial development should be pursued because of assumed "prohibitive costs of urban growth", see ch.19, para. 19, p.399.

1.127   In a survey of five urban areas of varying size conducted to test such assumptions, annual and capital costs for city sizes between 48000 and 1070000 were compared: see, MATHUR, O.P., SWAMY, M.C.K. and MORSE, R., 'Costs of Urban Infrastructure for Industry as Related to City Size in Developing Countries', prepared for US Aid, 1968, mimeo. The authors considered that "unit capital cost per Rs.1000 value added declined significantly with increase in city size to 132,000 population, slightly to the next size city and then stabilized instead of showing a rise. Expressed in Rs.1000 value added, çapital cost in the smallest city was 7.4% higher than in the largest city . . . highest direct industry cost per Rs.1000 added were observed for the smallest city size. Whilst the largest city size was the most economic in terms of unit costs for direct industrial infra-structure", pp.325-8.

1.128 This conclusion is reached in particular by BETTLEHEIM, C., in *India Independent*, MacGibbon and Kee, London, 1968, p.237.

1.129 Recent United Nations statistics indicate that Shanghai is at present the largest city in the world, with Peking not far behind. (See *United Nations Demographic Year Book*, 1970). Neither are these two cities isolated examples of rapid urban growth; SHAO, K., ('Industrialization and Urban Housing in Communist China', *Journal of Asian Studies*, May, 1966, p.381) has estimated that between 1949 and 1960 the average annual growth rate of the urban population as 7.6% and between 1957 and 1960, it was a high as 12.2% per annum; BUCHANAN, K., (*The Transformation of the Chinese Earth*, G. Bell, 1970, p.271) claims that by the early 1960s the number of million-plus cities had increased to seventeen, containing approximately one-third of China's population. Whilst these statistics cannot be regarded as reliable, it does seem relevant to conclude that China has experienced continuous high growth rates in its urban areas, which have not been significantly reversed by the policies of urban decentralization and rural development.

2.1 World Bank Sector Paper, *op.cit.*, p.14.
2.2 *Ibid.*, pp.14-15.
2.3 MCGEE, T.G., *The Urbanization Progress in the Third World*, *op.cit.*
2.4 World Bank Sector Paper, *op.cit.*, p.16.
2.5 SOVANI, N.V., *op.cit.*, pp.112-113.
2.6 AVCIOGLU, D., Turkiye 'Nin Duzeni', Ankara, 1969, p.587.
2.7 TRIBE, M.A., 'Some Aspects of Urban Housing Development in Kenya', mimeo, pp.4-5.
2.8 HARVEY, D., 'Social Processes, Spatial Form and the Redistribution of Real Income in an Urban System', in CHISHOLM, M., (Ed.), *Regional Forecasting*, Butterworth, 1971, pp.270-300; also in STEWART, M., (Ed.,), *The City*, Penguin, 1972, pp.296-337.
2.9 STEWART, M., (Ed.), *ibid.*, p.304.
2.10 DWYER, D.J., *People and Housing in Third World Cities*, *op.cit.*,
2.11 World Bank Sector Paper, *op.cit.*, p.17.
2.12 *Sunday Times*, July 15, 1973; *Straits Times*, May 10, 1973.
2.13 ANDREWS, D., *et al*, *op.cit.*, pp.16-25.
2.14 DWYER, D.J., 1975, *op.cit.*, p.19.
2.15 World Bank Sector Paper, *op.cit.*, p.17. This is also confirmed in the Calcutta Basic Development Plan, CMPO 1966, p.27.
2.16 ROSSER, C., 'Housing for the Lowest Income Groups — The Calcutta Experience', *Ekistics*, 31, 183, February, 1971, pp.126-121.
2.17 VERGHESE, B.G., 'City and Industrial Development', *Hindustan Times*, April 1, 1973.
2.18 These account for 61% of dwellings according to a survey by RAMACHANDRAN, P., 'Housing Situation in Greater Bombay, Report No. 2', Tata Institute of Social Sciences, 1972, mimeo, p.83, table 3.1.
2.19 AMATO, P.W., 'Elitism and Settlement Patterns in the Latin American City', *Journal of the American Institute of Planners*, 36, pp.96-105.
2.20 DWYER, D.J., *op.cit.*, p.22.
2.21 NILSSON, S., *New Capitals of India, Pakistan and Bangladesh*, Scandinavian Institute of Asian Studies, Monograph No. 12, 1973.

2.22    BERNIER, F., *Travels in the Mogul Empire, AD 1656-1668*, Westminster, 1891, 1, p.230, and passim. Quoted in NILSSON, S., *op.cit.*, pp.32–35.

2.23    FONSECA, R., 'The Walled City of Old Delhi', in OLIVER, P., (Ed.), *Shelter and Society*, Barrie and Rockcliffe; The Cresset Press.

2.24    FONSECA, R., *Ibid.*, p.108.

2.25    *Ibid.*, p.110.

2.26    *Ibid.*, p.106.

2.27    MABOGUNJE, A.L., 'The Pre-Colonial Development of Yoruba Towns', *op.cit.*, pp.26–33.

2.28    BRAY, J., 'The Craft Structure of a Traditional Yoruba Town', *Transactions of the Institute of British Geographers*, 46, 1969, pp.179–195. Reprinted in DWYER, D.J., (Ed.), *op.cit.*, pp.142–158.

2.29    ABRAMS, C., *Housing in the Modern World — Man's Struggle for Shelter in an Urbanizing World*, Faber and Faber, 1966, p.69.

2.30    MACINTOSH, D., 'The Politics of Primacy: Political factors in the development of Equadors largest city, Guayaquil, Columbia University Thesis, 1972, mimeo, p.30; RAY, T.F., *The Politics of the Barrios of Venezuela*, University of California Press, 1969; RAYMAEKERS, P., 'Le Squatting à Leopoldville' *Inter-African Labour Institute Quarterly*, Review of Labour Problems in Africa, VII, pp.22–53; LEGATES, R., 'Reform and Revolution in Chilean Housing Policy', University of Santiago, 1973, mimeo, p.10; TURNER, J.F.C., 'Barriers and Channels for Housing Development in Modernizing Countries', *American Institute of Planners Journal* Vol. 33; 3, May 1967, p.171.

2.31    ABRAMS, C., *op.cit.*, pp.23–24; PAYNE, G.K., 'Functions of Informality', *Architectural Design*, August, 1973, pp.494–503.

2.32    LEGATES, R., *op.cit.*, p.10.

2.33    ABRAMS, C., *op.cit.*, pp.23–24.

2.34    SOLAUN, M., FLINN, W. and KRONUS, S., 'Diagnosis and Solutions for Squatter Settlements — the Case of Los Colinas', Mid-West Universities Consortium for International Activities and the Graduate Research Board, University of Illinois, 1971, mimeo.

2.35    MCGEE, T.G., *op.cit.*, p.143.

2.36    See GOODMAN, R., *After the Planners*, Simon and Schuster, New York, 1971; also Penguin, 1972, to name just one obvious indication.

2.37    Report of the Working Group on Housing for the Fourth Five Year Plan, 1969–1974, New Delhi, Department of Works Housing and Urban Development, Government of India Press, 1968.

2.38    National Sample Survey, March-August, 1957, No. 67, Tables with Notes on Housing Conditions, Cabinet Secretariat, Government of India Press, Table 2.2, p.48.

2.39    ROSSER, C., *op.cit.*, p.126.

2.40    *Journal of the Indian Institute of Town Planners*, 1955, quoted by DWYER, D.J., 1975, *op.cit.*, p.102.

2.41    It has been calculated by the Working Group on Housing for the Fourth Five Year Plan that the cost of solving India's housing deficit would be in the region of Rs.330000 million, Working Group on Housing for the Fourth Five Year Plan.

2.42    Bannister has cited a 1971 Working Paper by an urban development consultant, projecting a cost of Rs.43970 millions, BANNISTER, J., *op.cit.*, p.31.

2.43    MANCHAR, 'An Approach to Realistic Housing Policies and Programmes', National Building Organization, Government of India and United Nations

Regional Housing Centre (ECAFE), Paper No, 15,196, mimeo, cited by BANNISTER, J., *op.cit.*, p.31.

2.44 TURNER, J.F.C., 'Barriers and Channels', *op.cit.*, p.168.

2.45 JUPPENLATZ, M., *Cities in Transformation*, University of Queensland Press, 1970, pp.117-147; also quoted in DWYER, D.J., 1975 *op.cit.*, pp.78-83.

2.46 *Malay Mail*, December 14, 1973.

2.47 *Sunday Times*, July 15, 1975; *Straits Times*, August 3, 1973 and May 10, 1973. There were, however, some more sympathetic articles.

2.48 *Times of India*, August 7, 1971.

2.49 PAYNE, G.K., *Squatter Housing and Urban Growth in India*, Social Science Research Council Monograph, 1973, p.91.

2.50 ABRAMS, C., *op.cit.*, p.126.

2.51 LIM, W., *Equity and Urban Environment in the Third World*, DP Consultant Service PTE Ltd., Singapore, 1975, preface.

2.52 NAIR, R.L., 'Why Chandigarh?', 1950, quoted in SCHMETZER, H., and WAKELEY, P., 'Chandigarh Twenty Years Later', *Architectural Design*, June, 1974, pp.350-351.

2.53 WAKELEY, P. and SCHMETZER, H., *op.cit.*, p.352.

2.54 For a full analysis of the spatial morphology of Indian cities, see BRUSH, J.E., 'Spatial Patterns of Population in Indian Cities', *Geographical Review*, 58, pp.362-391.

2.55 WAKELEY, P., and SCHMETZER, H., *op.cit.*, p.353.

2.56 GUPTA, S.K., 'Chandigarh — a Study of Sociological Issues and Urban Development in India', *Architectural Design*, June, 1974, p.364.

2.57 *Ibid.*, pp.363-364.

2.58 World Bank Sector Paper, 'Housing' IBRD, 1975, p.14, Table 2, annex 5, p.66.

2.59 Contained in a special issue of *Architectural Design*, August, 1963.

2.60 TURNER, J.F.C., 'Lima's Barriadas and Corralones: Suburbs Versus Slums', *Ekistics*, March, 1965, pp.152-155.

2.61 *Ibid.*, p.154.

2.62 MANGIN, W., (Ed.), *op.cit.*, p.xxix.

2.63 STOKES, C.J., 'A Theory of Slums', *Land Economics*, 1962, pp.187-197.

2.64 TURNER, J.F.C., 'Barriers and Channels for Housing Development in Modernizing Countries', *op.cit.*

2.65 MANGIN, W., (Ed.), *op.cit.*, p.xxxiii.

2.66 See, for example, World Bank Paper, 'Urbanization', *op.cit.*

2.67 TURNER, J. F. C. and FICHTER, R., *Freedom to Build*, Macmillan, 1972.

2.68 *Ibid.*, p.156.

2.69 *Ibid.*, p.157.

2.70 *Ibid.*, p.158.

2.71 *Ibid.*, p.172.

2.72 *Ibid.*, p.154.

2.73 TURNER, J.F.C. and ROBERTS, B., 'The Self Help Society' in WILSHER, P. and RIGHTER, R., *op.cit.*, pp.126-137.

2.74 *Ibid.*, p.133.

2.75 MANGIN, W., (Ed.), *op.cit.*, p.xxiii.

2.76 TURNER, J.F.C., *Barriers and Channels, op.cit.*, p.170.

2.77 TURNER, J.F.C. and FICHTER, R., *op.cit.*, p.ix.

2.78 TURNER, J.F.C., 'Uncontrolled Urban Settlement: Problems and Policies', in UN Seminar Report on 'Development Policies and Planning in Relation to Urbanization', Pittsburgh, 1966, Chapter 4, also in TURNER, J.F.C., 'Barriers and Channels', *op.cit.*, p.170.

2.79    It must be stated, of course, that there is a great deal of variety in the types of
        barriada settlement and in the socio-economic status of their inhabitants.
        However, the ideas which have been used to formulate 'self-help' concepts
        are generally, as Fichter acknowledges, based upon the more fortunate
        groups.

2.80    *Ibid.*, p.171.

2.81    The location of each income group, as at 1970, is shown in TUREL, A., 'A
        Study of the Residential Location Pattern of Different Income Groups in
        Ankara', Middle East Technical University, Ankara, MCP Dissertation,
        1972.

2.82    HARVEY, D., 'Social Justice and the City', *op.cit.*, p.134.

2.83    *Ibid.*, p.135.

2.84    LAVE, L., 'Congestion and Urban Location', Papers of the Regional Science
        Association, No. 25, pp.133–153; quoted in HARVEY, D., *Ibid.*, p.135.

2.85    *Ibid.*, p.125.

2.86    *Ibid.*, p.135.

2.87    *Ibid.*, pp.139–140.

2.88    WILSHER, P. and RIGHTER, R., *op.cit.*, pp.138–151.

2.89    *Ibid.*, p.138.

2.90    *Ibid.*, p.146 (emphasis added).

2.91    *Ibid.*, p.137.

2.92    *Ibid.*, p.136; *Architectural Design*, November, 1975, pp.658–659.

2.93    BOSE, A., *Land Speculation in Urban Delhi*, Institute of Economic Growth,
        1969, mimeo, p.37.

2.94    WARD, B., quoted in WILSHER, P. and RIGHTER, R., *op.cit.*, p.220.

2.95    The importance of this factor was acknowledged in the second session of the
        United Nations Committee on Housing, Building and Planning, which
        subsequently initiated a series of regional studies to evaluate its
        significance; see for example, Official Records of the Economic and Social
        Council, 37th Session, supplement, No. 12, paragraph 114; Seven volumes
        on Urban Land Policies and Land Use Control Measures, United Nations,
        1973.

2.96    A point also made by DWYER, D.J., 1975, *op.cit.*, p.212.

2.97    JUPPENLATZ, M., *op.cit.*

2.98    DWYER, D.J., 1975, *op.cit.*, p.201.

2.99    KHAN, Z.A., 'Population Growth of Karachi, the Example of a Large City in
        Developing Countries', *Pakistan Geographical Review*, 24, p.128; quoted
        by DWYER, D.J., 1975, *op.cit.*, pp.201-203.

3.1     MITRA, A., *Delhi, Capital City, op.cit.*, p.7.

3.2     *Ibid.*, p.7.

3.3     In 1956, refugee households constituted 35.9% and other in-migrants; see,
        RAO, V.K.R.V. and DESAI, P.B., *op.cit.*

3.4     DELHI DEVELOPMENT AUTHORITY, Draft Master Plan for Delhi, 1961, p.115.
        This also relates in part to the effect of the land freeze discussed by Bose: see
        2.93.

3.5     SINGH, SATWANT., 'Rehabilitation of Slum Dwellers', Paper presented to
        Seminar on Housing Management, Delhi, March 1969, p.3.

3.6     See, for example, the evidence presented by CORREA, C., in WILSHER, P., and
        RIGHTER, R., *op.cit.*, pp.139–140.

3.7     The Delhi Draft Master Plan itself estimated that 42500 houses would need
        to be built each year to meet existing and future needs. The Authority,
        however, only aimed to build 16000 units a year and actually completed a
        mere 4700 units during 1968–69. In 1970–71, only 5606 units were finished

of which only 60% were for the low-income group.

3.8 At 1971 rates, low-income units in Delhi cost on average Rs.12500–Rs.15000 according to the DDA pamphlet *Delhi Housing*. Yet the Master Plan, noting that the average per capita income for the city was Rs.188, observed that the ability to spend 10% of income on housing would not even pay for a single room dwelling. To meet the full requirements of official deficit estimates at existing standards would have cost approximately Rs.15–20 million at 1973 prices.

3.9 GOHAR, R.D., 'A Study of Squatters in Delhi', Institute of Town Planners, India, Dissertation, 1969, mimeo, p.263.

3.10 SINGH, S., *op.cit.*, p.11.

3.11 RAO, V.K.R.V. and DESAI, P.B., *op.cit.*, p.287.

3.12 RAMACHANDRAN, P., *op.cit.*, pp.36 37.

3.13 SOLAUN, M., FLYNN, W.L. and KRONUS, S., *op.cit.*

3.14 The field work of this study and the methods used were evolved and undertaken in conjunction with Richard Weiss of the School of Architecture, University of California, Berkeley.

3.15 It is unfortunate that almost all existing housing projects, whatever the income group they are intended for, fail to acknowledge these basic phenomena of Indian domestic life and instead provide house units of a type and specification one would expect to find in the temperate climate of Britain. The fact that this traditional solution is achieved within the extremely basic provisions incorporated into the Rouse Avenue settlement would indicate that private open space is a basic requirement of any successful housing project in this area.

3.16 A traditional form of village council which consists of village elders (or elected officials), whose job it is to settle disputes within the local community. The institution is frequently found in the more stable squatter settlements and is the link between the community and the wider urban social structure. Members are normally well-versed in urban politics and often use their council as a springboard for a political career, though if they are successful, there is pressure to stay within the community on whose votes they rely, rather than to move to fresh pastures, no matter how attractive.

3.17 The term 'scheduled caste' is used to include those low caste groups otherwise referred to as 'harijans' or 'untouchables' because of the ritual pollution considered to be involved in contact with them.

3.18 These are made almost completely by the user. Only the legs are made by specialists and they are normally elaborately turned and coloured, horizontal members are fixed into them and the job completed by weaving a basic supporting corase rope. The completed bed costs only a few rupees, and has the advantage of being custom-made.

3.19 These are based upon more detailed descriptions contained in PAYNE, G., *Squatter Housing and Urban Growth in India*, Social Science Research Council Monograph, 1973, pp.162–181.

3.20 For a more complete explanation of what is called *satisficing decision theory*, see SIMON, H.A., *Sciences of the Artificial*, MIT Press, 1969, pp.54–65, 75–76. Simon argues that most design problems in the real world are resolved by satisficing rather than optimizing, simply because constraints and the limited set of alternatives demand it. The same approach is closely paralleled by that of the rural subsistence farmers of Kavathe. See LIPTON, M., *op.cit.*

3.21 It has been estimated, for example, that Delhi consumes over half the national supply of building cement, see, Sondi, R., 'Delhi's Building Industry', *Times of India Weekly,* October 1, 1972.

3.22    Specific clauses quoted refer to the Contract Conditions of the Himachal Pradesh CPWD Regulations, but are representative of requirements in Delhi and other regions.

3.23    VESTBRO, D., 'Social Life and Dwelling Place', University of Lund, Report No. 2. 1975.

4.1    WILSHER, P. and RIGHTER, R., *op.cit.,* p. 1966. This problem however, did not prevent a United Nations urbanization study from making analogies between Sweden and Malaysia; see, 'Urbanization — Development Policies and Planning', International Social Development Review, No. 1, United Nations, 1968.

4.2    World Bank Sector Paper, *op.cit.,* p.11.

4.3    See, for example, BOSE, A., 'Land Speculation in Urban Delhi', *op.cit.*

4.4    TURNER, J.F.C., in WILSHER, P. and RIGHTER, R., *op.cit.,* p.136.

4.5    *Ibid.,* pp.143–144.

4.6    LEGATES, R., *op.cit.,* pp.24–25.

4.7    This is shown on the urban plan of Delhi, see PAYNE, G.K. 'Functions of Informality', *op.cit.,* p.503.

4.8    TURNER, J.F.C., 'Housing by People', *Architectural Design,* September, 1975; February, 1976.

4.9    MITCHELL, M., 'Shanty Cash — a report on Shanty Settlements and Co-operative Subsidy in the Metropolitan Region of Ghana', Architectural Association, 1975; mimeo.

4.10    *Ibid.,* pp.33–34.

4.11    The Co-operative also provided a mechanism by which the government could channel credit into secure forms. *Ibid.,* p.40.

4.12    This approach to urban administration is the subject of current research by the author.

4.13    LEGATES, R., *op.cit.,* p.8.

4.14    CROOKE, P., Paper presented to the Town and Country Planning Association Summer School, 1973; abstracted in *Ekistics,* 38, 229, July, 1974, pp.9–12.

4.15    UNITED NATIONS, 'Improvement of Slums and Uncontrolled Settlements', Report of the Inter-region Seminar, Columbia, March, 1970, United Nations, 1971, p.13.

4.16    *Ibid.,* p.162.

4.17    *Ibid.,* pp.164–165.

4.18    TYRWHITT, J., (Ed.), *Patrick Geddes in India,* Lund Humphries, 1947, pp.24–31.

4.19    *Ibid.,* pp.40–59.

4.20    *Ibid.,* p.11.

4.21    ABRAMS, C., *op.cit.,* pp.124–126.

4.22    The lack of enthusiasm exhibited by town planners regarding self-help projects has been discussed by BANNISTER, J., *op.cit.,* and by VAN HUYCK, A., the housing threshold for lowest income groups', in HERBERT, J. and VAN HUYCK, A., (Eds.), *Urban Planning in Developing Countries,* Praeger, 1968, pp.64–107.

4.23    An excellent review of Clinard's book, which expresses concern over the possible clash of interest between the residents and the housing agencies is by MUELLER, S., *American Journal of Sociology,* 73, 1967–8; pp.118–119.

4.24    ORTEGA, A., RYBCZNSKI, W., AYAD, S., ALI, W., and ACHESON, A., *The Ecol Operation.* Minimum Cost Housing Group, McGill University, 1972.

4.25    See, for example, UPPAL, I.S. and VASUDEVA, P.M., 'The Role of Stabilized

Soit in Low-cost Housing Construction', Paper presented to the 11th
I.F.A.W.P.C.A. Convention, Seminar on Low Cost Housing Delhi, 1971.

4.26    A project is well advanced in the research laboratories at Auroville Ashram,
Pondicherry, India, to develop solar stills.

4.27    Proposals contained in some reports sometimes appear like low-key
versions of the 'American Dream', with space even provided for car ports'.
See the report prepared for the Agency for International Development
entitles 'Proposed Minimum Standards for Permanent Low-cost Housing
and for Improvement of Existing Sub-standard Areas', Ideas and Methods
Exchange Series, No. 64, 'Housing Codes and Standards', Office of
International Affairs, Department of Housing and Urban Development,
Washington, May, 1966, p.48.

4.28    VAN HUYCK, A., 'Planning for Sites and Services Programmes', Ideas and
Methods Exchange Series, No. 68, prepared for the Office of International
Affairs, Department of Housing and Urban Development, Washington,
July 1971, p.37.

4.29    *Ibid.*, p.37.

4.30    KLEEVENS, J.W., *'Housing and Public Health in a Tropical City — a Study
of Singapore,* Medical Series No. 223, Van Goldum and Co., 1971,
pp.99–100.

4.31    ROMANOS, A., 'Squatter Housing-Kipoupolis; the significance of
Unauthorized Housing', *Architectural Association Quarterly*, 2, No. 2,
April, 1970, pp. 14–26.

4.32    ANDREWS, P., CHRISTIE, M. and MARTIN, R., *op.cit.*, pp.16–25.

# Index